TEACHING FOR
MASTERY

— MARK MCCOURT —

First Published 2019

by John Catt Educational Ltd,
15 Riduna Park, Station Road,
Melton, Woodbridge IP12 1QT

Tel: +44 (0) 1394 389850
Email: enquiries@johncatt.com
Website: www.johncatt.com

ISBN: 978 1 912906 18 5

Set and designed by John Catt Educational Limited

CONTENTS

2019001172

PROLOGUE

The book that follows is a conversation. A dialogue. The dialogue came into existence as a way of speaking carefully and deliberately to myself about some ideas that have been important in framing my views and beliefs around the nature of knowledge, the purpose of education and the most effective models of schooling that can be deployed in order to achieve that purpose.

I write as a way of articulating my own thoughts back at myself. Doing this allows me to have a conversation with myself – to argue, justify, correct, see where I have a lack of insight, find ways forward and continue to grow.

There are errors in this book. Lots of them. Some of those errors are errors because the truth is not yet known. Some of those errors will, happily, be put right as our profession and those professions that support education continue to learn more and more about learning. The assertions I make in this book are included because, right now as I sit here, I believe them to be true based on everything I have experienced and the knowledge I have available to me at this moment in time. Some of the errors are errors because I have made a mistake. I can't see those mistakes at this point – I have re-read the words and suggestions in this book and, at this moment, believe the book does convey my sincere beliefs accurately. The words in this book are written in good faith to myself as a conversation with myself.

I have always written for this purpose. I find that having such a dialogue with myself helps me to become increasingly enlightened. Sometimes, I share these conversations in interviews, articles, speeches, debates and blogs. In 2015, when I first wrote down the conversation that would later become this book, I began to share parts of it through my own blog. The response to this sharing helped me to better articulate my thinking, which I have attempted to do in speeches across the UK over the last few years. Each interaction and debate with teachers and educators again helps me to grow. Quite a few people suggested to me that the thoughts and ideas I was communicating in those blogs and speeches might be usefully condensed into a single narrative. This is what I attempt to do here.

As with all books, the very moment this book is published, it will be out of date. I adore learning and am absolutely addicted to it, so I will continue to play with the ideas I express here and those ideas will continue to evolve.

My writing approach has always been the same process. It is an informal discussion with myself. I write from memory – quickly and off the top of my head – and want my writing to be a conversation with the reader too. This book is not intended to be a dry academic tome. Much of what is written here, by the very nature of it being off the top of my head, exists in my memory as a connected story. Sometimes, I don't know where that story has come from. I write as a single narrative, not as a research paper. I have recently gone through the story and attempted to retrospectively reference and credit ideas and quotes, but a great deal of the writing is simply composed of things that I know and the origins have been lost in the haze of life. I am always happy to be reminded of conversations, lectures, articles and so on that may have been the genesis of some of my thoughts.

I believe that all children can learn all things given the right conditions. That belief was key to me deciding to become a teacher. In my career in teaching and education, I have attempted to learn all I can about learning and how schooling can most effectively lead to all children learning all things expected of them by school curricula. I hope that my own learning will continue throughout my life and I am sure there will come a time when I look back on some of my words from today and wonder how I could have known so little. But we all know so little, don't we? Our knowledge is just the sum of everything we've experienced; and in the grand scheme of things, our experience is very limited. We can't move beyond our own experiences, so we can only learn more as we experience more – and there is always more to experience. This is why different ideas resonate with all of us at different stages in our lives.

Through this learning about learning, I have, over many years, come to formulate a phased approach to educating, which I believe all human beings pass through from the point of meeting a novel idea to the point at which it can truly be considered to be understood.

I have been greatly influenced and guided by the canon of knowledge that exists in education – created by all the educators who have come before and all those who now continue to add to and enrich that canon – and have reflected seriously and with purpose on the implications of the canon, in the pursuit that I might add some new thinking to it. The phased model I propose is, I hope, not controversial. I see this phasing as a logical conclusion of a synthesis of well-thought-through, tried, tested and observed approaches and outcomes carried out and measured by educators over many, many years.

In proposing a phasing of 'TEACH, DO, PRACTISE, BEHAVE', I have necessarily had to settle on a choice of word for each of those phases. I gave these words time to evolve in my mind, particularly after debates with other educators regarding their suitability. Some agree; others do not. The choice of the word 'Behave' appears to be particularly contentious and I understand the reasons why. In the end, I believe the words do work and carry the meaning that I intend to convey; but if they bother you, why not simply swap them out for another word of your choosing in your mind.

Encountering the work of John B. Carroll (which led me to meet the work of Benjamin S. Bloom and, subsequently, Carleton W. Washburne) years before even thinking about becoming a teacher was an enormous stroke of luck. I don't think I would have entered teaching without that inspiration. I know I certainly would not have remained an educator without their insight.

Mastery is an entire and complete model of schooling. There are many, many models of schooling. They come and go, in and out of fashion, exist at different times in history and in different jurisdictions around the world. Some models work, some don't. Some have high impact; others take pupils backwards. Mastery is one of the models we know to be highly impactful, which is why it has endured over the years and why I continue to espouse its use.

I hope that some of the ideas in this book resonate with the reader and that they give the reader pause to think seriously and with purpose about a mastery model of schooling and the implications such a model has for one's own schools, classrooms and communities. The mastery model of schooling is subject-agnostic and I hope that this book is useful to teachers of any subject. Although I have used my own subject, mathematics, to illustrate and exemplify the approach, this book is not solely for the teacher of mathematics – the messages are aimed at any educator. However, as someone who is truly in love with mathematics, I do hope that the mathematical examples used in the book serve not only to give additional clarity to the mastery model but also to engage the reader, regardless of subject specialism, in learning some new mathematics. Sorry, I just couldn't help but take the opportunity to teach maths. Enjoy.

PART I
DEVELOPING A MODEL OF SCHOOLING

The early players

At the turn of the 20th century, Carleton Washburne would have appeared an unlikely hero. Born in Chicago, Illinois in 1889, Carleton led an unremarkable early life. His school career was reasonably average for the son of well-educated professionals, but he did not excel. Plodding through life and looking for a path to follow, Carleton turned to his father's love and attempted to follow in his footsteps by studying medicine at the University of Chicago. Things did not go well. His grades fell and his interest waned.

Now, frustrated with his university life and left with very few options open to him, Carleton gravitated instead to his mother's interests.

Carleton's mother was a strong-willed, politically active woman, untypical of the age. She was a friend to the famed progressive educator John Dewey and would regularly engage with him over many issues. The parlour would buzz with passionate debate about the purpose of education and how it might be bettered as the young Carleton listened eagerly while he played. From the very beginning, Carleton's life was one steeped in education theory and policy.

As a child, Carleton attended a Dewey school – Francis W. Parker School, Chicago – and would later go on to become a founding member of the John Dewey Society and president of the Progressive Education Association.

Carleton dropped out of UoC and headed to a new university that was starting to establish itself in California: Stanford. No longer pursuing medicine, he chose to study education.

As with all young men in the final year of a degree course, Carleton would have needed focus and dedication to his course to be truly successful. However, in that same year, Carleton fell deeply in love with Heliuz Chandler and all thoughts of studying took second place. Their first child was on the way. Despite this, Carleton did manage to scrape through and graduate.

A mediocre university degree in hand and with no real direction in life, Carleton turned his focus to becoming an entrepreneur. Enthused by what he believed to be a sure-fire business success, Carleton borrowed money from any source he could and invested it all in his new idea. It failed. Badly.

Now unable to support his family and with no other options in life, Carleton was faced with only one route out of penury: he reluctantly became a teacher.

Carleton's first post was as a teacher of science in an underachieving school in a poverty-stricken settlement in California. Today it is the city of La Puente (which means 'the bridge' in old Spanish), approximately 20 miles east of downtown Los Angeles, and continues to struggle economically, despite a brief period of prosperity in the 1930s when the area gained international fame for its fruit and walnut groves. La Puente was home to the world's largest walnut-packing plant and for a time looked likely to find a way out of poverty, but the industry collapsed and today its 40,000 inhabitants live in a fully urbanised city with median income significantly below the state average.

The experience at La Puente changed Carleton forever.

Unlike the comfortable, educated and supportive family life that Carleton had experienced and thought the norm, he was now faced with disengaged children from families failed by the education system. He began to see that the model of schooling prevalent in the United States acted as a harsh filter: the entire population was pushed into the system at the beginning, but year by year, the system 'filtered out' huge swathes of children, which it destined never to become educated. The system and society at large truly believed that some children were capable of learning whilst others, of low 'aptitude', were not.

This had a profound impact on Carleton. He began experimenting with his approaches, drawing on the experiences of his own Dewey education and the regular espousing of a progressive education he absorbed as a child. Carleton questioned whether it would be possible to create an education system that resulted in every single child being successful, rather than just the small 5% who appeared to be the result of the filter that he saw as the US education system.

He became obsessed with conceiving and implementing an approach that could achieve what he saw as the best practices of teaching an individual in a one-to-one tuition scenario but applied at scale to a group of pupils.

* * *

Aristotle was a pupil of Plato, but following Plato's death in 348 BC, he moved from his beliefs in Platonism to becoming dedicated to developing a new epistemological model, which would later become empiricism. He immersed himself in empirical studies and sensory experience became central to his view of epistemology. When, in 343 BC, King Philip II of Macedon asked Aristotle to become the tutor of his son, he carried this view of epistemology into the methods he deployed as a tutor, knowing that he required multiple approaches for teaching any particular idea so that the young boy in pupilage would always, in time, be able to learn the fact or skill at hand.

The son was to become, of course, Alexander the Great. As his tutor, Aristotle was afforded great wealth and opportunities to establish vast amounts of educational resources. He established a library at the Lyceum and brought about the publication of many hundreds of books, including tomes on the nature of knowledge and approaches to tutoring and pupilage.

The methodologies of Aristotle formed the basis for the approach to be widely adopted in delivering a classical education. A one-to-one tutoring, where the tutor and pupil are intricately linked such that the tutor is always aware of the pupil's level of knowledge and how to build upon the knowledge or to correct wrong thinking before moving on.

This approach to individualised instruction remained the dominant model for teaching for centuries to come.

* * *

Carleton was well aware of the success of the Aristotelian approach. He recognised that individualised tuition was the best method of teaching a child. It was clear that the ability to notice a pupil's misunderstanding immediately (such that the tutor could take action in the moment) was key.

But how could this be achieved when a single teacher is faced with not one individual following a pupilage, but a large group of children, all with different backgrounds, in a classroom setting?

Carleton began to trial approaches in the classroom aimed at integrating aspects of individual instruction, such as immediate feedback and intervention. He was determined to educate the 'whole child'.

* * *

'Adaptive learning' has become an important phrase in education in recent years. Around the world, venture capitalists and large education publishing companies are investing billions of dollars into trying to build distance learning

11

web applications that can guide pupils through a course without the need of a teacher. The technology is in its infancy, despite the rather outrageous claims from some EdTech companies to the contrary. Nonetheless, the need for large-scale individualised instruction grows ever more as the world's population increases and the demand for education seems insatiable. The sixty million children in the world today who do not go to school and will never meet a teacher could potentially be reached by a technological solution.

Frederic Lister Burk was born in 1862. Following a career as a journalist in the San Francisco Bay area, Frederic paid for himself to attend graduate school at Stanford University by taking on temporary teaching jobs in a variety of private and public schools across San Francisco, before embarking on a full-time career in education.

Throughout the 1890s, Frederic refined an innovative model for self-instructed learning, in which the pupil received only very minimal input from a teacher. A staunch progressive and follower of Dewey, Frederic believed the school system that had emerged in the US and much of the Western world was failing pupils and needed to be overturned. He devised new pedagogies that aimed to adjust to pupils' personal needs and progress. Instructional materials were also created to allow pupils to move forward without the assistance of a teacher.

Along with Mary Ward, a former student of his in San Francisco, Frederic conceived and produced sets of self-paced, self-instructional learning materials aligned with extensive and intelligent self-assessment materials, which allowed learners to progress at a rate that was completely individual.

Frederic Burk had invented distance learning a century before it would capture the imagination of return-hungry investors.

The model proved such a success that it piqued the interest of educators across the state. Frederic and Mary tried to spread the impact of the approach by publishing their findings and the materials that supported the programme, but were stopped from doing so by the California courts with a ruling that only the State Board of Education could publish printed instructional materials.

An entire and complete curriculum – proven to be successful, with all the materials already authored and available, and which would have saved countless teachers countless hours of work and research – was prevented from spreading and becoming embedded at scale because bureaucrats at the State Board of Education could not stomach the fact that Burk and Ward had produced instructional materials without their input. This small-minded act would hold back the growth of an important model for schooling in a way that those public servants had not even considered.

Frederic would later go on to become president of San Francisco State University; but it was in 1914, when Frederic was president of the San Francisco State Teachers College, that he spotted the work of a new teacher in a run-down school in La Puente.

* * *

Carleton Washburne admired Frederic and was keen to accept the job offer that he made. Carleton left La Puente and headed to the San Francisco State Teachers College to work alongside Frederic Burk in an associated elementary school linked to the college. He spent five years at the school as head of science, whilst also studying for a PhD in education at the University of California, Berkeley, making Carleton one of the first ever recipients of a doctorate of education.

* * *

When woolly mammoths migrated across what is now modern-day Illinois in the last ice age, 12,000 years ago, the hunters who occupied that area used the Green Bay Trail to track and kill their prey, feasting on the plodding giants. The Potawatomi tribe continued to use the Green Bay Trail for thousands of years before the arrival of Europeans, when early settlers moved west towards Chicago. In 1832, the trail became an official post road by an Act of Congress.

In 1836, Erastus Patterson and his family arrived from Vermont and opened a tavern to service passengers on the Green Bay Trail post road between Chicago and Green Bay. The first houses were erected and the birth of the new village of Winnetka had begun. Winnetka, incidentally, means simply 'beautiful place' in Potawatomi.

The village grew into the affluent town of 13,000 inhabitants that it is today. Winnetka is now the second wealthiest town in the United States and at its heart stands the Carleton W. Washburne Middle School.

* * *

In 1919, Frederic Burk became aware of an opening for superintendent of Winnetka School District 36. He recommended Carleton for the role, and so began Carleton's leadership of Winnetka's schools, which lasted until he finally resigned in 1943 to help the war effort by opening schools for displaced children in occupied Italy.

Carleton now had the opportunity he needed to implement his ideas at scale. As superintendent, he was able to develop a new model for schooling and roll it out across all of the schools in the district. He called it 'The Winnetka Plan'.

The Winnetka Plan

Inspired by John Dewey's work at the University of Chicago Laboratory Schools and those formative experiences in the troubled La Puente school, Carleton set about developing a model for schooling that would bring success to all children. He drew on the teachings of Aristotle and the work that Mary Ward and Frederic Burk had undertaken on individualised courses, bringing together the most powerful aspects of these approaches into his new blueprint for education.

The Winnetka Plan set out a system of individualised instruction in an ungraded setting (no year group structure, mixed-age classes), which aimed to develop the 'whole child'. Carleton split the curriculum into two strands: the 'common essentials' (reading, writing, number skills, history, and geography) and 'creative group activities' (such as art, music, literature, and physical education). The grade work divided into specific tasks to be learned by each child individually. Subject material was arranged in a journey through the learning, with distinct steps to be taken. Only when pupils showed 100% success on tests could they move on to the next step in learning the subject. Carleton recognised that, in an Aristotelian model, the pupil would always be progressing at a pace unique to themselves and that Ward and Burk had already created the means to make this possible. The 'common essentials' tests could be taken at any time and the pupil could continue their journey towards what Carleton termed **'mastery'**.

Carleton was convinced that every single child could be successful in the 'common essentials' in this 'mastery model for schooling' because he could use Frederic's instructional and assessment materials to ensure that all pupils at all times could progress with minimal input from the teacher. Rather than putting 'gifted' pupils into higher-level classes, the pupils struggling with schoolwork were given special 'corrective' support to immediately address those individual problems. Most of the time, the struggling pupil received one-on-one help from a teacher. Carleton had finally created a means for freeing up the time that a classroom teacher needed to work in the tutor-pupil manner, so favoured by Aristotle and millennia of educators.

It was clear to Carleton that, rather than accelerating a small group of so-called gifted children, the purpose of schooling should be to ensure that every child is extended and successful.

The programme would present learning material in a logical and tested sequence, with the course broken down into small steps. After each step, the pupil is given carefully designed questions which test their understanding and knowledge. The materials are designed with complementary solutions and explanations such that the pupil receives immediate feedback, allowing both the pupil and teacher to notice and act in real time, rather than allowing deep-rooted misconceptions to go unnoticed and fester. This approach later became known as 'programmed instruction'. Carleton wrote, 'With the development of the achievement test movement, we may now make units of achievement the constant factor, varying the time to fit the individual capacities of the children.'

Henry Clinton Morrison was a contemporary of Carleton's working at the University of Chicago Laboratory Schools – the John Dewey-founded private school in Hyde Park, Chicago – who was particularly influenced by the Winnetka Plan. Morrison further developed the idea of immediate intervention, formulating 'a variety of correctives' which included 're-teaching, tutoring, restructuring the original learning activities, and redirecting pupil study habits'.

Morrison continued to test and iterate on the complete curriculum materials developed by Frederic and Carleton. He worked with numerous schools for many years, refining the model and producing more and more materials which could easily be adopted by schools at scale.

By the early 1930s, the model was becoming mature.

It is important to note that this 'mastery model for schooling' only applied to the common essentials, which Carleton believed were the bedrock of leading an autonomous and fulfilling adult life. The creative activities had no achievement standards: each pupil did as much or as little of these as they chose and no tests were ever given.

Carleton implemented the Winnetka Plan from 1921 across all schools in the district. He knew that changing a model of schooling is a significant task and would take several years to yield results – true education improvement takes time, intellect and commitment to long-term reform. He observed, measured, tweaked and improved the model year after year, with the help of Morrison and others. Attainment in Winnetka schools rose and rose and rose.

Soon, Winnetka and Carleton began to draw national attention. Not only was attainment rising, but pupil engagement and satisfaction also soared. For the first time, 'aptitude' was not defined as whether or not a child had the capacity to learn, but instead viewed simply as how long that child would take to learn. Every child would learn eventually, always. Increasingly, schools imitated the approach that Carleton had developed and **mastery** became a dominant model for schooling across much of the United States throughout the 1920s and 1930s.

The formulators and the validators

Benjamin S. Bloom passed away in 1999 at the age of 86 in Chicago, Illinois. I met him only once, but his enthusiasm and wisdom were immediately infectious. In his lifetime, his work became one of the single biggest influences on educational models and policy. In 1981, a survey of educators found that Benjamin was already a significant influence on curriculum structures and approaches to delivery. Unfortunately, this influence largely stems from his work *Taxonomy of Educational Objectives: the Classification of Educational Goals*, outlining a classification of learning objectives which he began writing in 1956, with many volumes to follow throughout his life. Known to most teachers as Bloom's taxonomy, this weighty tome was repeatedly reduced to a single pyramid diagram:

But the pyramid does not come from Bloom. It was first used as a presentation tool by an educationalist in the 1980s who was attempting to deliver a speech about Bloom's work and created the diagram as a way of summarising what he thought Bloom was saying. It is a gross oversimplification of Bloom's theories and a misrepresentation of what he proposed.

The tiers of the pyramid strike a chord with most people – they **feel** good – and so, as is so often the case in education, schools and teachers en masse implemented their own versions of the taxonomy from simply reading the titles on the diagram without once reading the book. The trouble is, Bloom's taxonomy in the form of the pyramid diagram, wonderful though it seems, is somewhat bunkum.

Many in education belittle Bloom because of 'that bloody pyramid', which sadly means that a large number of educators have gone no further with his work or even bothered to read the book that inspired it.

Regardless, *Taxonomy of Educational Objectives* is not Bloom's magnum opus. His greatest work lies elsewhere.

In the late 1950s and into the 1960s, Bloom became increasingly interested in the seminal work that Carleton had carried out some decades earlier and was keen to build on the success shown in those schools throughout the 1930s. It was in 1963, after reading an article by the Harvard University professor John B. Carroll, that Benjamin formulated a clearer view of Carleton's mastery model. Carroll's article 'A Model for School Learning' debunked the widely held belief that some children are good learners and some are poor learners. He argued instead that pupil aptitude more accurately reflects an index of learning rate. In other words, that all children can learn well but differ in the time that they may take to do so.

Of course, this was not a new way of thinking: Aristotle would have recognised it and it was a principle commonly held by Comenius, Herbart and Pestalozzi. And it was the bedrock of Carleton's work.

Bloom was encouraged by a model in which, if a child was allowed the right amount of time, and spent that time 'appropriately', then the child would always attain the required standard.

At around the same time, the American psychologist and behaviourist Burrhus Frederic Skinner had further developed Carleton's work and coined the phrase 'programmed instruction'. Other behaviourists took the work even further, creating a programme similar to Carlton's mastery model, with a focus on the role of feedback and individualised learning, allowing pupils to move at their own pace and receive instant feedback on their current performance.

It was Fred S. Keller in the mid-1960s who took the behaviourists' ideas and theories and applied them practically. The Keller Plan (often referred to as the Personalised System of Instruction or PSI) is reminiscent of the work that Frederic Burk and Mary Ward had carried out years before in that Keller and his team actually produced the instructional materials required to implement the approach with real pupils. Keller created written texts which were broken into units of content that were arranged so that the pupil engaged with prerequisite content, new learning, then elaboration of sufficient complexity as to be effectively infinite in its scope. The units would be studied at the pupil's own pace, much like the units that Burk and Ward had authored. Each unit required pupils to demonstrate that they were ready to proceed to the next. A proctor would certify whether or not the pupil had achieved the required level of understanding before moving on. These proctors were often teachers or other expert adults, but Keller also suggested that older, more expert pupils could act as proctors for their younger peers.

The nature of some of the key influential works that led Carleton and Benjamin to their formal setting-out of the model often leads to the misconception that a mastery approach is one in which the teacher plays a minimal role. Researchers have often read the individualised and self-paced nature of the work of Frederic Burk and Fred Keller, often with no teacher input, to imply that Carleton and Benjamin's models must follow suit. This could not be further from the truth. Both Carleton and Benjamin fundamentally recognised that in order to make a mastery model successful, the teacher – like an Aristotelian tutor – is the key.

* * *

The scene was set: Bloom was poised to formalise and codify mastery.

What followed in the coming decades was not only Bloom's true magnum opus, but also one of the most important lifetime's works of any educator to date.

A mastery model for schooling

Benjamin S. Bloom pulled together the essential features of the mastery model and spent much of his life refining the instructional and assessment materials, the pedagogies and didactics, and the methods of deploying the model at scale in a practical way (for example, through non-graded schools). He continually tested its efficacy and integrated advances in technology for achieving greater impact.

Just as Carleton was driven to develop the model by an emotional experience – teaching deprived children in La Puente – so too was Bloom determined that his work in education should achieve good.

Knowing that, while pupils may vary in their learning rate, all pupils could learn well given the right amount of time, Benjamin was heartbroken that what he saw around him was an education system that consigned the majority of the population to a life of subordination.

He knew that if teachers could allow the **right** amount of time for each pupil to learn and could provide all pupils with the appropriate conditions to learn, then every pupil could learn well.

Benjamin was a pragmatist. He knew that there was little point in an educational model that could not be embedded at scale; and in the US system of the day, that meant a system where pupils were taught in group-based classrooms. Looking around, he saw that schools would break curriculum journeys into small units, which would be delivered at the pupils and then tested. The results of these tests would be used to grade and rank pupils. The next unit would then be served up.

* * *

Giving a speech for Cambridge University some years back at the British Library, I described my sadness at the fact that England, in common with most Western countries, had firmly embedded what I coined as a 'conveyor belt model for schooling'.

The conveyor belt starts when children enter schooling. Identifying the age of the children, the conveyor belt serves up content determined correct for that class – these children are aged 8, so they get aged 8 content; these children are aged 14, so they get aged 14 content – regardless of where those individual children actually are in their development in learning the subject. This conveyor belt is rigidly expressed in national curricula and often strengthened by school inspection systems.

When a unit of content is complete and the pupils are labelled with a grade, the conveyor belt simply keeps on rolling. It takes no account at all of whether the pupil was successful in learning the unit or not; and because the conveyor belt cannot be stopped due to teacher fear of 'falling behind the curriculum', the pupil never again has the chance to demonstrate what they have learned or to put right those ideas they have failed to grip.

* * *

Benjamin noted the same sadness decades before as he observed that the end of unit assessment marked the end of the time that pupils were required to keep working on a concept or idea. The assessment, used only to rank and label, brought nothing at all to the learning of the pupil.

Just as Carleton had rejected the 'filter', Benjamin recognised (and proved) that this approach resulted in only a small number of pupils learning well.

He represented the population of pupils as having attainment very close to a normal distribution curve.

Bloom knew of the success of the Winnetka Plan. His friend J. H. Block had already been exploring the results of the Plan and would later report on the impact of the 1930s schools in his 1971 book, *Mastery Learning, Theory and Practice* (Block and Airasian, 1971). So, Benjamin set out to document and further refine Carleton's work. He knew that the model would have two key features:

1. The crucial, successful elements of one-to-one tutoring, which could be transferred to a group-based environment

2. The dispositions of academically successful pupils in a group-based environment

Excellence is never an accident. It is always the result of high intention, sincere effort, and intelligent execution; it represents the wise choice of many alternatives – choice, not chance, determines your destiny.

Aristotle

It was clear that both one-to-one tutor and classroom teacher could, if they chose, use assessments as real opportunities to enhance the learning process rather than to simply label pupils.

Washburne, Burk, Ward and Morrison had all shown that carefully designed assessment materials could be used to identify specific areas of misunderstanding. Furthermore, they had shown and developed 'correctives' that could be deployed by the teacher to close those gaps in knowledge or skill.

This is precisely how an expert tutor works with a pupil.

Bloom noticed that academically excellent pupils regularly follow up on their own mistakes that they have made on quizzes or assessments. They seek out their own correctives by asking the teacher to explain again and help them see where they have misunderstood. They often look up work again in textbooks, try questions over and over, search for other sources of information and repeat work so that they will not make the same mistakes in future.

Beginning to pull everything together, in 1968, Benjamin S. Bloom published a strategy that combined the use of feedback and corrective procedures, entitled 'Learning for Mastery' (Bloom, 1968).

The core elements of a mastery model

Aristotle himself would have recognised the features of the model. A mastery model has the following core elements (Guskey, 2010):

- Diagnostic pre-assessment with pre-teaching
- High-quality, group-based initial instruction
- Progress monitoring through regular formative assessment
- High-quality corrective instruction
- Second, parallel formative assessments
- Enrichment or extension activities

Diagnostic pre-assessment with pre-teaching

Key to learning a new idea is the underpinning knowledge that makes it possible to do so. In a mastery model, teachers use carefully designed questions, surveys, quizzes or activities to reveal the readiness or otherwise of each individual child in the class.

These questions are incredibly difficult to design, as Burk and Morrison discovered – each taking many, many years to refine their materials. But given that the body of knowledge for many subject areas is, in large part, unchanging, once the questions have been created, schools can re-use them. Question design of this type – where the question or activity itself is carefully structured to reveal misconceptions or knowledge gaps – therefore becomes a key skill for the profession as a whole.

Where gaps or misconceptions are identified, the teacher directly and purposefully teaches the individual or individuals the knowledge or skill that they are deficient in. The intention is to ensure that all pupils have the necessary foundations for new learning before the group teaching of a new idea commences.

Leyton (1983), Deshler and Schumaker (1993) and Vockell (1993) all confirm the positive impact of even a relatively brief pre-teaching for pupils whose prerequisite knowledge and skills are not secure.

When first beginning to implement a mastery model for schooling, teachers often express concern that those pupils who demonstrate they are ready to proceed with new learning could be held back by the fact that the teacher must spend time directly teaching pupils whose prerequisite knowledge is deficient.

This concern stems from teachers existing in a current system where concepts or ideas are limited in scope by national curricula or state-wide programmes of study. However, given that ideas are infinitely broad in their scope, it is appropriate for the pupil who is ready to proceed to spend time instead taking the prerequisite idea beyond the curriculum. In a mastery model, many pupils find that they spend a great deal of their time on what would, in a conveyor belt system, be thought of as extension or enrichment work.

A pupil's readiness to proceed would be determined by their attainment on the prerequisite quizzes or tests. Carleton had argued that pupils should attain 100%, but Bloom more reasonably set the threshold at 80% to account for normal human fallibility, which does not necessarily indicate a lack of understanding, knowledge or skill.

High-quality, group-based initial instruction

A mastery model for schooling emphasises the importance of engaging all pupils in high-quality, developmentally appropriate, evidence-informed instruction.

To ensure the highest chance of impact across a group of pupils, the instruction should be varied in approach, resource, task and metaphor. The subject-specific knowledge and pedagogy of a teacher is central to the success of a mastery approach, since they now need to have multiple ways of communicating and teaching each and every concept or idea. Teachers adapt their instruction according to the knowledge, skills, dispositions, and background characteristics of pupils.

The teacher models approaches to solving problems or addressing ideas. They also give pupils extensive materials for deliberate practice so that they are able to embed and consolidate what took place in the classroom.

Progress monitoring through regular formative assessments

The key reason that the teacher asks questions or requires pupils to undertake activities or tasks in the classroom (in their presence) is so that they can notice and act. The type of assessment does, of course, vary with subject; but at its heart, a formative assessment is any device that a teacher uses to gather information about an individual pupil's level of understanding.

The assessment process itself also serves to reinforce what is expected of the pupils, giving them the opportunity to identify what they have learned well and what they need to improve.

The teacher carries out formative assessment continually, using carefully designed questions, prompts, quizzes and so on. If they notice something about a pupil, they are then able to act and intervene immediately. It is this immediacy that drives the impact of the approach. Feedback is in the moment and contextualised. Rather than waiting a term or so and then administering an exam, teachers are noticing in real time the needs of the individual pupils in the class and immediately intervening through the use of high-quality correctives.

Regular, low-stake quizzes also provide pupils opportunities to practise and consolidate knowledge and skills.

High-quality corrective instruction

It should be self-evident that moving on with teaching an idea that relies on one or more other ideas that pupils do not yet understand will only result in failure, but as Bloom noticed, that is exactly what was happening (and it is still prevalent today in many education systems). A mastery model for schooling uses formative assessment extensively to notice gaps. The teacher then provides high-quality corrective instruction, designed carefully such that it will remedy the issue.

Correctives are not the same as simply re-teaching an idea, where teachers often deploy precisely the same practice to teach a concept, skill or knowledge again but more slowly. Re-teaching is ineffective because the approach did not work with the pupil before – they were not able to 'meaning-make' – and so it is highly unlikely to work as a repeat. Correctives are mindful of the way in which a pupil was taught a concept previously. The teacher considers their own practice, thinks about how they acted previously and then, with deep subject-specific pedagogical knowledge, is able to deploy different approaches to address the issue.

In a mastery model for schooling, whether a pupil is successful in learning or fails to grip an idea is not seen as a result of some inherent capacity to learn. Here, the pupil learning (or not) is an outcome of the teaching. All pupils can learn all things, given the right time and appropriate conditions – and those conditions include impactful teaching. So correctives are a key tool in the teacher toolbox. Clearly, there are great implications for teacher training, but I shall turn to those later.

Block, Efthim and Burns (1989) showed that corrective activities typically add 10%–20% more time to a learning unit than a teacher would predict (having previously been using a conveyor belt approach). This can be disconcerting for teachers when embedding a new model for schooling; but Bloom argued that this intense, individualised assistance, offered early in an instructional sequence, would drastically reduce the time needed for remediation in later units.

Again, this appears self-evident. When the teacher wishes to introduce new learning, the pupils will now be in a position that the prerequisite knowledge, ideas, concepts or skills are far more likely to be secure and able to be built upon. Thomas Guskey (2008) showed that initial instruction in later units can proceed more rapidly, allowing teachers to cover just as much material as they would do when using more traditional methods.

It is common that small groups of pupils within a class will have the same identified needs, which means that corrective instruction can often be carried out in small groups. Recent studies exploring tutoring have confirmed that one-to-three tutoring can be as impactful as one-to-one.

Again, the issue arises around what pupils who do not require corrective instruction will be doing while the teacher is engaged with those who do. This is where deep subject knowledge becomes important once more, so that there is an understanding within the teacher that any given idea, concept or skill they are teaching is infinite in its scope. One does not 'master' anything in life, but one can become increasingly more expert.

Although the '10,000-hour rule' does not really stand up to rigour, the idea behind it – that an individual must spend a very large amount of time on any given skill before becoming an expert – is a useful analogy here. Taking my own subject area, mathematics, it would be easy for a teacher in a conveyor belt system to convince themselves that a pupil can **do** some mathematical skill. For example, that a child understands counting. But counting is, for practical purposes here, pretty much an infinitely broad topic (for example, it is not unusual for first-year mathematics undergraduates to be taught the pigeonhole principle, which is essentially the same concept as counting but extended to a new height). Without needing to move on from the idea at hand, the teacher is able to extend pupils well beyond the demands of the year group or school curriculum, so there is **always** something for the pupils to be engaged with. As mentioned earlier, in a mastery model, most pupils will find themselves engaged in extension material at some point.

Similarly, most pupils will also find that there are occasions when they are in need of corrective instruction. This is to be celebrated. In a mastery model, there are no thick kids or bright kids. Because human beings meaning-make in different ways and the time to learn any new idea is a variable (even though all will learn in time), moving from learning unit to learning unit will typically see different pupils learn quickly and different pupils need support. Teachers explicitly tell pupils that making a mistake on the regular, low-stake quizzes, tests or activities is not a cause for dismay, but something to celebrate – 'I now know something new about you. That's fantastic. It means I can help you nail it right here, right now. You will always be successful in time.'

Second, parallel formative assessments

Unlike conveyor belt systems, where pupils get only one chance to show how well they have learned, in a mastery model, assessments are ongoing and everyone involved – teacher, pupil, parent – is aware that they help the pupil to learn well. Following corrective instruction, the teacher will carry out a further assessment of the pupil in order to work out if the new approach to teaching has had the desired impact. This gives the pupil a new opportunity to show they have learned well and the teacher a new opportunity to celebrate their success. If the pupil still has not gripped the idea, then the cycle repeats. Imagine the analogy of learning to drive – an excellent example of a mastery model – where the learner fails the driving test. They are not then consigned to the scrap heap; they try again, they learn again, they listen to different approaches and they take the test again (and again and again) until they have passed. Once they do pass, they are as valid as every other driver on the road. Teachers treat learning the same in a mastery model for schooling – all will pass eventually and when they do, we celebrate it. There is no penalty for taking more than one attempt to pass – these pupils deserve the same standing as the pupil who flew through the tests first time.

The driving test is also a useful analogy in highlighting the fact that the intention is not that a pupil masters a skill, but that they achieve a level of understanding or competence that they can reliably build new learning upon. We all know that passing the driving test does not indicate one has mastered driving! It is merely a step in becoming more expert at driving – a journey that continues throughout one's life.

Enrichment or extension activities

The cyclical nature of the unit delivery in a mastery model means that the teacher is engaged in different activities with different pupils – they may be teaching, assessing, correcting or stretching.

This means that teachers provide activities, tasks or questions that allow pupils to take the idea into much greater depth and well beyond the expectations of the statutory school curriculum.

These pupils gain additional insight into the subject and are able to build new schemata for exploring the idea. Learning is not a linear process and all pupils benefit from extensive deliberate practice and consolidation, which can also be part of the enrichment process.

This type of approach allows the teacher to remain within the same instructional sequence, but at the same time extend the learning to much deeper levels. The enrichment and extension activities take a great amount of time to devise and develop – it is a complex process to ensure that an enrichment activity is truly valuable. Again, this becomes the collective responsibility of the profession and these activities should form part of the professional body of knowledge for each subject area.

It is crucial that weak activities are rejected – having pupils who are ready to learn more simply biding their time on some superficial filler task disguised as enrichment is both damaging and morally objectionable.

A diagrammatical summary

In 2015, I produced a diagram to summarise the steps detailed above, which Oliver Caviglioli kindly made into a poster. The poster can be downloaded from Oliver's fantastic website: olicav.com.

The cyclical nature of the mastery model for schooling is even more evident in the diagram.

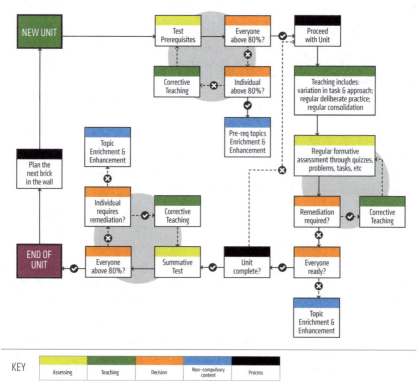

PART II
IMPLEMENTATION

Embedding the model

Benjamin S. Bloom had further developed Carleton Washburne's definitions to result in the list of core elements of a mastery model for schooling, which, in summary, are:

- Diagnostic pre-assessment with pre-teaching
- High-quality, group-based initial instruction
- Progress monitoring through regular formative assessments
- High-quality corrective instruction
- Second, parallel formative assessments
- Enrichment or extension activities

None of these elements, as a way of working with pupils, is necessarily impactful. It is in the combining of the elements into the cyclical model that brings about the impact. For example, a pre-assessment alone makes no difference to learning unless it is followed by an action. And similarly, formative assessments do not improve learning; rather, it is the action immediately **afterwards** that truly matters.

Each element is therefore like a tool in the teacher's toolbox, to be used at the correct time for the appropriate job.

As discussed earlier, both Carleton and Benjamin knew that the model would bring about the combination of:

1. The crucial, successful elements of one-to-one tutoring, which could be transferred to a group-based environment

2. The dispositions of academically successful pupils in a group-based environment

The core elements take one step to addressing the first point, but there is a final detail to be added: time.

Unlike a conveyor belt approach, which assumes time to be a given, in a mastery model for schooling time is **the** key variable. A teacher who plans a unit of work in a conveyor belt scheme will label that unit with a year group, perhaps the term or, worse still, the week and lesson number, and state how long that unit will last. The teacher is assuming that the instruction will be fully presented in the time stated and that it will be a result of the pupils' 'aptitude' as to whether they learn well or not. The teacher will then move on. This is compounded in many Western countries by the perception that a national curriculum is rigid and prescribed. During my time as a school inspector, I would often hear teachers talking about their concern that **they** were not keeping up with the curriculum, yet rarely hear teachers talking about whether or not the pupils were.

This conveyor belt approach is like the old joke:

A: I taught my dog to whistle.

B: I don't hear him whistling.

A: I said I taught him; I didn't say he learnt it.

The teacher is assuming that the unit of work, **presented at** the pupils in the allotted time, is sufficient. It isn't.

In a mastery model for schooling, since time is the key variable, teachers are no longer obsessed by what they have **taught**; rather, the focus is on what the pupils have **learnt**.

I have always viewed the words 'taught' and 'learnt' as synonyms – that is to say that, like Aristotle, I do not consider something to have been taught unless the desired learning has taken place. But conveyor belt approaches have falsely removed the connection between the two words, particularly in Western school systems, where it is common to find teachers talking about 'getting through the curriculum' as though it were some race to tick off a list of lessons.

In a mastery model, the viewpoint is very different: if a pupil has not learned what I, as the teacher, want them to, then the conclusion must be that my teaching has not yet been effective. So, celebrating the fact that the pupil has revealed their lack of understanding or skill, I notice that my practice did not achieve what I wanted it to. I look carefully at my own practice, like an outside observer, and question myself: what pedagogies and didactics did I deploy and how might I now change these? This means that, for every concept I am teaching, I must have multiple approaches available (or at least be able to find information about alternative approaches quickly and without burden) that I can pivot to as and when necessary.

There is, therefore, a significant need for teacher professional development to allow for the successful implementation of a mastery model for schooling. Teacher training should focus on ensuring that a subject teacher has multiple approaches for every concept they will be required to teach. This becomes the profession's body of knowledge. The canon of how to teach.

It is a long and complex process for a school or system of schools to change the embedded model. Carleton and Morrison understood this clearly and were patient in their work, taking over a decade to get to full implementation. More recently, countries such as Japan and Singapore have followed suit, working slowly and deliberately throughout the 1980s and 1990s to gradually shift their national approach to a mastery model. It is clear, given the scale of the challenge and the CPD implications, that the model cannot be implemented without first producing the courses, the assessments, correctives and curriculum structures. Furthermore, because teachers are required to have multiple approaches for the teaching of any given idea, concept or skill, the subject content and pedagogical knowledge of the workforce must meet these demands. Where cohorts of teachers have been trained in conveyor belt systems – which generally train teachers in just one approach for any given concept (or indeed provide no subject-specific training at all!) – the successful implementation of a mastery model for schooling will require the re-training of those cohorts.

This is a long but worthwhile process. A mastery model for schooling cannot simply be transplanted into a new system – it is a fallacy to think that one can end the school year in July, having followed a conveyor belt approach for decades, and then suddenly switch to a mastery model in September after a day or two of in-school training. Education systems – which are largely short-termist in their administration – often fall into the trap of cherry picking certain aspects of models, which they then attempt to implement in a superficial manner. Such attempts repeatedly fail. Rather, the implementation of a different model of schooling takes careful long-term planning, building slowly towards a move to a fully embedded approach.

A headteacher can, however, choose a long-term vision for schooling and move towards a mastery model. The starting point is to share the model (perhaps using the diagram above) with all teachers and to explore the cyclical nature of the approach. It is key that all teachers appreciate that all pupils can learn all things expected of them given the right amount of time and the appropriate conditions. This often represents a paradigm shift for many teachers as well as reframing epistemology itself. This is possible to achieve given the right professional development. In our 2010 work, 'Epistemological Transformation', Jean McNiff and I set out the strategies and processes we carried out in Qatar over a two-year period, which resulted in the shifting of teachers' (often deeply held) beliefs around the nature of knowledge and knowledge acquisition (McNiff and McCourt, 2010). We were lucky in that we had complete carte blanche to do what we knew would work and that the Supreme Education Council of Qatar (SEC) required every school in the country to take part in the programme. SEC was, and is, in the process of implementing 'Education for a New Era', a 30-year, long-term reform programme. With such a long-term approach, it is possible to ensure that the entire workforce receives sufficient professional development and that new entrants are trained in such a way that they arrive into the profession prepared for the chosen model for schooling. (In this case, the country was not choosing to move to a mastery model – there are many models of schooling which a country or system can try to adopt – which I felt was a missed opportunity.)

A countrywide adoption of a different model for schooling requires long-term, consistent support from government. The short-term focus of many governments around the world makes this impossible to achieve. However, at a smaller scale, an individual school or group of schools working together can take a long-term view.

Having shared the vision, a headteacher can begin the process of moving towards a mastery model for schooling by supporting their subject experts to build the body of knowledge required for their subject area. This is a laborious task if starting from scratch, which is why it is crucial to recognise that all of those intelligent questions, correctives, assessments and teaching approaches are already defined and exist within the teaching profession. The task is really one of collating the knowledge.

Subject experts need to know and have access to the entire journey through learning their subject.

Carleton Washburne was a science teacher and science is, largely, a hierarchical subject. This is true too of mathematics, grammar, languages, economics, the dispositions for studying history (though not the content itself) and some of the humanities. Hierarchical subjects are easier to define as a curriculum journey, but it is also the case that the less structured subjects can be plotted out for the particular country and school system in question.

Schools should not aim to reinvent the wheel; these journeys already exist and there is a moral imperative to act as a true profession, in which we use the professional body of knowledge that the workforce has created over time. We do, of course, build on this body of knowledge and continue to learn as a profession, but it is unwise for a school or group of schools or country to try to exist in a silo, ignorant of what has gone before.

With curricula defined in a way that ensures each new idea rests on top of the necessary foundations of prerequisite ideas, a unitised approach can then be plotted out and the correct starting point for any group of pupils diagnosed and defined. There are no hard and fast rules regarding how long each of these units might last – after all, time is the key variable – but work carried out by Bloom, Guskey, Kulik and others repeatedly points to units of between one and three weeks as being typical and impactful. These short units ensure that the teacher does not progress too far down the line before holding themselves to account and asking if their teaching is having the desired result.

The reason for this unitised approach is to carefully build new schemata in pupils' minds as the map of the subject is gradually revealed to them and they can make new connections, revisit ideas and build on their previous understanding, and to ensure that both factual and procedural knowledge are gained in the correct order to allow pupils to grip new ideas, ask questions and follow lines of enquiry and, in the broadest sense of the phrase, solve problems.

Turning to my own subject, mathematics, for a moment: I often describe the subject as being like one massive Jenga tower. Each brick in the tower represents an idea, concept, skill or leap in knowledge. It is glaringly evident that the main reason that pupils fail to acquire all of the knowledge expected of them by the end of schooling is not that the bricks at the top of the tower are somehow beyond them, but that the bricks lower down are loose, wobbly or missing entirely. Attempting to learn a new mathematical idea without the necessary foundations in place is pointless.

Carleton noted that not only did pupil attainment rise in the mastery model, but so too did pupil satisfaction and engagement. It feels good to be successful and human beings love to overcome, love to solve, love to learn something new. Success leads to motivation.

However, although curiosity seems universal in humans and the brain rewards us when a problem is solved (a quick hit of dopamine), thinking can be incredibly frustrating if the problem cannot be solved because the pupil does not have the toolkit to overcome it.

When pupils are learning a new idea, teachers must therefore ensure that the challenge is **just right**. There is no point whatsoever in asking pupils to carry out tasks if they have no way of becoming successful in time. The layers of the Jenga tower must be firm and secure before building on top, otherwise pupils will only become frustrated and damaged.

This is also true of problem solving. There is little point in asking pupils to engage in critical thinking if they have nothing to think about! The unitised approach that Carleton, Burk, Morrison, Bloom and others plotted out is designed to ensure that pupils have access to the background information required before engaging with a problem. They will draw on their long-term memory to engage with problems in a meaningful manner, which in turn will enable them to become more expert.

Becoming more expert

Carleton recognised that the study of an idea is, in practical terms, infinitely broad. One does not end learning; rather, an idea can grow and develop, make new connections and make new meaning as it is set in new schemata as a child acquires new knowledge of interrelated ideas.

For each idea or leap in understanding that a child is required to make by a curriculum, there is a never-ending journey of extension and enrichment that they can pursue. An idea is not 'mastered', but one does become more expert (and sometimes less expert – learning is not a linear process!).

Becoming more expert can be defined in terms of attention: as one becomes more expert, one does not have to attend to the idea as much. That is to say that a pupil can stop thinking so much about what they are doing with an idea that they have become expert in.

This is true of all learning. Rather than having to think, the brain uses the much less demanding process of drawing on the long-term memory. Because the pupil does not then have to attend to the new idea as strongly, they can turn that attention elsewhere and this allows the pupil to make new connections or take the idea way beyond the demands of a school curriculum document.

Take, for example, the process of commuting to work. Suppose this involves a drive through a city. When one first takes the drive, there is a lot of new information to take in – which way to go, what lane to be in, how the traffic flows, and so on – so the brain is engaged in thinking and the journey seems long and tiring. But, of course, as any regular commuter will know, it soon becomes the case that the journey seems to happen almost on autopilot. How many times have you arrived at work with almost no memory of the journey? This is because the brain is now using long-term memory, rather than thinking about the journey. Memory is a much easier process for the brain. The driver now no longer has to attend to the journey and so the brain can attend to other things: what's for supper this evening, making plans for the weekend, going over today's lessons and so on. The journey has been practised repeatedly and so no longer poses the brain any significant challenge.

As another example, consider a child learning to play the piano. She will spend a lot of time learning about the structure of the keyboard, the relationship between the keys, perhaps learning the scales and some simple melodies. At first, hammering out even the simplest of tunes seems an impossible task. The child must think incredibly hard to make her hands move in the correct way, to strike the correct notes, to keep in time. I guess most of us remember this feeling: learning to play 'Frère Jacques' as a child and the serious concentration it requires. She will knock out an awful rendition, thumping the correct keys eventually, but barely recognisable as the famous ditty. However, with practice and repetition, she gradually becomes more expert. Rather than thinking hard about where her fingers should land, she uses memory. This allows our fictional child to attend to other things, such as timing, perhaps using the foot pedal, and eventually even composing. And so the journey towards expertise continues.

Becoming more expert means the pupil is able to attend less to the idea and can progress in learning new ideas. They are committing factual and procedural knowledge to long-term memory, which can be retrieved with far less effort from the brain, meaning the expert appears to be able to carry out a task with very little effort. Committing knowledge to the long-term memory is vital if one is to be able to learn well.

Carleton knew that pupils arrived at school with differing levels of knowledge. The experience he had at the school in La Puente shook him to the core – he had never before witnessed such poverty, both financially and educationally. The pupils he met there were fundamentally different human beings to the ones he had grown up with. Here, the children had experienced a great deal less by the time they arrived into the school system. They knew fewer words, had visited fewer places, understood less about the world, did not have access to books, had never visited a museum or attended the theatre. He knew that his mastery model would, therefore, need to take careful account of the pupils' individual starting points and build from there.

This becomes the key challenge of the teacher in a mastery model: identifying the starting point and filling in the gaps. Carleton believed, and John B. Carroll later proved, that all pupils could learn well. All have the ability to commit to long-term memory the factual and procedural knowledge that is needed to unlock learning new ideas and concepts.

Figuring out how to get pupils to commit knowledge to the long-term memory then became a key question, and the answer forms a key component of the teaching profession's body of knowledge. It can be shown that knowledge and the ability to retrieve it from the long-term memory is a result of a pupil attending to a task. This seems obvious, but its importance is profound. Only by ensuring that a pupil pays careful and precise attention to a task will they actually think about the meaning of the concept, idea, problem or material. Ward and Burk were interested in getting pupils to really think, forcing the pupil to bring consideration of the facts or ideas to be learnt to their conscious thinking (generally referred to today as the 'working memory'). Carleton suggested that tasks must therefore be varied to promote as many thinking opportunities as possible. Repetition is also important, which is why Carleton built in the need for sustained, regular and deliberate practice.

A key characteristic of the expert is that they no longer have to think about a procedure in order to undertake a task; rather, they rely on the ability to retrieve the relevant knowledge and techniques from their long-term memory.

The unitised approach ensures that pupils have to think about ideas repeatedly over the years, giving additional practice and opportunities to learn more about the original concept in the framework of new schemata. This also gives new opportunities to commit ideas to the long-term memory, since it is very difficult to guarantee knowledge is stored following a single attempt.

Laying out the journey through a discipline in this unitised manner gives the teacher more opportunities to spot and act, filling in the gaps and creating new connections in subject matter for further depth of understanding.

Using the journey

So, subject leaders will now have at their disposal an entire journey through their subject and multiple approaches to tackling each concept, backed up with the relevant course and assessment materials (probably taking a couple of years to collate and refine). A headteacher taking a long-term strategy towards a mastery model for schooling can now begin the process of implementing the model in the classroom.

In parallel with subject leaders and their teams producing the journeys and materials, a headteacher will ensure that all staff are engaged with sustained, high-quality professional development targeted to their own subject-specific knowledge and subject-specific pedagogies and didactics. Much of this knowledge will already lie within the staff: individual teachers will have refined different approaches for teaching the same concepts, which they can share with each other, test (preferably through lesson study) and accept or reject from the canon. Of course, it is crucial to engage with other outside sources, such as research, books, debates, conferences, subject experts and associations. This CPD must be long term and focused on the impact it has in the classroom.

As these two parallel tasks begin to intertwine and mature, a headteacher finds himself positioned to begin implementation of a new model of schooling. Reaching this point takes a great deal of time, but the headteacher now has the following two strands:

1. Subject departments equipped with detailed course, assessment and corrective materials

2. Subject teachers equipped with the subject knowledge and pedagogical insight such that each teacher knows multiple ways of teaching every concept

Only when this point is reached can implementation begin.

It is obvious that the work involved here is substantial. For the initiative to be successful, a school or group of schools must have constant leadership from a driving force who is relentless in ensuring both strands are achieved. The Winnetka Plan was only possible because Carleton, as superintendent, was able to provide long-term vision and see it through with long-term leadership and delivery. Having these two strands in place is just the start of the journey. Carleton knew not only that he would need to create courses with the transferable ideas of one-to-one tutoring, but that it would also require pupils to have the dispositions of those who succeed in group-based models. These dispositions include being self-directed, seeking out new opportunities to learn, following up on misconceptions, determination and being open to trying again and again. In other words, for the model to work, the onus is not just on the adults in the school but also on the pupils: they must work really hard.

As schools move through the process of designing courses and training or re-training teachers, they must also develop pupils into, in many cases, quite different people. The pupil needs to know, understand and, crucially, believe that they can learn all things given the right amount of time as long as the conditions are appropriate. They need to be clear that these appropriate conditions include effort on their part. During the period of planning and development, headteachers can work carefully with all teachers, pupils and parents to shift the perceptions of those who believe that being able to learn well is somehow the result of luck of the draw. Learning is simply a result of thinking appropriately – so all pupils need to know that they must engage and think if they are to be successful.

Carleton noticed a huge change in the attitude of the pupils in Winnetka when they were exposed to this revelation. It might seem obvious, but pupils really do respond better to being told they will always get there in the end rather than being labelled as someone who cannot learn well.

The pre-implementation process described so far is likely to take at least two to three years.

For many headteachers, the leap of faith is just too much. With perceived pressure on school leaders to focus on annual high-stake test results and their position in league tables or comparison against largely arbitrary nationally set targets, many headteachers do not feel it is within their ability to take a sustained, long-term view. Without this, however, implementation is never successful.

PART III
LESSONS FROM COGNITIVE SCIENCE

Understanding the human mind

Throughout my years as an undergraduate, I lived with Steve – a lazy, disorganised social sciences student. I could never understand his aversion to hard work or his bizarre attitude to deadlines, but alongside his indolence, he was also charming, funny, kind and really good company. I liked him a great deal. One afternoon, Steve told me that he was going to be kicked off his course and would have to leave university because his main assignment for the term was due in a few days and he hadn't even begun to think about researching and writing it. This was pretty much the norm for Steve, who was completely dedicated to having a good time at the expense of any kind of academic experience that university might have to offer. So, not wanting to lose him and always up for a bit of madness, I offered to write his assignment for him. I had no idea about the subject matter or how to go about authoring a social sciences essay, but assumed it would be possible to overcome such trifling matters.

The assignment was to research and write an authoritative discourse on the phenomenon of homicidal somnambulism. I was instantly fascinated by the task and squirreled myself away in the library for 48 hours of research and writing. It struck me, as I read more and more about cases in the 1800s, that at the heart of the matter must be the very nature of sanity, psyche, thoughts, knowledge, morality and control. This led to me scouring the library for every book I could find that discussed the human mind. I had written a fair proportion of what would become the final document and had mapped out a clear way forward for the rest of the essay – I was making good progress and knew the assignment would be completed on time. But then, I stumbled across a book written in 1956 by Benjamin Lee Whorf: *Language, Thought and Reality*. I read the book cover to cover and was transfixed by Whorf's central thesis that the very nature of reality – our perception of the lived experience – was not fixed but rather that there are myriad realities. Whorf argues eloquently that the way in which we structure and use language deeply influences reality and our thoughts. Reading this book was the beginning of my obsession with psychology and cognitive science. The book begins with two warm up acts: firstly, a foreword by Stuart Chase; and then an introduction to the life of Whorf and his thinking by his friend, the American psychologist John B. Carroll.

John B. Carroll was born in 1916 in Hartford, Connecticut. He graduated summa cum laude from Wesleyan University, where he had majored in classics, before heading to the University of Minnesota as a doctoral student under the supervision of B. F. Skinner. Carroll pursued an interest in psychometrics and embarked on a lifetime of work that would add to the canon of knowledge that all teachers should know. And he did so in such a significant way that I consider Carroll to be the father of cognitive science as related to education and in its implications for classroom teachers.

Having read Caroll's introduction to *Language, Thought and Reality*, I spent the evening searching out and devouring other writings by him. And this is when I first met his 'Model of School Learning', an article written in 1963, in which he concisely and persuasively posits that all children can learn well if given the right conditions. Carroll's insight paved the way for the further development of the mastery model of schooling.

It was this random series of chances – living with someone so lazy and also happening to like him; his impending doom; my silliness of offering to do his work for him; the subject matter of the assignment; and the books that happened to be available to me over those two days in our library – which brought me to discover all of my education heroes: Carroll, Bloom, Block, Guskey, Skinner, Burk, Ward, Morrison and, of course, Washburne. For that, I am eternally grateful to my laid-back friend and his 'couldn't-care-less' attitude to deadlines. In return, I completed his essay, which he submitted to an unsuspecting, kindly old professor, who allowed him to stay on his course and enabled me to keep his amusing and surreal company for a little longer.

It is worth me pausing here to recommend to all teachers that they acquire a copy of 'The Carroll Model: A 25-Year Retrospective and Prospective View', which Carroll published in 1989. This phenomenal piece of writing is a must-read for anyone involved in education. Additionally, his 1993 tome, *Human Cognitive Abilities*, is a clear and exhaustive description of what was known at the time about how the human mind is structured and how it operates.

What we know about the architecture of the human mind – and how, in particular, the success or otherwise of both memory and retrieval can be influenced – can and should play a central role in how we design our schooling models, how we organise learning, how we schedule the revealing of a discipline over time and how we, as teachers, act in the classroom. The mastery model that emerged through Carleton's endeavours to improve educational outcomes for all quite rightly continues to evolve and improve as we learn more about learning. Being able to lever the benefits of a deeper and deeper understanding of human intelligence and cognition means we are able to continue Carleton's mission of educational improvement for every single child.

* * *

By taking Aristotle's one-to-one model of educating, where a tutor works with his pupil, Carleton Washburne was able to create the mastery model of learning. Central to these ideas, as demonstrated by Burk and Ward in the 1910s, was that all pupils can learn all content if they are starting at the right point and given the right amount of time. Morrison further emphasised the importance of considering all pupils individually with his introduction of correctives to Carleton's model in the 1920s.

It is critical that teaching should start from what the pupil already knows. The new learning will build on this and be just beyond already-embedded knowledge and understanding. This makes the mastery model of schooling incompatible with non-homogenised groupings of pupils. That is to say, mixed-ability and mixed-attainment classes where the gap between highest and lowest attaining is too large are anathema to the mastery approach.

All pupils can learn well

The mastery model espoused by Carleton stood the test of time and was generally accepted as being impactful, but it was not until Bloom picked up the story that the rigour of research and evidence was able to confirm what he had asserted those decades earlier.

Bloom was introduced to the idea of mastery and the potential impact by his friend, John B. Carroll. Carroll argued that all pupils can learn well given the right conditions. In 1963, he embarked on a lifetime's work to prove this was true. Carroll's 'Model of School Learning' showed that ability is simply an index of learning rate (Carroll, 1963). He also emphasised the importance of instructional design and resource design, which needed careful thought and planning if a pupil's attention was to be drawn to the relevant information and ideas.

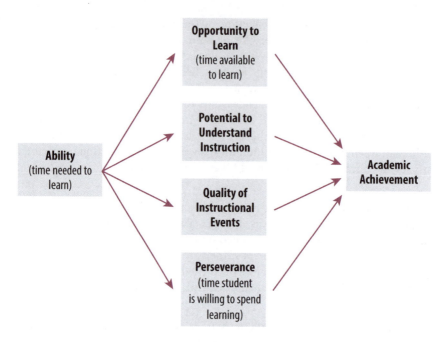

In addition to the quality and type of the instruction and materials, Carroll highlighted the same key ingredient that both Aristotle and Washburne had insisted on as being essential for learning to take place: effort.

The results of successfully implementing a mastery approach are profound, with much greater numbers of pupils learning well than previously. Carroll, Bloom, Block, Guskey and others find similar results: a significant shifting of the distribution of those who reach particular levels of attainment.

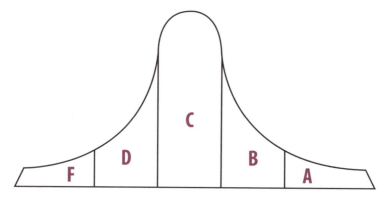

The distribution of attainment in a traditional setting broadly follows a normal curve; but in mastery settings, the distribution is significantly skewed towards greater levels of attainment.

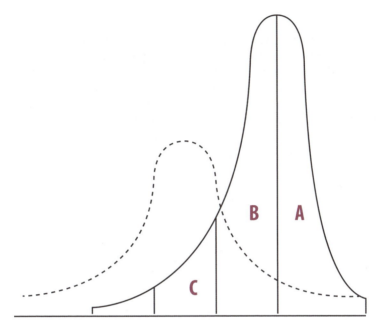

As discussed previously, we are interested in long-term memory. The challenge is to ensure that as many pupils as possible learn well. The mastery cycle describes the logistical issues in running the approach, but inherent in the approach is that all teaching results in learning. That is to say, all teaching results in such a change to the long-term memory that 'far transfer' is possible and likely. This must be the case in all 'learning episodes'. (I will discuss '**far transfer**' and the idea of a 'learning episode' later in this book.)

Later, I will explore some important and useful lessons we have learned from the discipline of cognitive science over the last century or so. But first, we must be clear with our language.

Establishing a common vocabulary

Many of the words we use in education are also commonly used in day-to-day language. This often results in confusion and mixed meanings. But the words we use in the science of education are well defined and have specific meaning. Before continuing, to avoid ambiguity, I will set out some key words and their definitions.

Learning

Learning is the bringing-about of some change in the long-term memory. When tasked with enabling a pupil to learn a novel idea, skill or information, as teachers we are concerned with changing their long-term memory. First of all, in terms of embedding the novel idea in the long-term memory in the form of some mental representation that can be thought about; and secondly, in assimilating this new mental representation into the schema of knowledge and ideas that already exists.

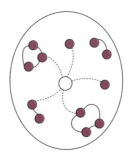

Attention

Dan Willingham's phrase 'memory is the residue of thought' is a handy reminder to us that we are seeking to change the long-term memory. But 'thought' is too loose a definition. When faced with, for example, a mathematical problem, scenario or task, a pupil may well be 'thinking' about it – but they may just be thinking, 'This is crap.' Instead, it is a very specific aspect of thinking that results in a change in the long-term memory: attention. Attention is focused and deliberate. We are interested in what pupils are attending to, not just what they are thinking about. When presented with a novel mathematical idea, we want pupils to be attending purely to the mathematics (or as purely as is achievable in reality) and the mathematical structure. We also want to draw attention to how the mathematical idea relates to knowledge they already have in their current schemata.

Giving attention is difficult; it requires focus and a belief that what is being attended to is important. This hard, deliberate process is how the long-term memory is changed.

Expert

Expertise relates to layers of attention. As one becomes more expert, one can attend to higher layers of attention. For example, when I was a child, I learned how to play the piano. When learning to play the piano, one needs to give huge amounts of attention to the position of one's hands, their movement, the pressure each figure is exerting, the meaning of musical symbols, and so on. As one becomes more expert at playing the piano, one can attend to higher-level aspects. Nowadays, when I play the piano, I have absolutely no idea where my hands are or what they are doing. I can attend to higher levels such as melody, composition or beauty. The process of learning is the process of becoming more expert. It is never ending; there is always more one can attend to. What a sad state of affairs it would be if, one day, one simply closed the lid of the piano and said, 'Well, that's the piano finished!'

Mastery is about becoming more expert, not about 'mastering' things. Crucial to the mastery approach is the recognition that there is always more to learn.

Fluency

We consider someone to be fluent in a technique, procedure, idea, concept or facts at the point at which they no longer **need to** give attention. It is important to note that fluency is simply the state of attention not being necessary in order to perform, but this does not mean that one couldn't, if one wanted to, choose to give attention. Considering the piano example again, although I don't know where my hands are or what they are doing (because I no longer need to give attention to that aspect of performing), I can **choose** to give attention to it. I might, for example, see another pianist do something with their hands and think, 'Wow, that's interesting, how did she do that?' I can then give deliberate attention to that lower-level aspect. Quite often, when learning mathematics, great new insight comes from choosing to give deliberate attention to an area of mathematics one is already fluent in. So, fluency is when attention is no longer necessary. Attention is hard; it is effortful. Fluency is effortless. When learning to manipulate algebraic expressions, for example, pupils need to give a lot of attention to the rules and conventions in order to carry about even simple rearrangements; but as they become fluent, this becomes effortless and they can attend to other, higher-level aspects such as what the underlying relationships between variables are.

Understanding

Let us imagine mathematics as a complex web of interconnected ideas.

Often, understanding is described in quite a woolly way. People will say, for example, it is the number of connections or the ability to use the idea in another area of mathematics. But understanding has a much more precise meaning.

The mathematics is **understood** if its mental representation is part of a network of representations. The degree of understanding is determined by the number and strength of its connections. A mathematical idea, procedure, or fact is understood thoroughly if it is linked to existing networks with stronger or more numerous connections.

Hiebert and Carpenter, 1992

Mathematical ideas are connected and, as pupils mature, they assimilate new ideas into their schemata in the form of mental representations. These representations form a map of mathematics that can continue to grow – there is no limit to the number of connections we can make. Understanding is about the reasons why the connections are true. Again, there is no limit to the depth of reasoning one can make, so understanding can be thought of as infinite.

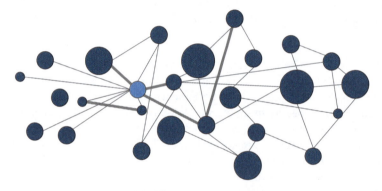

The depth and strength of the reasoning why connections are true is what we define as understanding. This has a beautiful corollary: understanding never ends; there is always more that we can understand about ideas.

Understanding is not a dichotomous state, but a continuum ... Everyone understands to some degree anything that they know about. It also follows that understanding is never complete; for we can always add more knowledge, another episode, say, or refine an image, or see new links between things we know already.

White and Gunstone, 1992

Near and far transfer

This web of connected ideas and the reasoning behind those connections enables pupils to address problems that are not isomorphic to the examples and problems they have worked on previously.

I shall use the term 'near transfer' to refer to a pupil's success on a problem that is similar in form to the examples they have been shown by a teacher or worked on independently. When a pupil can go further to recognise underlying principles in a problem, linking it to examples they have been shown or worked on but that appear different in structure to the new problem, and apply these methods to successfully overcome the new problem, then we can say they have 'far transfer'.

Far transfer is the key aim – it is when knowledge and understanding become truly useful. The pupil is able to deploy a learnt technique like a tool in their toolkit, using it on any problem of any type that they recognise the tool is suitable for.

Attainment

Attainment is the point that a pupil has reached in learning a discipline. It can change; pupils can unlearn as well as learn. It is not precise. But it is very useful in determining appropriate points on a curriculum from which to springboard pupils to new learning. We, as educators, continually assess these attainment points so as to best ensure the curriculum we are following can adapt and flex to what has been understood or forgotten. Knowing the prior attainment of pupils (rather than what has been previously presented at them) is crucial if we are to ensure pupils are learning appropriate new ideas and concepts.

Ability

Ability is an index of learning rate. It is the readiness and speed at which a pupil can grip a new idea. It can change: as with all human beings, pupils will make meaning from some metaphors, models or examples, more readily than they will of others. In mathematics, for example, we often see pupils quickly understanding some numerical pattern, say, but then taking a long time to grip a geometrical relationship. An individual can have a high index of learning rate during some periods of their life and a low one at others. Again, as educators, we are continually assessing ability so that we are best able to judge the amount of time, additional practice, new explanations or support that a pupil needs in order to really grip an idea. Knowing the ability of a pupil (rather than woolly ideas of engagement or enjoyment) is crucial if we are to ensure that pupils are learning new ideas and concepts for the appropriate amount of time (rather than some arbitrary amount of time presented on a scheme of work).

A common misconception is that pupils who are low attaining are also low ability. This misconception arises when 'conveyor belt' approaches to curriculum are deployed rather than a mastery approach. In conveyor belt systems, the focus is on coverage rather than learning. Teachers race through objectives and teach all pupils the same content as mandated by a scheme of work on any given week or day. This results in low-attaining pupils being asked to learn material they are simply not ready for. The gap from their true starting point to what they are being asked to grip is a severe handicap, so they appear to be slow learners. But, in a mastery approach, where we ensure that all pupils are learning the right level of content for the right amount of time, low-attaining pupils are being taught content just beyond their current understanding and so can assimilate and connect the new learning much more readily, leading to fluency and then understanding. When taught at the right level, all pupils can learn at pace.

Enquiry

Mathematical enquiry – asking questions as to the nature of the mathematical structures at play – can happen at any stage in learning mathematics. Pupils can specialise, conjecture, generalise, follow the logical implications of their thinking, test their hypotheses and pursue interesting, open-ended problems to a logical resolution through fluent use of mathematical thinking, skill and knowledge.

Inquiry

Mathematical inquiry – asking questions in to the nature of the mathematical structures at play – takes its natural prerequisite step of enquiry much further. In addition to enquiring, inquiry is a significant process of exploration, examination, discovery and the internal creation of additional insight. Beyond the generalising stage that enquiry can result in, inquiry demands more: it is not enough to find a resolution; inquiry additionally consists of robust and defensible reasoning as to why connections and relationships hold true; and then, critically, inquiry includes a period of reflection, during which the inquirer notices how they have changed as a human being as a result of the substantial thinking and growth that inquiry demands. Because inquiry includes reasoning and reflection, it necessarily requires mathematical maturation. We shall discuss the maturation process later in this book, but suffice to say here, this means that inquiry cannot happen at any stage – the implication is that inquiry cannot occur with novel ideas.

A brief discussion on
mixed ability vs mixed attainment vs setting

It is central to the idea of a mastery model of schooling that time is the key variable and that all pupils are able to move through the learning of a discipline at pace because they are working at the right level of demand. An implication of the mastery cycle – with its aim of ensuring every pupil grips every idea through careful instruction, diagnostics and responsive correctives – is that the groups do indeed become highly homogenised. The implementation of the mastery model from the very start of schooling removes the need to debate how to react when attainment gaps are large – they have been removed by design.

However, given that many readers of this book will not be in a position to implement approaches from day one, it is worth taking a moment to pause and consider why the arguments around the grouping of pupils are so fierce and what the implications might be.

The discussion around how to group children when learning mathematics is as old as maths teaching itself. It is quite right that we should ask which is more impactful. Numerous studies and meta-studies have looked at the question and there is a wealth of published research on the issue. What does it find? Well, broadly, that there is little difference in outcome. Some studies suggest a slight improvement for low-ability pupils in mixed-ability groups; some suggest high-ability pupils achieving worse results. Some suggest high-ability pupils doing better in setting, with low-ability pupils doing worse. Some highlight the common practice of 'teaching to the middle' in mixed-ability classes. Some studies show no impact at all. It is fair to say the broad picture of evidence in the debate is really rather fuzzy and the evidence certainly weak.

The main weaknesses in the data come from the tendency of studies in this area to conflate very different issues. Most studies looking at ability grouping combine the practice of setting with other, non-analogous, practices such as streaming and other groupings. Prima facie it is clear that setting and streaming are in no way relatable for the purposes of a robust study. The second weakness is the common practice of carrying out these studies without considering the subject-specific nature of pedagogy, didactics and hierarchy. Studies tend to look at pupils across many subject areas, rather than commenting on the differences within studies. Where studies have gone further – for example, Ireson and Hallam (2001), which looked at mathematics separately – the results are often quite different (in this particular case, showing setting improves outcomes in mathematics slightly).

There are some interesting studies underway, including a particularly notable one in the UK funded by the Education Endowment Foundation (EEF), which should bring some more clarity to the subject-specific part of the debate (though perhaps not to the differentiation between setting and streaming, which would be a great shame). This will make for interesting reading when the study reports back.

For the moment, though, the evidence remains pretty much as it has been for a couple of decades: mixed and unreliable.

So, why change?

In England, from the point of coming to power in 1997, the Labour government repeatedly published commentary stating that schools should set children by ability unless there were extraordinary circumstances to justify mixed-ability teaching. So strong was the belief in the efficacy of setting, both in terms of attainment and social justice, that Labour asked the school inspectorate, Ofsted, to penalise schools where mixed-ability practices were deployed.

The government published statements making clear their belief that mixed-ability teaching can work, but only in cases where the teachers delivering were exceptionally good at doing so. For over a decade, the government maintained its view and made clear its beliefs to all schools. It is no surprise, then, that the majority of maths lessons in England's secondary schools occur in setted classes. As a result, most maths teachers have learned their craft in teaching mathematics in non-mixed-ability classes. The workforce is set up to teach groups of children set by ability.

Given there is no new evidence to suggest a system shift towards mixed-ability teaching, it is curious that the notion is gaining traction. It is even more curious that some proponents of mixed-ability teaching are including in their justification for doing so a description of a mastery approach, failing to mention that all successful implementations of a mastery model of schooling have included grouping pupils based on their current level of attainment. In many examples, such as those that Washburne and Bloom worked with, this included further steps to even more closely homogenise groups by operating non-grade settings. In non-grade settings, pupils can be set across age groups, giving schools even more scope for creating groups with narrower attainment gaps. Many jurisdictions, today and historically, have achieved these elements of non-grade settings by not allowing pupils to graduate from one year group or grade to the next unless they can demonstrate they have fully gripped the necessary ideas to make such a step up successful.

Throughout my career as a maths teacher, I taught some classes that were setted by attainment and some classes that were so-called mixed ability. I loved every minute of it. It was by pure luck that the first school I landed in as a trainee teacher was a utopian, hippy kind of place. The maths department (by far the best maths department I have ever known) was staffed by huge intellects, all of whom were over the age of 50. Their combined knowledge on the teaching process was immense. Classes were truly mixed, which meant I had to learn how to deliver mathematics lessons with the lowest-attaining and highest-attaining, lowest-ability and highest-ability pupils all in one room. It was a blast. The intellectual challenge was huge and I relished it. Every member of the maths team truly believed in mixed-ability classes and had become masterful in their practices and pedagogies specific to mixed-ability teaching to ensure they had high impact. Those are the pedagogies and practices I developed too and I remain thankful for that.

The Labour government's claim that mixed ability is only impactful with very specific types of teachers resonates with me. I have watched so many teachers being forced to teach mixed-ability classes without having had suitable professional development and time to develop necessary practices, and it has always resulted in sub-optimal lessons. Often a complete waste of time for everyone involved. As a young teacher, this used to upset me greatly, wondering why the outcome was so bad. Of course, as one learns more about teaching, one comes to realise that shoehorning a teacher into a pedagogy is always a disaster.

Social justice

An oft-wielded argument in support of mixed-ability teaching is the 'education for social justice' angle. I loved that my mixed classes were not segregated, loved that my pupils had equality of opportunity, loved the social interactions and what, as a young teacher, I believed to be the removal of stigma. But the social justice argument just doesn't stand up to scrutiny. Real social justice comes from becoming learn'd, from becoming autonomous and being able to lead a purposeful and meaningful adult life.

Yet, the evidence tells us that mixed-ability practices don't result in greater gains in terms of achievement at the end of schooling.

But what about those pupils who would be placed in bottom sets? Surely they feel more included and less stigmatised? Yes, some do. But, also, some don't. Where mixed-ability teaching is forced upon teachers who have not developed necessary practices, the tendency to 'teach to the middle' leaves the lowest-attaining and lowest-ability pupils adrift, alienated and, most importantly, unable to learn. This returns us to the Labour government argument of mixed-ability teaching only being defensible with appropriately skilled teachers.

And what about the highest-ability pupils? Clearly, 'teaching to the middle' fails them. But, I have seen many mixed-ability classes where high-ability pupils are stretched and challenged because the teacher has sufficient subject knowledge and developed pedagogies to enable them to take a mathematical concept further and deeper than the aspirations of the national curriculum. This is wonderful to watch. Sadly, this is not common practice for two reasons. Firstly, most teachers have been trained to teach in a setted situation, where it would appear on first look that the content can be constrained to a fairly narrow inspection (more on that fallacy later). Secondly, the subject knowledge of teachers is not always sufficient to understand how to stretch a concept. This latter point is driving some of the worst practice I have witnessed in England's schools, which is also a result of official bodies erroneously spreading the myth that all pupils should learn the same content, namely the practice of keeping high-ability pupils on mundane work for months on end. An increasing number of teachers and parents are telling me about their frustration at this practice, with many going further to say that officials have told them they are 'not allowed' to let the pupils progress further up the curriculum no matter how secure they are in the concepts they are being kept on. We do, of course, want to give pupils as many opportunities as possible to behave mathematically, so once an idea has been gripped, it is desirable to give the pupil opportunities to explore the concept further and more deeply, making connections and solving problems. But there is a point where pupils should move on. The idea that all pupils should be kept on a concept arbitrarily is simply wrong.

So, the social justice argument doesn't appear to be the driver either. After all, the Labour government was very committed to education for social justice too.

Ability or attainment

There is a current movement arguing that the term 'ability' is damaging and should be replaced instead with 'attainment'.

There is a slight problem with this argument: as discussed earlier, the words don't mean the same thing.

Emotive language is used to try to advance this mind-numbing claim, with some people asserting that the word 'ability' is 'dangerous'.

This attempt to redefine language is a common tactic when trying to create a deliberate dark age and gain control for ideological reasons.

The greatest problem with the mixed ability vs setting debate is the fanatical tribalism of those at the extremes of both sides (sides that the evidence suggests there isn't a modicum of difference between). Trying to discuss mixed ability or setting is often difficult because the debate is shut down by no-platformers, who will not accept any challenge to their beliefs, no matter how unsupported by evidence they are. Using words like 'dangerous' is a way of shutting down debate. Who would want to be a 'danger' to children?

Ability is not a dangerous word; it is a very helpful one. As is attainment. The difference between these words, in an education discussion, is really important and formative.

Current attempts to abolish the word 'ability' from education's lexicon are deliberate in trying to remove nuance from the debate. The fanatics do not like nuance.

All classes are mixed attainment and mixed ability

One issue with the practice of setting pupils is the assumption that those setted classes are now homogenous. They are, of course, not. Setting is merely a way of narrowing the attainment range within a class. With a narrower attainment range, teachers may focus their attention on fewer aspects of a concept and spend a greater amount of time with a greater number of pupils on the crux of the matter. The class will still contain pupils who need to access the concept at a lower entry point and those who have already gripped the focus of the lesson and can be stretched further in their thinking. The teacher must still be aware of the prerequisites and the possible areas for extension. The narrowing of the attainment range is a mechanistic way of maximising teacher focus. The range of abilities in the class is also always present in setted classes. Pupils will grip ideas at different speeds through different metaphors and explanations. This is true of the highest attaining and of the lowest. A common misconception is that pupils in low sets have very similar indices of learning rate. They don't. There will still be pupils who grip ideas very quickly because the ideas are being pitched at the right level for the pupils and the examples or models have resonated. Similarly, there will be very high-attaining pupils in the top set who take a long time to grip an idea because the way in which it has been communicated has not allowed them to make connections to already known facts and ideas. The teacher must be aware of these attainment and ability ranges when working with pupils arranged in sets. The effective mixed-ability teacher appears to be more alert to these differences; the ineffective mixed-ability teacher ignores them and teaches to the middle. There are pros and cons in both approaches.

The impact of attainment range

Advocates of mixed-ability teaching will often argue that the attainment gap does not matter – it can be any size. This is easy to dismantle reductio ad absurdum: would one advocate a class containing an individual who cannot number bond to ten and another who is red hot at advanced Fourier Analysis? Of course not, so there is a range where the defence falls apart. The debate is really about how wide that gap can be and still maintain efficacy with a highly expert teacher. Those who refuse to engage with the nuance of the debate, choosing instead to maintain a fanatical stance of insisting the range can be of any size, serve only to weaken the argument for mixed-ability teaching. I see many schools addressing the issue through logistical solutions such as having a top set and bottom set, but then six mixed-ability classes between. This hybrid approach is a way of taking some account of the normal distribution nature of a year group. I would welcome research on these hybrid approaches so the impact can be better understood.

How big can the range be? This is really the question. We know that all classes are actually mixed attainment and ability, and that setting is simply a way of reducing the attainment spread to bring about efficiencies for teaching. The typical attainment range in mathematics at aged 11 in England is seven years of learning. Every secondary teacher knows this; we all know 11-year-olds who can do some pretty sophisticated mathematics and some who can't yet count to ten reliably. Should these pupils be in the same class? Should these pupils be forced to be in the same class with a teacher who does not subscribe to the approach and has not been trained to be impactful in such a setting? Is it possible to be impactful across all pupils when the attainment range is seven years? These are the questions schools need to ask.

Thinking of changing?

The outcomes in both mixed ability and setting can be great. The outcomes in both can be awful. It is the practices, structures, logistics and pedagogies that bring about efficacy or not. But do not for one minute believe there is any requirement upon you and your school to change. There isn't. The national curriculum is quite clear in its aspiration that the majority of pupils should learn the same content. Of course they should. The population of pupils is a normal distribution, so the majority around the mean are broadly similar in both attainment and ability. But majority simply means any number larger than 50%. Not all. There are many, many pupils who should be learning different materials, either because they are not yet equipped to learn the material of the majority or have far surpassed the majority.

I really loved teaching mixed classes. But I have a pedagogy and you have a pedagogy and they are not the same and they do not have to be the same. If, as a whole maths department, you decide you want to teach your classes in sets, do. If, as a whole maths department, you decide you want to teach your classes in mixed-ability groups, do. But, with either of these decisions, it is crucial that you understand and take seriously the huge burden of professional learning that must come first. Just like moving your model of schooling from conveyor belt to mastery, moving from setting to mixed or mixed to setting takes years of careful planning, dedicated professional development, resourcing, profound changes to pedagogy and an adherence to the principles of making the model work effectively. Sadly, I increasingly come across schools where a grand pronouncement has been made – 'From September we will move to mixed-ability classes' – without a single thought for the consequences. A school making such a significant change to their model of schooling without the required focus and effort of the years of professional development it takes to transition successfully is simply setting teachers and children up to fail. When I meet headteachers who tell me they are changing to mixed ability at the start of the new school year, I always respond, 'Wow, that's amazing. The commitment and forethought you must have given this five or six years ago and the funding you must have invested in all of your staff over those years to develop their pedagogical approaches sufficiently is really commendable. Can you tell me about it?' Those headteachers who look at me sheepishly and reply 'We took the decision last week and will have a few days professional development in the summer' really have no right to be leading a school.

Parental views and better evidence

The evidence in support of setting or mixed is highly varied, highly unreliable and tells us nothing of value. For every report supporting setting, another supports mixed. The methodology behind the research is very often designed to find precisely the outcome that the researcher or the funder of the research wished to find. The argument around how to group children is so fiercely driven by deeply held ideologies that it is almost impossible to unpick anything useful from the research.

The ideological beliefs surrounding the grouping of children are also strong in the population of parents. It is important for schools to understand the position that the parent body holds if they are to transition smoothly from one model to the other.

Schools can survey parents and prospective parents to garner their opinion.

As a quick litmus test, I posted two polls on Twitter. Clearly, such polls do not stand up to rigour since no attempt is made to stratify the sample or account for social media presence and following. However, the sample size is large enough to at least begin a discussion.

Which grouping policy would you prefer for your own children in mathematics lessons?

32% Mixed ability

68% Setting

1722 votes · Final results

When given only the option of mixed ability versus setting, a significant minority of parents voted for mixed.

PARENTS: HOW WOULD YOU PREFER YOUR CHILDREN TO BE GROUPED IN MATHS LESSONS?

Please retweet for large sample.

12% Mixed ability throughout

27% MA then sets from Year 4

45% MA then sets from Year 7

16% MA then sets from Year 10

669 votes · Final results

But when given a slightly more nuanced choice, support for a completely mixed-ability approach plummets. There appears to be a strong belief that there is a right time for pupils to be set in mathematics lessons. This is certainly the feedback I have received from parents over the years too.

The debate around how to group pupils will, undoubtedly, continue for many years to come (and perhaps will never be resolved), particularly while the research into the issue remains so unreliable.

I have a set of tests that I believe a study into mixed ability vs setting should be required to pass before it can be considered credible:

1. The study must not conflate grouping types. Setting, streaming, banding, in-class grouping, etc. cannot be treated as a single case.

2. The study must be subject specific. Hierarchical subjects and non-hierarchical subjects cannot be measured together. Individual subjects must be investigated separately.

54

3. The study must take account of teacher quality. A study that claims to find impact of mixed ability or setting by treating such impact as univariate is of no value. The issue of pupil outcomes is complex and the study must be multivariate.

4. The study methodology must be designed by a disinterested party. A proclivity towards either mixed ability or setting biases methodology design.

5. The study must be funded by a disinterested party.

6. The study must stratify results on the basis of the attainment gap that exists in the observed cases and look at variance in outcomes.

7. The study must include analyses of teacher demographics in the case study institution, particularly experience level of subject management.

8. The study must report on prior grouping practices encountered by the pupils and timeframes in shifting to the current model.

9. The study must report on length of experience case study teachers have in teaching particular grouping types.

Research into this issue has not yet met these tests. Studies almost always conflate grouping types and combine results from different subject areas. Crucially, studies have not taken any account of teacher quality, which I view as the single most important variable at play here. Researchers often object that designing studies that address the issue of teacher quality is too difficult to achieve, particularly given the challenges of generalisabilty from small-scale experimental design. But, without addressing this issue, the claims made by such studies are farcical. A complex, univariate issue cannot be distilled to a simple sound bite focused on one variable.

In discussion about this issue, Dylan Wiliam commented: 'I actually think that it is difficult to overplay the issue of teacher quality, since the impact of teacher quality is likely to be an order of magnitude greater than the effects of ability grouping policies.'

I hope that the research community will, at some point in the future, be able to provide the teaching profession with better-informed, multivariate analyses on the issue of how to group pupils for the greatest gains. Until then, schools should ensure any move they choose to make reflects the requirements of the families they serve and is supported thoroughly with pre-emptive, significant professional development over a substantial time period for all teachers who will be involved in the change.

From the perspective of this book, the issue of grouping fades away. When a mastery approach is adopted and fully embedded from the very start of schooling, the diagnostic and responsive cycle of the mastery model results in groups of children becoming highly homogenised, with the teacher ensuring that no child is left behind. This homogenisation of pupils ensures, with expert teaching, that all classes can move through the learning of a discipline at pace and with success. This success drives motivation and the cycle becomes virtuous.

For schools considering the move towards a mastery model of schooling with older pupils, it is a case of carefully working out the broad starting points of each pupil in the cohort and then grouping the pupils such that the attainment gap is not too great. These groups can then be treated as normal in the mastery cycle, but with the teacher ever mindful that pupils' ability and attainment is not fixed and may require the fluid movement of pupils between groups.

Types of professional knowledge

Many teachers enter the profession with high levels of subject content knowledge. This knowledge is connected to, but not the same as, subject-specific pedagogical knowledge. Knowing how to bring about learning is complex and requires many years of professional learning to acquire. Some of this knowledge can be studied, reading the best evidence (**propositional knowledge**); some of it can be acquired through hearing about practice – perhaps a teacher giving a presentation at a CPD event (**case knowledge**); and, most importantly, some of this knowledge only comes about by teachers experiencing events themselves (**strategic knowledge**). This strategic knowledge involves teachers thinking about and considering propositional and case knowledge, which they then develop further based on actual practice in real classrooms.

What is set out in here has had to pass the test of the three types of knowledge. Propositional knowledge is incredibly useful and stimulates professional enquiry, but many aspects of education research cannot be replicated beyond laboratory conditions, so, although theoretically interesting, those ideas do not form part of the mastery approach. I have chosen to include in this book only testable ideas that are able to be applied to real classrooms and that I have had first-hand experience of in real schools with real pupils.

The importance of effort

Both conceptual understanding and procedural fluency are necessary in learning mathematics, but they are not sufficient. As Kilpatrick et al. (2001) remind us, pupils must also have strategic competence (the ability to solve problems), adaptive reasoning (the capacity for reflecting and reasoning, which leads to understanding) and, critically, productive disposition (a belief that one's own effort matters)

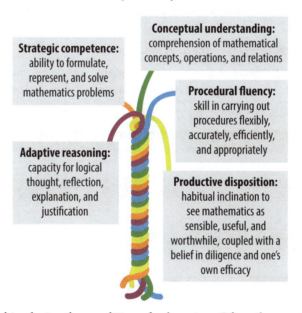

Interrelated and intertwined strands of mathematical proficiency.

Strategic competence: ability to formulate, represent, and solve mathematics problems

Conceptual understanding: comprehension of mathematical concepts, operations, and relations

Procedural fluency: skill in carrying out procedures flexibly, accurately, efficiently, and appropriately

Adaptive reasoning: capacity for logical thought, reflection, explanation, and justification

Productive disposition: habitual inclination to see mathematics as sensible, useful, and worthwhile, coupled with a belief in diligence and one's own efficacy

These combined give the conditions for learning. Often the most important of these – effort – is shied away from to great detriment. Schools avoid honest conversations with pupils and parents, yet it is this honesty that can bring about huge gains in learning. Families and pupils need to understand that their success is a result of their effort and their failure is a result of their laziness. A pupil can have the worst teacher, be at the worst school, and have shoddy books, yet still learn well because they put in great effort. Conversely, a pupil may attend the best school in the world and be under the instruction of an amazing teacher who uses the very best materials, yet completely fail to learn because they expend no effort. Effort matters. A lot.

Washburne's mastery model was based on the teachings of Aristotle. Central to the model is the recognition that effort matters and, further, that pupils understand that it is their own effort that determines their success.

Where pupils recognise this, the impact is profound. Generally, in Western countries today, pupils and families have surrendered their agency. Pupils routinely blame their failure in a lesson or on a task or test on their perception of the quality of the teacher, rather than realising they are the key driver.

Attitudes and beliefs around which factors influence success vary wildly around the world.

Mindsets eclipse even home environment in predicting student achievement.

Predictive power by catergory of variable by region, % share

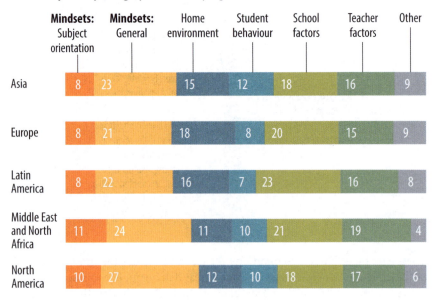

From McKinsey Analysis, OECD PISA (Dorn et al., 2015)

Where pupils understand that the main factor in success is their own effort, the impact on attainment is significant. A McKinsey analysis (Dorn et al., 2015) of attainment against self-efficacy showed pupils in the most disadvantaged circumstances, and who believe their own effort is key, outperform pupils in the most advantaged settings who believe success is a result of external factors.

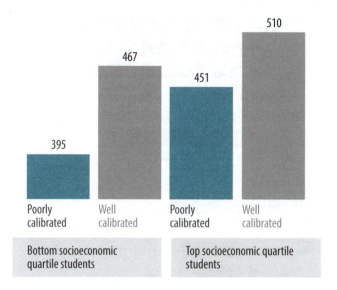

From McKinsey Analysis, OECD PISA (Dorn et al., 2015)

By examining subsets of pupils who have undertaken PISA tests, John Jerrim found that children of East Asian descent attending Australian schools far outperformed those of Western European descent. In his paper 'Why do East Asian children perform so well in PISA? An investigation of Western-born children of East Asian descent' (Jerrim, 2014), Jerrim concludes that the hard work ethic of these children is a key factor in them outperforming native pupils by two and a half years of learning. This conclusion is similar to that of Feniger and Lefstein (2014).

Figure 2. Average PISA maths test scores: a comparison of second-generation Australian immigrants to children in other countries

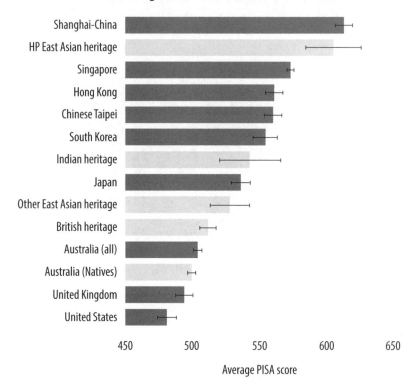

Figure 2 from Jerrim, 2014

The Nuffield Foundation research paper 'Values and variables: mathematics education in high-performing countries' (Askew et al., 2010) again points to the importance and impact of a culture of self-efficacy.

This belief in hard work and the transformative impact that effort makes is central to the mastery approach. It is therefore incumbent upon educators to be direct and honest with pupils and their families that they play an active (not passive) role in their learning.

Blending approaches

Mastery is an entire and complete model of schooling. There are many models that exist, having varying degrees of impact both in terms of the currency they give to pupils (school grades) and long-term engagement in a subject or discipline (for example, whether or not pupils pursue mathematics at higher education or enter mathematical careers later in life). Much debate occurs around which model to adopt.

Two models that might be seen as being at the extremes are inquiry learning and teacher-directed instruction. At the extremes of these lie discovery learning and direct instruction (here I take 'direct instruction' to mean the scripted intervention programme arising from Project Follow Through (Engelmann, 2007)). Advocates of both often take the view that the approaches are mutually exclusive. Washburne rightly understood that education is nuanced and rarely are such fanatical positions helpful.

It has long been an element of the mastery cycle that instruction is varied in order to allow as many opportunities for meaning-making as possible. The approach very much embraces teacher instruction, but also includes time for inquiry. It can be shown that, at the extremes, direct instruction does indeed lead to good outcomes in terms of pupil performance on tests, but not optimal performance. As models move towards teacher direction in all lessons, performance passes a plateau and begins to reduce.

Impact of teacher-directed instruction
Average PISA science score with different amounts of teacher-directed instruction

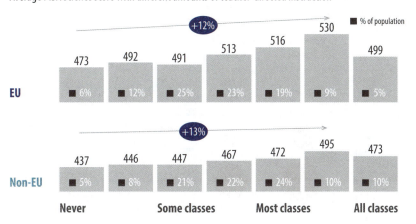

From McKinsey Analysis, OECD PISA (Dorn et al., 2015)

Equally, by increasing the opportunity for pupils to undertake suitable inquiry, performance initially increases, but quickly begins to worsen.

Impact of inquiry-based teaching
Average PISA science score with different amounts of inquiry-based teaching

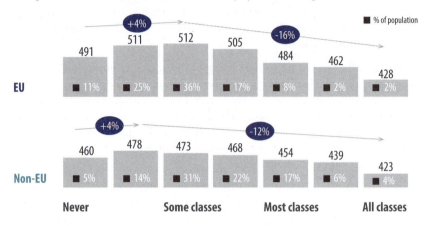

From McKinsey Analysis, OECD PISA (Dorn et al., 2015)

By blending both direct teacher instruction and appropriate opportunities for inquiry, pupil performance increases.

Impact of teacher-directed and inquiry-based combinations
Average point increase in Europe PISA science relative to baseline

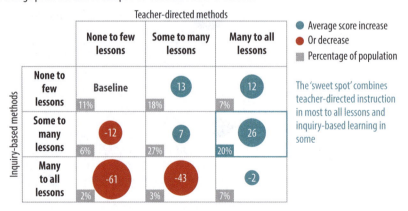

From McKinsey Analysis, OECD PISA (Dorn et al., 2015)

We are seeking to strike a balance between teacher-directed methods and inquiry methods. Getting the recipe right consists of several key considerations – namely: the type of instruction in each, the order in which the instruction happens, and the ratio of the methods used.

The pedagogic choices made when phasing teaching have a significant impact on pupil outcomes.

The importance of knowledge

As discussed, inquiry is a critical element in learning mathematics. It is the stage where reasoning, conjecturing, generalising and reflecting occur. These are all important in revealing underlying relationships and bringing about understanding, which greatly increases likelihood of long-term recall.

Unfortunately, inquiry is often conflated with 'discovery learning', where pupils are expected to discover and create their own new knowledge. Inquiry is not this. Inquiry is an intellectually demanding process, forcing pupils to give deliberate and sustained attention to ideas, concepts and connections. When carrying out inquiry, pupils draw on embedded knowledge and understanding. It is true that from this existing knowledge, with carefully constructed inquiry, pupils can and do construct new meaning and even new knowledge, but this is an incredibly inefficient process (see later). Rather, we improve the gains from inquiry when we first ensure that the required knowledge is already in place. After all, it is incredibly hard to think about something when one doesn't know anything!

Phasing the teaching process such that prerequisite knowledge comes before inquiry is key. Furthermore, the required knowledge should be embedded through maturity, meaning the inquiry process may take a couple of years before it really draws on some information or idea being learnt today.

The disastrous meta-study effect sizes often quoted to diminish the importance of inquiry arise from meta-analyses conflating inquiry with discovery learning or from including studies that do not take account of the importance of correct phasing and maturation. It is easy to paint inquiry as having no impact if we ask pupils to carry out inquiry without having the prerequisite knowledge or to carry out inquiry with novel ideas that they have not yet assimilated into their schemata. But, carried out well, inquiry does not only greatly advance understanding: it is also the key to improving long-term memory of mathematical ideas.

It cannot be said too often: knowledge comes first. But inquiry must come too if we are to move from knowing to understanding.

Inflexible knowledge

Because of the polarised nature of education debate, radical advocates of knowledge often sneer at inquiry and radical advocates of inquiry sneer equally at knowledge. These two camps have established themselves as though ·'never the twain shall meet'. They position inquiry and knowledge as mutually exclusive. This is clearly ludicrous. Education is complex. The debate is never so black and white; there is always nuance. Both knowledge and inquiry matter. It is the phasing and proportion of each that needs to be got right.

The more extreme inquiry promoters paint a picture of knowledge as being about rote learning. In fact, very little knowledge is rote knowledge. Usually, when talking about rote knowledge, people are really describing inflexible knowledge.

Inflexible knowledge is a perfectly normal step in learning. Most of us, when learning something new, will acquire inflexible knowledge.

The oft-quoted example of rote knowledge from *Anquished English* (Lederer, 1989) is the pupil who gives the response:

'A menagerie lion running about the earth through Africa.'

What question is the pupil responding to? The pupil has been asked to describe the equator!

Clearly, this knowledge is not useful. They have misheard the sentence 'an imaginary line...' and have absolutely no concept of what the equator actually is. Furthermore, they have not tried to assimilate the sentence with known information and ideas, else they would surely spot the ridiculousness of the sentence. The pupil has simply remembered the line being said. This is rote knowledge. That is to say, this is memorising in the absence of meaning.

But rote knowledge is rare. Most things that are remembered do have meaning (even if that meaning is not yet understood). Consider, for example, the pupil who tells their teacher 'Eight take away five is three. But you can't do five take away eight.' Clearly, this has meaning. The model of subtraction they are using is one of removing – literally taking away. This knowledge is not rote. It is true that they don't yet fully understand subtraction, but the knowledge they have is useful and is a perfectly natural step in learning about subtraction. This knowledge does fit with other learnt ideas (removing objects, say). It is connected, but it is not complete.

We want our pupils to become creative problem solvers, but we should not despair at inflexible knowledge. Our job as teachers is to schedule the learning of mathematics such that the discipline is carefully revealed to pupils over time at the right stage of maturity.

Inflexible knowledge is very different to rote knowledge. It is meaningful. Inflexible knowledge is inflexible because the knowledge is tied to the surface structure – pupils can use it only in examples that are the same – but does not transfer to the deep structure of the idea. In other words, inflexible knowledge cannot transcend specific examples. In the above, the pupil is not able to say how the concept of subtraction could be applied to the case where the removing model breaks down.

Continuing our shared language

Surface structure

Particular examples, designed to illustrate the deep structure

Deep structure

A principle that transcends specific examples

Rote knowledge

Memorisation in the absence of meaning

Inflexible knowledge

A type of knowledge that has meaning, but is limited to specific examples. A natural step to deep, flexible knowledge

From a teacher's point of view, it is important to remember that knowledge tends to be inflexible when it is first learnt. This is a natural step. Don't despair!

Continuing to work with this knowledge – assimilating it into schemata of established truths – leads to fluency and expertise. The knowledge gradually shifts from being organised around surface structure (examples) to deep structure (principles).

In order to help pupils with this shift, we must use carefully considered examples, showing not only when the learnt idea will apply but also when it breaks down, along with non-examples. Teachers should be explicit in telling pupils when they have acquired rote knowledge and also open about inflexible knowledge. Learning a discipline is a leap of faith for the pupil; be honest with them when they have inflexible knowledge. Tell them that it is not complete, but will be built upon later. This honesty avoids one of the most significant problems in a conveyor belt, objective-led curriculum, where teachers are racing through objectives and are dishonest about inflexible knowledge. For example, it is not unusual to hear a teacher telling a pupil that 'multiplication makes things bigger' or that 'to multiply by ten, just add a zero'. These shortcuts enable a teacher to 'get through' an objective more quickly, but they embed serious misconceptions, which are very tricky to undo later. Instead, an honest approach is much more helpful. For example, when the pupil above says, 'You can't do five takeaway eight', we tell them that we understand why the examples they are using at the moment would make that seem true, but in fact it is possible and we will teach them how later in the curriculum.

At any given time, all human beings, including our pupils, know only what they know. Our schemata of knowledge and understanding are continually growing. Educators must appreciate that and celebrate that it is a natural step to deeper and deeper understanding of the universe.

Human cognitive architecture

The evolutionary psychologist David Geary has proposed a distinction between types of knowledge. He splits knowledge into biologically primary and biologically secondary knowledge.

Biologically primary knowledge is knowledge that we have evolved to be able to acquire easily, without the need for thought or attention. For example, speaking. Although we need to think about words and vocabulary, the act of speaking itself is untaught.

Biologically secondary knowledge is knowledge that we, as a culture, have generated. This requires attention and is difficult to learn as described earlier.

A simple example of the distinction is the fact that it is easy to learn how to speak, but difficult to learn how to read.

There is no need to teach biologically primary knowledge, so schools are concerned with the business of biologically secondary knowledge.

This secondary knowledge is the knowledge we, as a species and social collective, have created. It is our art and our music, our science and our literature, our pursuit of sport, our love of dance, our interest in history, our rich languages. Biologically secondary knowledge is our combined culture. I like to think of biologically primary knowledge as the knowledge that keeps us alive, but biologically secondary knowledge is the knowledge that makes it worth living.

One perhaps unexpected finding is that problem solving is biologically primary. We have evolved to solve complex problems, particularly those that increase chances of survival. But as mathematics educators, we are interested not in generic problem solving, but specifically in mathematical problem solving.

Is mathematical problem solving biologically primary or secondary?

When human beings are unable to obtain knowledge from others, they use randomness as an action for generating new responses, which can then be tested and lead to hypotheses or conclusions. This is known as the 'randomness as genesis' principle. This way of creating new knowledge is incredibly inefficient and prone to significant misinterpretation.

When faced with a mathematical problem, the randomness as genesis principle **could** apply. That is to say, it is possible to consider mathematical problem solving as biologically primary. Pupils **can** learn mathematical ideas and mathematical truths without being taught. They can use randomness as an approach – brute force is the method most pupils will resort to when faced with a mathematical problem that requires prerequisite knowledge they have not been taught. Through trial, testing, errors, re-trial, drawing conclusions and iterating, it is **possible** for pupils to construct new mathematical meaning. But this approach is inefficient and pupils only have a finite time at school. Instead, it is far more efficient and impactful to simply teach the pupil the knowledge they require. The process of problem solving is also something that can be taught.

Pupils become significantly enhanced problem solvers if they are explicitly taught how to tackle problems. To achieve this, the teacher can:

1. Prepare problems and use them in whole-class instruction.

2. Assist pupils in monitoring and reflecting on the problem-solving process.

3. Teach pupils how to use visual representations.

4. Expose pupils to multiple problem-solving strategies.

5. Help pupils recognise and articulate mathematical concepts and notation.

Woodward et al., 2012

So, I suggest that mathematical problem solving is both biologically primary and biologically secondary.

Key principles in cognitive science for learning

Cognitive science is a cross-disciplinary study of the mind with contributions from fields such as linguistics, computer science, psychology, artificial intelligence, philosophy, neuroscience, and anthropology.

Earlier, I discussed the three types of professional knowledge: propositional, case and strategic knowledge. The field of cognitive science offers much of use to educators. In 1963, John B. Carroll set out on a lifetime of work to uncover how an understanding of human cognitive architecture can help educators plan, design and deliver more effective learning episodes. Many have followed and added to the canon, with some remarkable and surprising results. Much of what is hypothesised in cognitive science remains at the propositional knowledge phase and has not been able to be replicated beyond laboratory conditions. In this next section, I seek to highlight just a few areas of cognitive science that we can draw on for improving the single aim of mastery: learning.

Working memory

Carleton Washburne suggested in the 1920s that the human mind can only cope with thinking about so much at once. This 'conscious thought' was to be defined as what one is immediately concerned with. Nowadays, this aspect of short-term memory is referred to as working memory. The working memory is responsible for temporarily holding information, so that it is available for processing. Most of us can cope with only a small number of pieces of information at any given time, typically two or three, perhaps as many as four or five.

Suppose you were asked to perform the following calculation in your head

$$287 \times 34$$

This is a trivial problem to solve with pencil and paper, yet asked to perform the same task mentally, most people struggle. This is because one is being asked to process too many pieces of information at once. The working memory can't cope.

Working memory is a limited cognitive tool both in terms of capacity and duration. It can be thought of as:

interconnected cognitive mechanisms that maintain newly acquired information and retrieve stored information to an active state for processing and manipulation

Pociask and Morrison, 2004

This limited tool plays a crucial role. It is where thinking takes place. It is in the working memory where complex cognitive tasks such as reasoning and problem solving occur.

The working memory acts as a bottleneck between the learning of a task and the long-term memory. In order to get into the long-term memory, the idea or information must first be processed in the short-term, working memory.

This makes placing things in the long-term memory difficult, which is very important from an evolutionary point of view. Imagine if one remembered every single thing one ever encountered! The bottleneck ensures that only important information – that is, information that one has given attention to – is able to pass into the long-term memory. The working memory is playing an important role as a buffer between all of the nonsense we encounter and what we remember as truth.

Cognitive load

Cognitive load is defined as the 'total amount of mental energy imposed on working memory at an instance in time' (Cooper, 1998).

Sweller et al. (1998) suggest that this overall cognitive load can be broken into three subcomponents:

Intrinsic cognitive load (ICL): the load imposed on the learner by the nature of the instructional material that must be processed and learned

Extraneous cognitive load (ECL): the load imposed by factors such as instructional strategies, message design, interface design, and the quality of instructional materials and learning environments

Germane cognitive load (GCL): the load imposed by cognitive processes directly relevant to learning

Clearly, from an educator's point of view, we should seek to maximise the latter. GCL is the energy being used when attending. Since attention is the only known way of making information and ideas pass into the long-term memory, this energy being exerted is desirable. Learning is hard.

Given the limited nature of short-term, working memory, we should also seek to minimise both ICL and ECL. Let the following colour coding represent each type of cognitive load:

Using this system, we can describe much current classroom practice as often placing great demands in terms of ICL and ECL. Learning episodes often look like this:

In this case, the very nature of the learning materials being used by the teacher creates unnecessary ECL burden. These resources may be muddled, verbose, contain unnecessary information or use confusing language or diagrams. As teachers, we can lessen the demand on the brain by presenting materials that are concise, accurate, clear and relevant.

In this typical scenario, ECL is taking up lots of mental energy. ECL is demanding when the way in which information is being communicated is long winded or irrelevant, or when the learning environment is competing for attention by containing other stimuli or distracting features. Again, it is a simple problem to solve. Teachers can communicate precisely, use appropriate media, and ensure that learning environments do not distract.

When ICL and ECL are taking up so much mental energy, there is less energy available for the desirable GCL. When we minimise both ICL and ECL, learning episodes can be more fruitful by giving greater energy to attending. A more appropriate load phasing could look like this:

It is worth noting that significant controversy surrounds the claim that ICL can be reduced. Mayer and Moreno (2010) outline the segmenting principle, which aims to reduce ICL by presenting information step by step. They claim that this helps pupils to better organise new information. Mayer (2005) suggests that ICL can be reduced by using the pretraining principle, where pupils are given information about the new content before starting the new learning unit. The intention is to increase the impact of a pupil's prior learning on the new material.

I believe the controversy is warranted. Both of these approaches, which do appear to reduce ICL, might better be considered as simply changing the task that pupils are meeting and so not actually reducing the intrinsic load of learning the idea at all. For this reason, most instructional designers concentrate on reducing ECL only.

Anxiety and cognitive load

It is worth considering the impact of anxiety, since there is good evidence to suggest anxiety takes up working memory and has detrimental impact on cognitive load (Ramirez et al., 2013).

Anxiety can arise in pupils when learning new mathematics if they have a poor grasp of earlier, prerequisite mathematics. A mastery approach mitigates this since, unlike conveyor belt approaches, in a mastery approach teachers homogenise pupil groups and choose appropriate starting points on the journey through mathematics such that all pupils are building on firm foundations. However, even with this approach, as mentioned earlier pupils will forget or unlearn as a natural part of the nonlinear journey through learning a discipline; and given that teachers are human beings too(!), we are all fallible and will make mistakes in judging the correct starting points. It is, therefore, important to continually consider this aspect of anxiety and to minimise it by always testing for prerequisite knowledge as shown in the mastery cycle diagram earlier.

Social cues also play a role in bringing about a feeling of anxiety in pupils who are learning mathematics. All mathematics teachers are familiar with the experience of hearing other teachers, parents or the media condemn mathematics as intractable and to be feared.

These fears take up working memory – literally, the pupil is thinking about their fears rather than thinking about the mathematics – so it must be addressed.

When dealing with deep structure rather than surface structure, pupils must attend to higher-order aspects such as underlying relationships and general principles. This requires more of the working memory. A result of this is that anxiety is disproportionately damaging to high-performing pupils. Their working memory is more disrupted because they tend to work on mathematics using deeper problem-solving approaches, rather than the simplistic, single-step approaches that lower-performing pupils tend to use.

Another aspect of anxiety that is crucial to understand is teacher anxiety. Many teachers who teach mathematics do, themselves, have underlying fears about the subject. In the UK, only around 24% of mathematics teachers have a post-school qualification in mathematics, so the vast majority of the workforce is non-specialist. Teacher anxiety is communicated to pupils and can lead them to embed those same anxieties. Studies show that teacher anxiety impacts on pupil performance, with a stronger impact on girls' performance.

Reducing pupil anxiety is therefore a goal of the effective mathematics teacher. This requires sticking to the mastery cycle, which ensures that fundamental skills are secure and assimilated before moving on and that continual formative assessment monitors for when prerequisite knowledge is forgotten or not fully secure.

Teacher anxiety can be reduced significantly through effective CPD. This CPD should focus on how to teach a concept, rather than the mathematical concept itself. When the focus is on how to teach, teacher anxiety lessens far more rapidly than when the CPD is really about teaching the teacher the mathematics.

Assessment types can be changed too. In mastery, as described earlier, assessment is not about labelling pupils; it is about working out whether or not one's teaching has been impactful yet. There is no need to time tests or to assign grades in a mastery approach. Removing both timing and grading significantly reduces pupil anxiety and has no detrimental impact on learning (quite the opposite, in fact!).

Finally, teachers should avoid consoling pupils. This may sound counterintuitive when talking about reducing anxiety, but consoling a pupil who has answered a question incorrectly is disingenuous and gives them no help to become secure in mathematics. Rather than saying, 'Well done, you tried your best, that's all that matters', teachers should use responses such as 'Yes, the work is challenging; but I know, with hard work, you can do it!'

The difference between novice and expert

As discussed, the more expert a pupil becomes, the greater the impact of anxiety, because experts work at a deep-structure level, whereas novices tend to work at the surface-structure level.

So, when designing instructional materials and modalities, it is important that the teacher takes account not just of the ICL-ECL-GCL relative proportions, but also of the type of audience they are instructing. Novices and experts learn differently and attack problems at different structural levels. The format of instructional materials suitable for an expert may not be appropriate for a novice and vice versa.

We have seen that as a pupil becomes more expert, they tend to consider mathematical ideas as general principles which they can work with across various problems and formats. But pupils do not begin with expertise; they begin with inflexible knowledge which they can use in only restricted examples. Their knowledge is superficial at this stage.

This is true of all learning. We all move from the surface level, superficial knowledge to expertise as we continue to learn. Take, for example, the trainee teacher. We were all once in that position. When observing a trainee teacher, we can see that their attention is focused on the superficial: 'What am I saying? How long do I spend on this? Where should I be standing? What resources should be on the table?' But the expert teacher is attending to much-higher-level principles, such as pedagogic choice. This expertise comes about by studying (propositional knowledge), networking and learning with others as well as articulating our own experiences for critique and development (case knowledge), and most importantly through actually teaching (strategic knowledge). This latter part is critical if one is to become an expert teacher. It takes a long time – perhaps around ten years – to experience enough real classroom encounters for this strategic knowledge to develop.

A key weakness of education systems in many Western countries is the lack of honesty and clarity about how long it takes to become an expert teacher. In the UK, a single year of teacher training, followed by a probationary year, results in qualified teacher status. The assumption of many is that this is the end of the training period and that the teacher is now a skilled educator. This is clearly nonsense. Teaching is an incredibly complex profession and is a skill that continues to develop throughout one's career. The learning never ends; one never completes the journey. There is always more to learn, always more expertise to develop.

Strategic knowledge is the most important. Experiential learning is necessary for us all to notice our own practice. Take again, for example, the trainee teacher. We all, as maths teachers, have to go through the experience of finding out that it is a really bad idea to place compasses and glue sticks on the table before the start of a lesson on constructing 3D shapes – because the kids bloody stab each other and stick the glue to their foreheads! These are things we have to experience, not simply read.

As expertise develops, the way in which knowledge is organised in the mind moves from disconnected, inflexible knowledge to a problem-based schema. Experts encounter problems and are able to connect both the content knowledge and the principles and procedures necessary for attacking the problem. In the novice mind, content information and problem-solving knowledge are separate.

This is why, as discussed earlier, novices attack problems with brute force trial and error. The expert, on the other hand, recognises features in the new problem that they can connect to problems they have solved in the past. They work from the known to the unknown.

Because knowledge is organised in different ways, the expert has efficient ways of addressing new problems. Their knowledge is connected, making it easier to search their memory for similar situations and the resolutions that followed. The novice mind, with its disconnected storage, is inefficient.

Recognising the differences between novice and expert is extremely important if teaching is to be successful. Teachers, who are typically expert in the mathematical ideas they wish their pupils to learn, will often forget the experience of being a novice and, in good – but misguided – faith, design instructional materials and learning modes suitable for experts (suitable for themselves!), leaving the novice pupil unable to access the meaning.

Generic cognitive skills and domain-specific skills

Human beings acquire generic skills without the need to give specific attention to the skill; they come automatically. Domain-specific skills are not acquired automatically, so teachers must instruct pupils in domain-specific skills if they are to be gained.

A common debate in education is whether or not skills should be the purpose of schooling. I suggest that if we make pupils bright – that is, by building their schemata of knowledge across multiple disciplines – they are able to think critically and creatively. There is no need to teach creative thinking – it is a by-product of being learn'd!

Information store principle

Human long-term memory is indescribably large – despite many efforts to determine the storage capacity (often in the language of computer science), no one has yet been able to find any limit to the long-term memory. In practical terms, it appears to be inexhaustible. Who we are, as human beings, in every sense can be thought of as the record of our experiences, emotions, encounters, and living histories. In a real sense human beings **are** their long-term memories.

Our long-term memory **is** our aptitude. The chess grandmaster is able to triumph not because of some generic problem-solving skill, but because they recognise configurations and the possible futures of those configurations. They remember them. They have encountered them in the past and can call upon them. This is the only reason they are a grandmaster.

To build exceptional competence in any discipline means to build up an enormous knowledge base in the long-term memory.

Using information from the long-term memory takes up no mental energy. Unlike using the working memory, which is extremely limited, to think about novel information, drawing on the long-term memory appears to have no bounds on the number of pieces of information that can be utilised at once.

Building this knowledge base is generally achieved by obtaining that knowledge from other people through borrowing, imitating, reading and storytelling.

For these processes to occur, the pupil must have a good relationship with the teacher.

Relationships

Learning is a social endeavour.

Too often, this aspect of education is ignored; yet, without good relationships, learning is unlikely to occur. Human beings have evolved over huge periods of time to borrow knowledge from those around them. For millennia, storytelling has been the key mode of knowledge transfer, with one generation handing down a body of knowledge to the next. As described earlier, the working memory acts as a protective buffer to prevent unimportant information getting into the long-term memory. So knowledge needs to be considered important by the pupil. Human relationships play an enormous part in bringing about this feeling of importance. The pupil will consider the information important when they have faith in the person telling them the new knowledge. The teacher must establish a relationship with the pupil such that the pupil trusts them and has belief in their assertions. In order to accept new knowledge as truth, the pupil first must believe that the teacher is a carrier of truth and is sincere in their desire for the pupil to become learn'd.

Too little emphasis is placed on the crucial role of human relationships between teacher and pupil (or, indeed, teacher and trainee teacher, mentor and mentee, headteacher and staff).

Avoid tricks and lies

A reason pupils lose faith in a teacher stems from the common practice of teachers lying to pupils. It is a feature of conveyor belt approaches – where teachers are racing through objectives and are more concerned with coverage than learning – that teachers will conceal truth about a mathematical idea. This truth is later revealed, thus exposing the teacher as a liar. Faith falls apart.

For example, our pupil who says, 'Eight take away five is three. But you can't do five take away eight.' It can be tempting for the teacher, who simply wished to 'get through the lesson objective' to agree with the pupil: 'That's right, you can't do five take away eight.' The pupil trusts the teacher and remembers this fact. Later, the same teacher will need to break this apparent truth. This happens continually throughout the pupil's life at school. They are told lies such as:

- **'To multiply by ten, add a zero to the right-hand side of the number.'**

- **'Multiplication makes things bigger.'**

- **'It is not possible to find the root of a negative number.'**

The experience of the pupil is one of continual disappointment in the teacher.

Rather than adopting these approaches (better still, scrap any aspects of conveyor belt in your practice), be truthful at all times. Teach everything correctly first time. Do not use examples that are not generalisable or metaphors that break as the concept develops. Rather than responding, 'That's right, you can't do five take away eight', tell the pupil, 'I can see why you think that at the moment, because we are looking at one type of subtraction; but actually, it is possible! Isn't that exciting! And later, as you learn more about subtraction, I will show you how.'

Narrow limits of change principle

When dealing with novel information, the human mind can only process very limited amounts of information at any given time. For most of us, the working memory limit is around three or four items of new information. As described earlier, the working memory is not only limited in terms of number of pieces of information, but also in duration. Most of us can hold something in working memory for a maximum of around 20 seconds before it is lost or replaced. These two protective devices ensure the long-term memory is not inundated with meaningless information. So, from an evolutionary point of view, the dramatic limits of working memory are necessary and helpful. However, from a learning point of view, these limits are inconvenient.

Working memory can also process information that is held in the long-term memory. When carrying out processing of information already stored in long-term memory, the operation of working memory is dramatically different: there are now no capacity or duration limits. The working memory can cope quite simply and without encumbrance with vast and varied pieces of information.

This can be utilised when learning new information. Take for example, the following list. Read the list of 20 letters and try to remember them:

X B B
C C I
A I T
V F B
I S A
S M F
I X

This is quite a tricky thing to do. This list is new, so the working memory struggles to cope with 20 pieces of new information at once.

However, I know that if something is already embedded in the long-term memory, we are able to work with any number of pieces of information and that the problem of duration goes away. Therefore, as a teacher, I can rearrange the information such that it draws upon already-learnt knowledge.

Suppose we think of the domain of mathematics as a complex web of interconnected ideas:

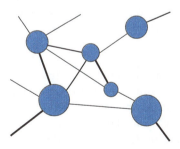

When learning a new idea, as teachers we know which previously learnt and understood ideas connect to the novel idea, so we can shine a light on the new idea from the perspective of established knowledge. This means the pupil can have far less demand on their working memory, since they are using information from their long-term memory.

Here is the same list again. Read it and remember it:

X

BBC

CIA

ITV

FBI

SAS

MFI

X

This list is much easier to learn. The information is the same, but the information is presented in such a way that it draws on already-learnt knowledge. Because the entity 'BBC' is a known idea, we can think of this as one piece of information instead of three. This 'chunking' is a useful way of partially overcoming the limits of working memory. As teachers, we must therefore ensure the scheduling of our curriculum is such that we can allow pupils to encounter new knowledge and concepts from the viewpoint of well-connected ideas that they have a good understanding of already.

Worked-example effect

During their time at school, pupils in the UK have approximately 1600 hours of mathematics lessons. In this time, they are to learn around 320 novel mathematical ideas. Of course, we will expect pupils to undertake a great many more hours of study and work outside of school; but the time they get to spend with an expert is limited by design. It is important, therefore, that the time pupils actually spend in the company of their teacher is used as effectively and efficiently as possible.

When asked to work on a problem, assuming the underlying knowledge is in place, pupils can go about addressing it. But, if the teacher first shows a worked example of such a problem, the pupil will then be able to address the problem far more readily. The time teachers invest in showing worked examples pays dividends.

In addition to the teacher working through the example with the pupil, there is also significant gain when a pupil is simply given a fully worked example to be able to study and reference when working on a problem. This finding is repeatedly demonstrated across many studies at the propositional knowledge stage (for example: Sweller and Cooper, 1985) – and, more importantly, at the strategic knowledge stage, where the gains predicted by laboratory studies have been able to be replicated in real classrooms (Carroll, 1994; Ward and Sweller, 1990).

Split-attention effect

This view of lessons having to be efficient is often railed against by teachers – they argue that learning is not a factory process and not about efficiency. While this is a valid argument on paper, the reality is what it is: they only get so much time with you; you have a moral obligation to make that time as impactful as possible.

Continuing, then, with the theme of efficiency, we come to the split-attention effect. When teachers are demonstrating worked examples or preparing tasks or questions for pupils to work on, it is worth considering the limits of working memory and ensuring that – at the point of learning new material – the information is presented as clearly and with as little burden on the working memory as possible. One very simple example of this is to remove the need for pupils to split their attention between diagrams and information. So, for example, when working on a problem involving angle facts, say, rather than having a diagram on one part of the page and then a few sentences explaining the angles, we can make the information much more unified by labelling the angles in the diagram. This integration of the information reduces the demand on working memory by removing the need to consider two separate sources of information.

For example, look at this diagram:

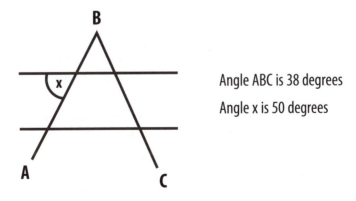

Angle ABC is 38 degrees

Angle x is 50 degrees

We can integrate its information like this:

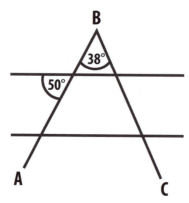

Redundancy effect

It should be noted, however, that it is not always necessary or desirable to integrate information into diagrams. Where the information is simply repeating what is on the diagram, there is no need to add it. That is, where the nature of the diagram itself already informs to reader, then adding information becomes redundant. Mayer (2001) uses the term 'coherence effect' in reference to this situation.

Another aspect of the redundancy effect to consider is the gains that can occur in learning when, rather than using two modes to communicate information, one is eliminated. For example, if showing a PowerPoint slide with text, it is beneficial to avoid reading the text aloud to the audience – let the audience read it.

Storage and retrieval

By design, the mastery cycle seeks to optimise learning by:

- ensuring all pupils are taught the right level of mathematics (just beyond what they already know), building on secure understanding of prerequisites.

- giving all pupils varied experiences with mathematical ideas that transition from doing to practising to behaving mathematically.

- ensuring that novel ideas are met carefully in such a way that they are seen as important and draw the pupil's attention in order to pass the gatekeeper of working memory and enter the long-term memory.

- continually checking that ideas are being gripped by an ever-present cycle of formative assessment and correctives.

- never moving on to mathematical ideas that require a current idea if it has not been fully understood and embedded.

All of this operates with the intention of changing the pupil's schema of knowledge and understanding, assimilating new truth in a logical way. With all this effort to ensure that a pupil's long-term memory is changed, we now face the next challenge: optimising the storage of that knowledge and making it readily retrievable.

It has long been known that the memory is the key concern of the educator; Washburne, Ward, Burk and others were discussing the role of memory in the 1910s. In 1943, Hull wrote about memory from two points of view. Firstly, what he referred to as the pupil's 'momentary reaction potential' – that is, the potential they have to use their prior knowledge in the moment through recalling learning. He noted that this varied from person to person. The second aspect of memory Hull identifies is what he calls 'habit strength'. Hull knew that some actions required no thought; they could just be performed. 'Habit' is a sensible description of this type of action since it reflects a common view of what it means to be able to do something habitually (Hull, 1943). Later, Estes (1955) refined Hull's work and talks about 'response strength' versus 'habit strength'. This takes the idea of what one can think about in the moment further and starts to apply the notion of there being a strength to this ability, which can explain the differences various people display. The idea of response strength also takes the debate towards the idea that this aspect of memory is not a fixed potential, but can be improved (strengthened). The research into these two aspects of memory continued for several decades, with a large number of experiments being carried out in laboratory conditions.

Enter Robert and Elizabeth Bjork. The Bjorks have dedicated much of their professional working life to furthering the understanding of human memory. In 1992, they went further and redefined the two aspects as 'retrieval strength' versus 'storage strength' (Bjork and Bjork, 1992).

We now have a view of the long-term memory as being able to be improved both in terms of how readily one can recall knowledge and how well that knowledge is embedded in the long-term memory.

Performance is not the same as learning

In its current incarnation, the formal examination system in the UK measures whether or not a pupil can perform on a certain bank of questions, of certain types, at a certain point in time. Performance is easy to measure, which is why national systems often resort to simplistic, mechanistic approaches for benchmarking the success or otherwise of the system.

Unfortunately, performance is not the same as learning and, more critically, is not even a good predictor of learning. Being able to perform at any given time is heavily influenced by local conditions – cues, predictability, recency – which can serve as crutches that prop up performance, but will not be there later when the knowledge might actually be useful.

We have known for a long time that current performance is a very poor predictor of long-term learning, yet schools are forced to operate in ways that reward pupil short-term performance over meaningful, long-term learning. This, of course, leads to poor design of learning episodes, which can be praised by an inspector or observer in the moment (all the kids had smiley faces; they all put their thumbs up at the end of the lesson; everyone could do the target question at the end; the pupils all made progress!), but are in fact not learning episodes at all – they are presentation and regurgitation.

The key driver of systems adopting poor assessment practices is the fact that they are easier and cheaper to implement. But there is another, serious reason why assessment that actually measures learning is not routinely used by national systems: cheating.

Rather than terminal performance examinations, we could instead choose an approach of continual assessment, where pupils are working very closely with their teacher, who builds strong relationships with them and gets to know them inside out. Pupils can build portfolios of evidence throughout their time at school, demonstrating mathematical understanding of deep-structure problems over sustained periods of time, as we spiral through the curriculum and pupils grow their schemata. This teacher assessment-led approach could discern what pupils truly do know and understand. So, why did we abandon such approaches (note, for example, that the ATM GCSE, which was abolished in the 1990s, had no terminal exam) and opt for systems that measure point-in-time performance only? Well, continual assessment is very hard to carry out and takes a great deal of time; it also requires teachers to have very high levels of professional knowledge around assessment and make accurate judgements over time that are free of bias; it comes with an enormous moderation burden; and finally, it relies on teachers maintaining their professional integrity and ethics whilst simultaneously working in a high-stakes profession. Alas, no system has ever been able to achieve all of this!

At a local level, however, there have been many excellent examples of continuous assessment working, including Carleton Washburne's own schools and pupils.

We work in a system that measures performance only and we need to be alert to the flaws of such a system and alive to the extremely weak practice it can drive. It can feel rather scary for the teacher in a high-stakes system to change their lesson design to focus on long-term learning rather than performance, but it is negligent not to do so.

Suppose a class has just had a one-hour lesson on Pythagoras' theorem. During the lesson, the teacher has repeatedly emphasised that the lesson is about Pythagoras' theorem and shown multiple examples. The teacher then gives the pupils similar questions to work on. The teacher is then pleased that the pupils can perform.

Well of course they can perform! They have just been given all the cues to do just that. They are replicating.

But what we, as teachers, want to achieve is for pupils to be able to encounter problems in the future that may or may not require the use of Pythagoras' theorem and for them to be able to recognise appropriate scenarios and put their learning to good use.

In other words, as teachers we should focus more on getting pupils able to know **when** to use an approach, rather than simply how to use the approach that day. As we will see in part 5 of this book, a learning episode phasing that includes only 20% new content and 80% previously learnt content helps with this, since the lesson is not then just populated with questions like the examples just shown.

The importance of forgetting

In the practical use of our intellect, forgetting is as important as remembering. If we remembered everything, we would most occasions be as ill off as if we remembered nothing.

James, 1890

We encounter huge amounts of information in our everyday lives. It is important (for one's own sanity!) that not all of this is remembered. Imagine if you could take a pill so you never forgot anything. It would be awful! If every single thing you had ever been told was continuously to mind, the impact would be literally maddening. So, forgetting is a really important evolutionary mechanism that protects the mind. Teachers should be alert to forgetting and phase their learning episodes such that important ideas and information are brought to mind again for the pupil at the point just before being forgotten.

Desirable difficulties

Learning is difficult, but we want our children to become learn'd. So removing as many of these difficulties as possible – such as by lessening the load on the working memory by removing distractions or giving clear instruction – is clearly a useful thing to do. But not all difficulties are unhelpful to the process of learning.

Many cognitive scientists, and in particular the Bjorks, have explored the impact on introducing difficulties during learning. This has included work on:

- asking participants to practise things that are not part of the criteria (e.g. throwing a ball five metres and three metres, when the test will be to throw it four metres);

- interrupting the learning through distraction (e.g. when learning about one idea, periodically diverting the learner to think about an entirely separate idea);

- and interrupting the learning episode (e.g. instead of asking a novice tennis player to learn everything about serving a ball first, the novice is asked to learn myriad of skills, intertwined in the same learning episode).

For a long time, much of this work focused on physical activity such as sport – and much of it has not been replicable beyond laboratory conditions. However, some work in the last 30 years in particular has shown encouraging results, which bring interesting implications for the mathematics teacher.

These difficulties that increase long-term learning are referred to by Robert Bjork as 'desirable difficulties'. Bjork outlines four key desirable difficulties:

- Varying the **conditions** of learning

  This could include varying the learning environment. Bjork looked at moving pupils between bright, clean, inspiring classrooms to dark, cramped basement-like ones. There is propositional knowledge and case knowledge regarding this desirable difficulty. However, in this book, I shall not be considering this area since I have never been able to find strategic knowledge of any impact (that is to say, I do not know of any real classroom examples).

- Distributing or **spacing** study or practice

  Typically, pupils practise a topic in one period of time and then are tested on the topic. Spacing the topic over a longer period, with gaps in the practice, has a significant impact on long-term learning.

- Using **tests** (rather than presentations) as learning events

Rather than only presenting new ideas, asking the pupils to answer a question about that idea first has a significant impact on long-term learning (even if they know nothing about it).

- Providing contextual interference during learning (**interleaving** rather than blocking)

Interrupting the learning of an idea with different ideas has a significant impact on long-term learning.

I will expand on each of the three desirable difficulties – which have all three levels of professional knowledge to support them – throughout the rest of this section.

The testing effect

Exercise in repeatedly recalling a thing strengthens the memory

Aristotle

Regular low-stakes or no-stakes quizzing is a key element of mastery approaches. Washburne (though really it was Ward and Burk's work) outlined entire curriculum journeys through each subject, punctuating the journeys with quizzes and tests.

In conveyor belt approaches, testing is used to label pupils as those who can learn well and those who can't. In a mastery approach, testing is used to enhance learning.

When faced with learning a novel idea, even when the learning episode is highly effective, pupils very quickly forget much of what was learnt. This is a protective mechanism for the human mind and evolutionarily important. The amount of content retained after a learning episode decays quickly. However, if that learning episode is brought to mind again, the rate of decay lessens and lessens. This is yet another reason why all mastery approaches embrace a spiral curriculum model.

Typical Forgetting Curve for Newly Learned Information

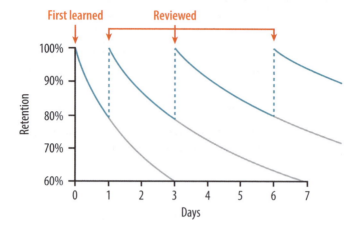

On the whole, the way in which teachers bring learning to mind again is to review it – perhaps through a re-teaching process or asking pupils to read their notes. This is a useful activity and does indeed improve retention by lessening the rate of decay.

A perhaps-surprising result, however, is that reviewing material in this way is less impactful than simply asking pupils to answer questions on the previously learnt content. Rather than studying an idea several times throughout the spiral, it is move beneficial to replace the repeated study with testing.

Here are some typical results from Roediger and Karpicke (2006), which is one of several studies to show this 'testing effect':

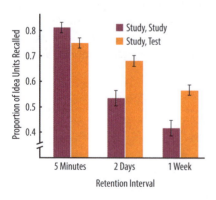
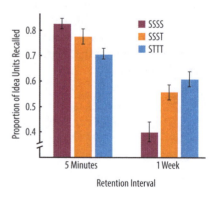

As you can see, those pupils who did two periods of study immediately before a test performed well. Those who did just one period of study followed by a testing exercise did not perform as well when the test proper was immediately afterwards (five minutes gap). This is what we would expect. The first group was engaged in cramming.

But when a longer period of time passes – one week in this case – the results are reversed. The crammers perform significantly worse than those who studied and were then tested.

On the right-hand side, another experiment shows the impact of three models. The first group had four periods of study; the second had three periods of study followed by a test; and the final group had just one period of study followed by three tests. The results are striking. The crammers perform well if the test is immediately afterwards, but their long-term recall is much worse. Now the group that had just 25% of the study time of the crammers, followed by three tests, far outperform all others.

The testing effect can feel counterintuitive: one would imagine that those who study for longer will have the greater long-term recall, but this is not the case. Testing instead of reviewing brings much greater long-term benefits. As discussed earlier, performance is not the same as learning. This is a clear example of that statement.

It is the act of asking a pupil to recall their learning (testing) that leads to greater retention.

Testing potentiates learning

Another powerful use of testing that the teaching for mastery teacher must be aware of is that testing **potentiates** learning. That is to say, testing a pupil before the teaching of an idea by asking them questions (on what has not yet been learnt) alerts them to the fact that learning must happen. By considering the questions, even if they can't answer any of them, pupils become more ready to learn the new idea. They are getting a glimpse of what will be expected of them and are able to recall previously learnt material that may connect to the new problem they are seeing. This makes the pupil more alive to learning the new idea and increases their potential to learn.

Marking and feedback

In my 2004 book, *On Being a Teacher*, chapter 18 is titled 'Marking books'. The chapter, in its entirety, reads: 'I wouldn't bother.'

Few practices in teaching take up such enormous amounts of time and energy as marking. If we are going to dedicate such a lot of these limited resources to an activity, we must be sure that there will be a significant impact on learning – and that this impact is greater than if the time and energy had been invested in undertaking a different activity. Marking books, grading papers, writing comments and other common marking and feedback policies that schools deploy simply do not pass this test.

Marking and feedback **can** have an impact if done extremely well and if, and only if, that marking and feedback is **genuinely** used to change the learning experience. In all practicality this is nigh on impossible for a teacher with 200 pupils, and what we see instead is marking and feedback to tick a policy box rather than any meaningful attempt to change learning. The time wasted to such ineffective practice is vast. This time could be spent on planning learning, creating questions, developing subject knowledge and making pedagogic choice. All of these have a greater impact on learning than marking and feedback (even if done well).

The TALIS report gives us a view of the scale of the issue. Teachers in the UK spend around ten hours per week on marking and administration related to assessment.

Hours Spent Per Week on Non-Teaching Activities

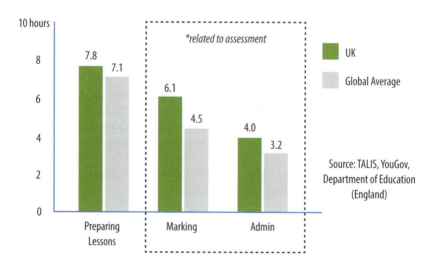

Furthermore, this wasted time is also a key factor in lowering professional satisfaction in teachers. Teachers regularly report marking, feedback and the recording of grades as a significant waste of their time.

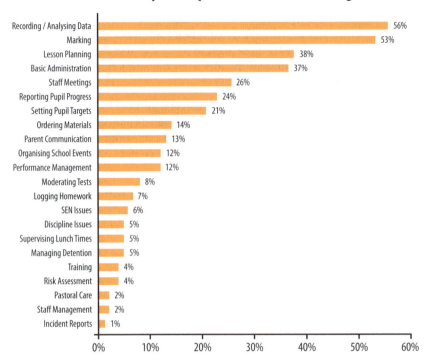

Tasks Teachers Say Take Up Too Much Time Percentage

Task	Percentage
Recording / Analysing Data	56%
Marking	53%
Lesson Planning	38%
Basic Administration	37%
Staff Meetings	26%
Reporting Pupil Progress	24%
Setting Pupil Targets	21%
Ordering Materials	14%
Parent Communication	13%
Organising School Events	12%
Performance Management	12%
Moderating Tests	8%
Logging Homework	7%
SEN Issues	6%
Discipline Issues	5%
Supervising Lunch Times	5%
Managing Detention	5%
Training	4%
Risk Assessment	4%
Pastoral Care	2%
Staff Management	2%
Incident Reports	1%

Marking and feedback are a very poor use of a teacher's time. Instead, use that time to think carefully about learning episodes and the materials and approaches you will use to communicate mathematical ideas.

If one must mark books, then finding time-efficient ways to enhance learning is key. I rather like a suggestion I heard from Dylan Wiliam: instead of ticking and crossing questions, a statement on the page along the lines of 'There are five wrong answers here; find them and correct them' can be a quick way of making the pupil undertake a useful activity. This creates a situation where the pupil, not the teacher, must locate and identify the incorrect responses they have given. When a pupil finds their own errors and corrects them, the gains are much greater than when they must correct an error their teacher has identified.

The hypercorrection effect

An area where feedback **might** be worth the time invested is to bring about a hypercorrection effect. Hypercorrection occurs when pupils respond to a question with an answer which they feel highly confident is correct, but then receive feedback revealing their response was in fact wrong.

The feeling of surprise a pupil has when discovering that something they firmly thought to be true was actually a misconception leads them to better correct the original problem and to be far more likely to remember the correction in future, improving long-term learning of the idea even though, following the original study of it, they had misunderstood.

Designing activities to bring about hypercorrection requires them to be such that feedback is given and takes account of the level of confidence the pupil had in their assertion. This could again lead to significant workload for the teacher and not give the gains in learning needed to justify such investment of time and energy.

Robert Bjork proposes a simple, yet powerful, alternative: better multiple-choice questions.

Better multiple-choice questions

Traditional multiple-choice questions are a quick and easy way for a teacher to glean a sense of the level of understanding in a class of pupils. When used at scale in technology products, these models are also useful for discerning trends in strengths and weaknesses in the population. But to bring about the hypercorrection effect, we must know something about the level of confidence associated with responses.

Erin Sparck, Elizabeth Bjork and Robert Bjork designed an approach to confidence-weighted multiple-choice questions that achieves this.

Rather than the pupil only being asked for their response, they must also indicate their confidence in their response. A scoring system is then used to heavily penalise confident wrong answers (Sparck et al., 2016).

Here are some examples (note the pupils do not see the associated scoring)

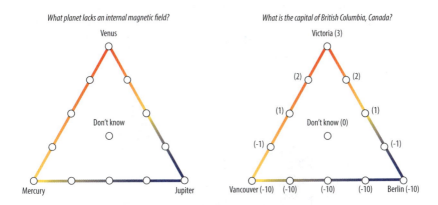

Figure 1 and Figure 3 from Sparck et al., 2016

As you can see in the two examples above, the pupil must choose between three possible answers to the question, but they can choose to place their response on the answer itself (confidently asserting) or between answers (equally or skewed towards one they feel more confident about), or to simply state they 'don't know'. Giving the correct response is the best score. Asserting confidently a wrong response is significantly punitive. This helps to bring about the emotional response we are looking for in order for the hypercorrection effect to occur.

The impact of this approach is significant.

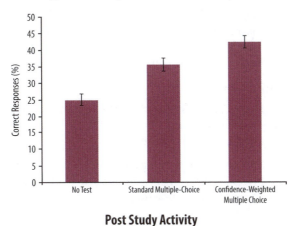

Post Study Activity

Figure 3 from Sparck et al., 2016

The confidence-weighted multiple-choice approach gives gains in long-term learning over a standard multiple-choice quiz. Sparck et al. also explored whether standard multiple-choice quizzes could be improved by asking pupils to state their confidence in their response.

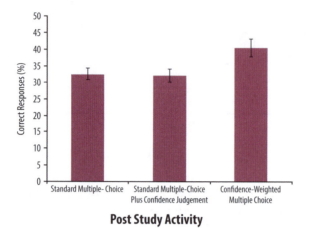

Post Study Activity

Figure 4 from Sparck et al., 2016

There appear to be no additional gains in learning from asking pupils to state the confidence of their response on a standard multiple-choice quiz. The impact would appear to be an outcome of the confidence weighting and scoring system.

Creating confidence weighted multiple-choice questions is a straightforward and quick task for the teacher. So, in this particular case, it does seem a good use of time to create these simple feedback mechanisms.

Massed vs spaced practice

There have been a great many studies into the impact of massed vs spaced practice. Here, I will use Rohrer and Taylor (2007) as the main example, since their study specifically focused on mathematics.

Briefly, massed practice refers to carrying out all of the practice on an idea, skill or concept in one period; whereas with spaced practice the pupil practises over a longer period with gaps between practice.

Rohrer and Taylor also look at the impact of 'light massing', where pupils still carry out all of their practice in one period, but undertake much less practice.

In one experiment, three groups were asked to carry out different types of practice, as below:

	Week 1	Week 2	Week 3
Spacers	Two problems	Two problems	Test
Massers	Four problems	Test	Filler task
Light Massers	Two problems	Test	Filler task

The 'spacers' worked on four problems, but spread out over two weeks; the 'massers' on the same four problems in one week; and the 'light massers' worked on just two problems in one week. Each problem was given the same amount of practice time.

The gap between completing practice and taking the test was the same for all groups: one week. The results of the test are shown below

B Test Performance

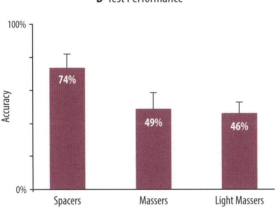

The spacers significantly outperform the massers. This result has been replicated many times across many disciplines.

Implications for overlearning

The results only consider participants who answer at least one practice problem correctly.

Note that, despite the 'massers' undertaking double the amount of practice than the 'light massers', there was no significant difference in their test scores.

93

Because the 'light massers' answered at least one practice problem correctly, this finding suggests no gain resulting from overlearning. This has an important implication for teachers who set pupils practice worksheets with dozens (or hundreds!) of minimally different questions or variation theory worksheets that focus on quantity of content over the need to discern underlying relationship. It appears that, as long as pupils get at least one question correct, there is no need for a vast number of practice questions. This is an unsettling finding for many educators who have long been wedded to overlearning as an important element in the learning episode. There is not enough evidence in Rohrer and Taylor's study to assert that overlearning is not effective, but it should at least raise the question when one is designing practice problems.

It is possible that overlearning might have significantly boosted test scores if there had been, say, a tenfold increase in the amount of practice rather than twofold; but given the constraints on time that teachers face, the gains from such overlearning might not be worth the amount of time needed to undertake the activity.

A null effect of mathematics overlearning was also observed previously in Rohrer and Taylor (2006).

Blocked vs interleaved practice

Blocked practice refers to the practice of learning about and practising one distinct aspect of a domain at any given time. Robert Bjork often uses the analogy of learning to play tennis under the guidance of a professional tennis coach. The trainee will be instructed on how to serve a ball and then practise this one micro-skill for weeks. Once deemed to have gripped this one aspect, the coach then instructs on the next micro-skill – say, backhand – and so on. Interleaved practice refers to the practice of skills or ideas in a phasing that is disrupted by the practising of other skills or ideas. These can be related or not. In the tennis example, the novice player now has practice sessions that include all of the micro-skills. The initial experience of this is confusion and difficulty for the new player, since they are being asked to get to grips with lots of unfamiliar and unconnected movements all at the same time. But, over time, the interleaved practice leads to some interesting results.

Taking another example from Bjork, he looked at participants trying to learn the style of some unfamiliar artists. Some participants were asked to study an individual artist's work all at once before moving on to the next artist (blocked practice), whilst others had to learn all of the artists' styles in a randomly presented sequence. For example:

From Bjork, 2009

Intuitively, most people think that learning the style of one artist at a time would result in being able to firmly grip the similarities in that artist's work and, therefore, being able to spot a painting by the same artist in future because it would contain those same similarities.

However, as we will explore later in further depth when considering variation theory, it would appear that discerning differences in styles, which is what the interleaved approach achieves, was more beneficial in terms of long-term learning.

To measure the learning, Bjork showed participants new paintings that they had not yet encountered and asked them to choose the correct artist.

The results of the experiment show a significant increase in performance by those who were asked to study the styles through interleaved (spaced) practice.

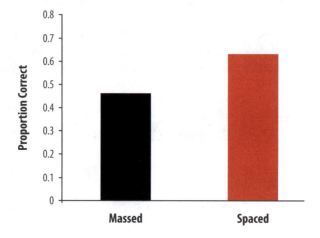

It is also interesting to note that the participants themselves strongly expressed that they would perform better using blocked (massed) practice over interleaved practice. This remains their belief even after they have been shown the actual results!

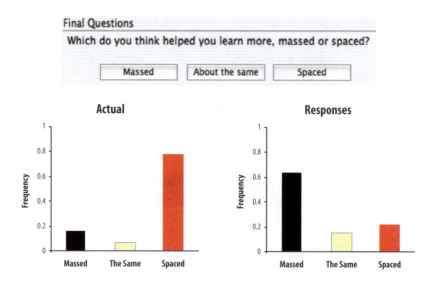

This strong bias for practising in a blocked way is likely a result of experience – after all, it is how almost all educators and trainers ask their pupils to carry out practice.

Given that interleaved practice leads to better retention, the implication for the teaching for mastery teacher is to be able to design practice sequences that highlight not just what is the same but also what is different. There is a strong link to variation theory here, which is about discerning underlying relationships and principles in and across ideas.

For example, the teacher who is trying to get their pupils to grip a sense of 'triangleness' should not only use examples of triangles, but should interleave these with examples of non-triangles.

Much of the research around interleaving is centred on physical skills, such as the tennis example; but we, of course, are interested in the evidence directly related to mathematics.

Let us turn again to Rohrer and Taylor. In their 2007 paper, 'The shuffling of mathematics problems improves learning', they considered these hypotheses using mathematical content.

Participants were taught and then asked to practise finding the volume of four different solids:

A **wedge** is the boldfaced portion of the tube.
Its bottom is a circle, and its top is a slanted oval.
Its volume equals $\dfrac{r^2 h \pi}{2}$

A **spheroid** is similar to a sphere.
But its height has been squeezed or stretched.
Its volume equals $\dfrac{4r^2 h \pi}{3}$

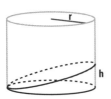

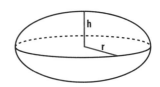

A **spherical cone** is the boldfaced part of the sphere. Its bottom is at the center of the sphere. The rim of the cone is on the surface of the sphere. Its volume equals $\dfrac{2\,r^2 h\,\pi}{3}$

A **half cone** is the bottom of a cone. Both its top and bottom are circles. Its volume equals $\dfrac{7\,r^2 h\,\pi}{3}$

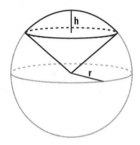

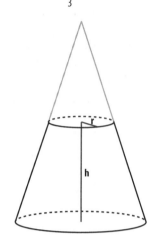

They were later tested, with questions looking typically like this:

Problem

Find the volume of a wedge with $r = 2$ and $h = 3$.
Write the formula in the box; write the answer in the oval.

Solution

$$\boxed{\dfrac{r^2 h\,\pi}{2}}$$

$$= \dfrac{\cancel{2}\cdot 2\cdot 3\pi}{\cancel{2}}$$

$$= \boxed{6\pi}$$

Figures from Rohrer and Taylor, 2007

Groups of participants followed different practice procedures, with one group undertaking interleaved practice and the other blocked practice.

A Practice Procedure

	week 1	week 2	week 3
Mixers	Set 1 interleaved	Set 2 interleaved	test
Blockers	Set 1 grouped	Set 2 grouped	test

From Rohrer and Taylor, 2007

The results reflected earlier studies of blocked vs interleaved practice, with a significant increase in performance from the interleaved practice group.

B Practice Performance

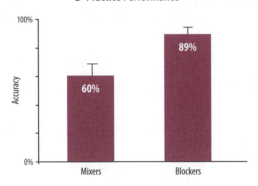

C Test Performance

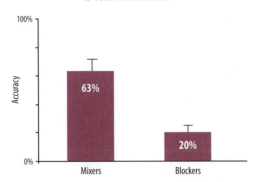

From Rohrer and Taylor, 2007

Just like the results of cramming shown earlier, immediate performance is better when the participants blocked their practice. But when tested later, the tables are turned, with the interleavers far outperforming the blockers.

Once again, the implication for teachers is to carefully consider the difference between immediate performance and long-term learning. Clearly a one-hour lesson containing blocked practice will look more 'effective' to the inspector or observer, since the pupils will perform well in that immediate time, but this common practice would appear to have poor results when it comes to long-term learning. The somewhat messy-looking interleaved lesson – certain to upset the inspector – is actually the desirable practice procedure to engage pupils with.

Rohrer and Taylor postulate that the superior test performance after interleaved practice is a result of requiring the pupils to know not only how to solve each kind of problem but also which procedure was appropriate for each kind of problem. This supports the point I made earlier that it is more important for a pupil to know when to use an approach rather than simply how to use the approach.

The generation effect

Malcolm Swan asked a large number of 14- to 16-year-old pupils to recall how often particular scenarios occurred in the classroom. Pupils, quite rightly, report that the most common scenario is that they listen while the teacher explains. This is, of course, a very good activity.

Here are the most commonly reported (Swan, 2005) activities that pupils say happen in mathematics lessons:

Statements are rank ordered from most common to least common 1 = almost never, 2 = occasionally, 3 = half the time, 4 = most of the time; 5 = almost always.	Mean (n=779)
I listen while the teacher explains.	4.28
I copy down the method from the board or textbook.	4.15
I only do questions I am told to do.	3.88
I work on my own.	3.72
I try to follow all the steps of a lesson.	3.71
I do easy problems first to increase my confidence.	3.58
I copy out questions before doing them.	3.57
I practise the same method repeatedly on many questions.	3.42
I ask the teacher questions.	3.40
I try to solve difficult problems in order to test my ability.	3.32
When work is hard I don't give up or do simple things.	3.32

What is even more interesting about the results is what pupils report as being less common. At the bottom end of the table we find:

Statements are rank ordered from most common to least common 1 = almost never, 2 = occasionally, 3 = half the time, 4 = most of the time; 5 = almost always.	Mean (n=779)
I discuss my ideas in a group or with a partner.	3.25
I try to connect new ideas with things I already know.	3.20
I am silent when the teacher asks a question.	3.16
I memorise rules and properties.	3.15
I look for different ways of doing a question.	3.14
My partner asks me to explain something.	3.05
I explain while the teacher listens.	2.97
I choose which questions to do or which ideas to discuss.	2.54
I make up my own questions and methods.	2.03

Routinely, pupils report that they do not have many opportunities to create their own questions. In other words, pupils report that they are not being asked to **conjecture**.

In the 1980s, teaching for mastery was generally referred to as 'diagnostic teaching'. Here are some excerpts from the teacher standards at the time (with my emphasis added):

- Explore existing ideas through tests and interviews, **before teaching**.

- Expose existing concepts and methods.

- Provoke '**tension**' or '**cognitive conflict**'.

- Resolve conflict through discussion and formulate new concepts and methods.

- Consolidate learning by using the new concepts and methods on further problems.

It was an expectation that teachers should provoke tension and cognitive conflict. That is to say, teachers would design problems and activities that led to pupils questioning something they had held as truth (much like the hypercorrection effect discussed earlier). An important part of this process is for pupils to conjecture, test, confirm, generalise and reason. In doing so, pupils follow their own lines of inquiry and ask their own questions.

The 'generation effect' tells us that if we give pupils minimal information and then ask them to generate a problem, they will retain the learning far longer than if we simply give them the problem to solve.

It is important that pupils believe they are generating their own problems, but of course, the teacher has designed the scenario such that the pupil will ask the questions we want them to ask. This is not discovery learning.

It is incumbent upon the teacher to ensure that the pupil will be able to succeed at generating appropriate questions by making sure the required knowledge and understanding is in place and by having a good view of what the pupil already knows and believes.

The implication for teachers is clear: the teacher should ask themselves how often they create opportunities for pupils to generate their own questions to solve and how to go about designing such opportunities. Some powerful examples include the use of 'always, sometimes or never?' prompts, asking 'What is the same and what is different?' and using the prompt 'and another… and another…and another…' to make pupils continue to generate new examples or counter-examples.

Performance is not a good proxy for learning

The trap of high-stakes systems is that teachers are judged on what can be observed. Unfortunately, what we can **observe** is performance, which is an unreliable indicator of learning. In the moment, for instance during an inspection, we can only **infer** learning.

We have seen that conditions of instruction that make performance improve rapidly often fail to support long-term retention and transfer, whereas conditions of instruction that appear to create difficulties for the learner, slowing the rate of **apparent** learning, often optimise long-term retention and transfer. This issue presents a real challenge to those who wish to judge the effectiveness of teaching through observation – that is, it's pretty much impossible to reliably do so! This type of inspection is both laughable and damaging, since it drives counterproductive teaching practices.

The reality is that teachers do exist in a landscape of inspection and this is not going to go away, so it is incumbent upon the profession to at least ensure inspection is as meaningful and formative as possible. This means training inspectors to make long-term inference rather than immediate performance observations. This is clearly a more intellectually demanding task to carry out, but there is surely no excuse for not trying to make inspection better reflect what we know about long-term, sustained and meaningful learning.

Teachers and pupils can be fooled

The lure of performance means that teachers become susceptible to choosing poorer conditions of instruction over better conditions and pupils to preferring those poorer conditions.

If teachers and observers applaud rapidity and apparent ease of learning during lessons over conditions that more readily lead to long-term retention, a system-wide preference and bias for poorer conditions of learning becomes the accepted norm.

Also, pupils do not appear to develop a nose for identifying impactful ways of learning. Rather, they are misled by indices – such as how fluently they process information during a re-reading of material – into believing in poorer conditions of learning.

This appears to be the case across several aspects discussed above, as several studies demonstrate:

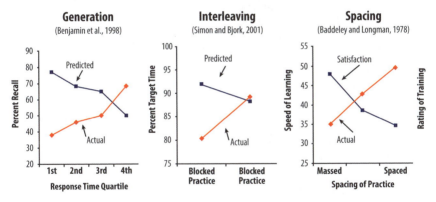

This unshakable misconception that we, as learners, carry is an important consideration for the teacher. Pupils are repeatedly biased towards modes of learning that actual results show to be less effective than the modes they determine to be unhelpful.

The teacher parable

Another finding – one I believe most teachers actually know in their hearts – that we must be aware of is that teachers themselves almost always overestimate the impact of their teaching (Newton, 1990).

A nice example of this can be found in Newton's experiment looking at the perception an instructor had about the impact of their teaching against the actual impact.

Newton created two groups of participants: tappers and listeners. The tappers were handed a card on which was the name of a popular melody (such as 'Happy Birthday to You'). The tapper then tapped out the melody on the table with their finger. The listeners then recorded the name of the melody they believed they had just heard.

The tappers were asked to predict how many of their melodies had been correctly identified by the tappers. Here are the results:

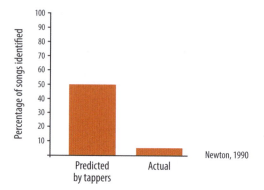

Adapted from Newton, 1990

As you can see, the tappers wildly overestimated their musical performance!

In the tapper's mind, the melody they are tapping out is part of the overall song they can 'hear' in their head. They hear the instruments and lyrics, the familiar tempo and all the richness of the music. So, to the tapper, it is **obvious** what melody is being performed.

The listener has none of this context, none of this background information. All they have is a novel set of tapping noises and rhythm.

This is often the case when mathematics is being taught too. The teacher has forgotten what it is like – intellectually and emotionally – to be in the position of a novice. They embark on the teaching of, say, introducing trigonometric ratios, with all the richness of background information and connections to other mathematical ideas (including ideas conceptually beyond this stage), and have a sense of ease about the new idea. This sometimes leads to ideas being communicated to pupils as though they are also expert. The teacher, believing their explanation to be clear, sensible and obvious, often gains a false sense of security in the impact of their teaching, just like the tappers did.

This is why in a teaching for mastery approach, continual assessment through questioning, discussion, listening, observing and quizzing is so important. The teacher must always be checking they are not falling into the trap of assuming that their intended meaning is being received by the pupils. Newton's experiment, known by educators around the world as 'the teacher parable' is an handy reminder to us all.

Antifragility

Parenting is pretty predictable, isn't it? With the first child, parents are super cautious: they panic about everything, worry that every pause in breathing is a sign of terror; they coddle their child constantly, find it heartbreaking when the little one gets a cold or cries in pain after bumping their head. The new parent goes to great lengths to ensure their precious darling faces no danger of harm or disease: they clean everything continually with antibacterial agents; they avoid playgroups when rumour of an ill child attending spreads around the other new parents they have coffee with. The child is wrapped in cotton wool and handled with care, like a fragile crystal doll.

And then the second child arrives. Oh, sod it. They can be thrown around, allowed to play in the dirt. A sneeze? Oh, well, they'll get over it quickly enough. Banged their head? They all do that, no need to worry, everything will be fine. The parent has learnt how malleable children really are and that there is no need to coddle and coo all of the time.

Children are not fragile.

Fragility describes those things that are irrevocably damaged or made useless by randomness, breakage, stress or being forced to operate beyond their current limit.

A wine glass is fragile. Drop it on a hard kitchen floor and it will shatter into countless useless pieces. Its function is completely destroyed by the damage it has endured. Fragile things are defined by the very fact that such out-of-the-ordinary events end their utility.

What is the opposite of fragility? Is it robustness? Robust things do not break when dropped or thrown around; robust things maintain their utility even under stress and even when attacked.

But the utility of robust items does not improve when out of the ordinary events impose stress, harm or damage upon them. They remain constant.

The opposite of fragility is not robustness; it is antifragility.

Antifragile things or systems **improve** when out-of-the-ordinary events impose stress upon them. The action of harming an antifragile system makes it stronger and even more useful than it was previously.

There are many antifragile things and systems. Take, for example, the human immune system. It is an incomplete system at birth – even though it is remarkably complex and sophisticated, the immune system is not designed to stop the attacks and potential illnesses it will face throughout a lifetime. Instead, the immune system is a learning, adaptive system. It must encounter randomness and stress before it can learn and adapt to overcome those stresses.

The enlightened new parent knows that wrapping the child in cotton wool only serves to make them weak, not strong. The enlightened new parent carefully and deliberately exposes their child to risk. They let them play with the child with chickenpox; they let them mess around in the dirt; they encourage them to climb trees and know that each small fall improves their ability to both assess and deal with the inevitable risks that will come along in life.

Children are antifragile, not fragile. They need to encounter problems and harm – carefully and deliberately and appropriate to their developmental stage – such that they learn to adapt and become strong, not weak, adults.

The parent drip-feeds risk and randomness into their child's life in a calculated and compassionate way. Antifragile systems become stronger through exposure to randomness and stress, but antifragile systems lose their utility and become weaker if the stresses imposed upon them are beyond their ability to adapt at that developmental stage. Exposing children to severe or sustained harm irrevocably damages them and the result is a weak adult who cannot cope with the demands of life. It is a heinous abuse of the child to deliberately impose severe harm upon them. But this should not be used as a case for treating the child as a fragile system, keeping them in a bubble away from all harm – such children will not be able to overcome the challenges that their life will undoubtedly present to them at some point. It is extremely unhelpful to treat children as fragile and it is disingenuous to attempt to justify such treatment by wielding the argument that abusing children is wrong. Of course it is wrong. But so is treating children as though the universe holds within it no harm or risk or randomness or stress.

Children are antifragile. This is true of their biological systems – sometimes bones get broken and when they do those bones reform stronger. Their immune systems grow more capable at defending them from disease by encountering disease. And it is also true of their cognitive systems.

In order to become sophisticated thinkers, children need to encounter randomness, stress, emotional shock and the stark fact that they are at times simply wrong. These encounters, handled correctly by the expert teacher, make children stronger. Over hundreds of thousands of years, humanity has, through great endeavour and pain, established profound thoughts and ideas. The civilisations humanity has built – along with all the arts, the music, the insights, the knowledge, the skills, the disciplines and the unquenchable thirst for new enlightenment – define our very souls. To engage with these ideas is difficult and requires sustained effort and the ability to overcome uncomfortable emotions.

Learning new ideas is hard. It requires a significant shift in the knowledge structures and schemata already embedded in an individual at the moment of meeting the new idea. Many new ideas are uncomfortable, particularly when they require us to re-evaluate our own beliefs. This discomfort is painful: most people do not find it easy to be told that they are wrong or to face tricky ideas that might take many years of very hard, very purposeful thinking to grasp.

The child who is treated as though their cognitive systems are fragile is the child who is always told they are correct. They are the child whose parents and teachers will pussyfoot around them, never wanting to ask them to do anything difficult, never wanting to question and correct their naïve beliefs. The fragile child is praised whenever they present an idea, no matter how foolish it is, no matter its utility. And this treatment is often justified by claiming it is compassionate, claiming that feelings are more important than thoughts and ideas. But it is not kind to praise the child who is incorrect: it serves only to make them ill informed and frustrated.

Children are antifragile. The expert teacher should carefully and deliberately manufacture scenarios for their pupils to meet tricky ideas and to feel discomfort in the moment for the long-term gain of enlightenment. The incorrect child should be told they are incorrect. This creates an emotional shock that alerts the child to the fact that they better listen really carefully to the correct knowledge that the teacher will now explain to them.

Teachers should seek to make children truly resilient. Children should be able to face tricky, sometimes hurtful ideas head on so that they can overcome and continue to learn. The randomness and stresses the expert teacher places on their pupils are calculated and careful, designed to make the child stronger and more knowledgeable. This is what resilience means – the child who can grapple with ideas, debate, justify, adapt to new knowledge or put right those who are wrong. The resilient child grows into the resilient adult who is not afraid of thoughts and ideas, who knows that harm exists but is ready to take up arms against it and help make humanity better.

There is nothing resilient or moral about the education that some pupils face in schools with policies that instruct teachers to always praise or never point out a child is wrong or to award every child a medal on sports day. There is nothing resilient about the child who has been conditioned to block out challenging ideas. The child who hits the block or mute button on their social media at the slightest hint of an opposing idea is not strong; they are weak and they will not cope well with the demands of life.

The case for antifragility was first put forward by Nassim Taleb (2012) in his book *Antifragile: Things that Gain from Disorder.* Taleb describes systems in economics, business and society that are antifragile, which led me to think about antifragility as applied to children and learning. More recently, Greg Lukianoff and Jonathan Haidt published *The Coddling of the American Mind* (2018). Lukianoff and Haidt also apply Taleb's thinking to children. It was attending a lecture given by Haidt last year that brought me to think further about the fact that children truly are antifragile and that this has been known in the teaching profession for a very long time as an item of simple common sense. Whenever I speak with teachers about antifragility, the response is always that it is clear that pupils must carefully encounter tricky situations if they are to become free thinkers capable of navigating through life with autonomy and a sense of purpose. Yet, so many schools and colleges have adopted policies that clearly position children as fragile. These policies are counterproductive and are restricting the beautiful and meaningful intellectual journey that all pupils could be taking if viewed as antifragile.

Knowing that children are antifragile has implications for how teachers work with ideas such as cognitive load theory, which we met earlier in this book. There has been an unusual unintended consequence to the increasing popularity of CLT – some teachers and schools have interpreted the theory as stating that the cognitive demand on pupils should always be kept as low as possible. But, not only is this not what the theory claims (we discussed the importance of hard thinking earlier when reviewing CLT), but if pupils are antifragile it is crucial that we sometimes provide deliberate and calculated barriers to their learning, which they must overcome through perseverance and the belief that hard work pays off. Children are capable of a great deal more than they are sometimes given credit for. Paving the way for a smooth and predictable path through all learning with no unexpected results or random challenges to their knowledge and beliefs, spoon-feeding pupils every micro-step of every problem so that all they have to do is replicate what the teacher has shown, creating a classroom where nothing is ever uncomfortable and no child is ever wrong – all of these things remove the need for the child to rise to the occasion and demonstrate the power and sophistication that they are capable of. Bjork's proposal of 'desirable difficulties' gives additional, purposeful opportunities for the teacher to deliberately and carefully move pupils out of their comfort zone.

Treat children as antifragile, not fragile.

Moving from propositional to strategic knowledge

Throughout my career in education, I have been implementing the strategies described in this book in my own classrooms and with schools I work with. Taking John B. Carroll's seminal work on cognitive science from the 1960s onwards, I have built the understanding with findings from many others over the years and tried to untangle those hypotheses that are not replicable beyond controlled laboratory conditions from those theories that have been shown to work in the classroom. I have been fascinated and am obsessed with finding answers to questions such as:

- How long passes before someone starts to forget something?

- What is the most effective period of time to allow to pass before using the testing effect to force a pupil to recall?

- When should old material arise again in the spiral?

- How much maturation must occur before a pupil can effectively use that prior learning and understanding in their own inquiry?

These questions have been intractable for many decades now. Experiments have been limited in scale and scope, meaning the data available to address these fundamental questions are not yet sufficient to give educators truly useful guidance.

Some years ago, along with a group of colleagues, I started to propose a large-scale data collection that might help to give new insight. We designed and built an online system, over several iterations in different countries, capable of capturing data on not just pupil performance, but also teaching decisions, curriculum planning, learning-episode phasing, pupil retention, forgetfulness and spiral intervals. We have now collected millions of data points, which are beginning to indicate patterns.

Of course, these are only very early indications at the moment and we are continually growing the community and waiting for the data bank to build up into the hundreds of millions of data points rather than just tens of millions.

I would like to end this part by sharing these very tentative results in our instructional design.

At the moment, most of the models indicate four sequential study-and-test encounters with the novel idea over four learning episodes.

	Idea 1	Idea 2	Idea 3	Idea 4	idea 5
Episode 1	Study				
Episode 2	Test	Study			
Episode 3	Test	Test	Study		
Episode 4	Test	Test	Test	Study	
Episode 5		Test	Test	Test	Study

As described earlier, the study of a novel idea takes as long as it takes. The next learning episode is concerned with a new idea and the pupils are studying that idea, but content from the previous idea is also contained in the lesson (though no teaching of this previous idea occurs), meaning pupils need to recall and answer questions on the previous idea (the testing effect). This continues to build up so that, by the fourth learning episode, the content of the episode is 20% study of a novel idea and 80% testing of three previous ideas (actually, older ideas are often included too in the form of the weekly, no-stakes quizzes that pupils undertake outside of class time, but this content does not appear in class time).

With this scheduling of study-test-test-test for each novel idea, future test performance appears to be greatly enhanced.

The second finding I would like to share here relates to the timing of study episodes. As discussed previously, every idea occurs again in the spiral so that pupils can consider the idea from the point of a more mature schema and see further connections and make further reasoning. These results are nascent and should be read as simply an interesting early finding and not used to change the scheduling of any curriculum.

We are seeing correlation with high rates of retention of test performance over time with the following spacing of study periods:

	Novel Idea
Day 1	Study
Day 2	Study
Day 6	Study
Day 31	Study
Day 90	Study

There do not, at this stage, appear to be any additional gains in studying the idea again after the 90-day study.

So, on early indications, each mathematical idea will have 5 study periods and 15 testing periods on the entire journey through mathematics.

In the coming years, we will continue to monitor, refine and expand our model to take account of effective trends. We will move more deeply from correlation to causation and, since our data set is live and vast, hope to be able to confirm some of the assertions that Carleton Washburne made a century ago and that cognitive scientists have been able to replicate in real classroom conditions at the small scale.

PART IV
A MATHEMATICAL DIVERSION

A final addition to our common vocabulary

In this part of the book, I will draw on my own subject to better exemplify some of the ideas I have already presented as well as some new ideas contained within this section. The mathematical ideas I will use have been chosen to be accessible to all, so there is no need to be a mathematician in order to read what follows. The reader will get the most out of this part if they really engage with the mathematics and examples – some of it might at first feel tricky to the non-mathematically inclined, but if you stick with it, I think you will find it surprising and rewarding.

Before talking about mathematics, we must first add the word to our common vocabulary.

Mathematics

I take 'mathematics' to mean a way of existing in the universe. Mathematicians are curious in all aspects of their lives. Mathematicians, when faced with a problem, enjoy the state of not yet knowing the resolution (indeed, knowing there may not even be a resolution). Because they are curious, mathematicians, when faced with a problem, ask themselves questions of it. They can specialise, pattern-spot, conjecture, generalise, try to disprove, argue with themselves, monitor their own thinking, reflect and notice how these new encounters have changed them as a human being. That is to say, mathematics is an epistemological model: a way of considering the very nature of knowledge.

Sadly, in many Western countries, children have been conditioned to believe that mathematics is about wading through questions, getting 'right' or 'wrong' answers. This is confusing to mathematicians, since it does not represent our domain at all. Mathematicians are not in the business of answering lists of questions. Rather, they meet scenarios and, driven by their curiosity, create their own questions and follow their own lines of enquiry. Many of these lines of enquiry result in unexpected results, but we do not consider these to be 'wrong', simply not what we thought would happen. Often, great discoveries in mathematics have resulted from lines of enquiry that lead to unexpected results.

Mathematicians enjoy being stuck. They revel in the initial apparent impenetrability of a scenario and understand that by attacking it in a structured way, enlightenment can arise.

Teach everything correctly first time

In 1995, the government in England embarked upon a major project in an attempt to raise standards in primary school mathematics. Following a general election in 1997, the National Numeracy Project was continued by the subsequent government, growing into the National Numeracy Strategy. A sharp increase in attainment quickly followed and the perceived success of the Strategy saw it extended into secondary education. The National Strategy continued until 2010, making it one of the most significant, large-scale and costliest initiatives to improve mathematics teaching that the world had ever seen. However, despite the positive and much-lauded improvements in primary mathematics, the effects did not appear to continue through to give similar gains in secondary school examinations.

A wide-reaching, large-scale professional development programme was designed and deployed across the entire country in order to train primary teachers in approaches to teaching mathematics. These approaches were comprehensively supported by extensive teaching and learning resources and even scripted and timed lessons.

It appeared baffling, then, that following such extensive support and the expected improvements in attainment at primary, the Strategy was having no impact on the critical exams that pupils would take at the end of secondary school.

One key reason for this strange outcome lay in the very training and support that all primary teachers were required to engage with. The approaches to teaching key mathematical ideas were very often sufficient for handling the level of mathematics that pupils encountered at the end of primary school, but did not hold true or did not generalise readily for use with higher-level mathematics. Many of the methods pupils were being taught were 'backward facing', suitable only to take them to a known end point rather than 'forward-facing' approaches to mathematics that plan for later mathematical ideas. This profound flaw in the design and implementation of the National Strategy resulted in a neglect for what is needed for mathematical progression.

An effective mathematics education system is one that focuses on teaching approaches that maximise subsequent progression, rather than a pursuit of short-term, superficial success.

Arranged as a coherent, long-term and unified journey through mathematics, the curriculum can drive a responsibility at each stage to prepare for the next. It is not the job of the primary teacher to get pupils to pass a primary mathematics test; rather, it is their moral duty to ensure that the mathematics they teach enables their pupils to continue to learn mathematics in secondary school. The secondary school teacher, too, has the same moral burden upon them – they must ready their pupils to be able to continue to study the subject at a higher level should they choose to do so.

In a conveyor belt system, it is all too understandable why, when faced with a pupil who is struggling, teachers often show the pupil a quick trick, rule or method that they can apply there and then in order to perform and 'get through' the lesson. These backward-facing methods often give a quick win – allowing the pupil to feel comfortable and perform – but they seriously hinder the pupil when, later, they are faced with a problem that requires a proper understanding of an approach rather than the limited trick they were shown some years back by a teacher under the erroneous belief that their job was to get through a curriculum rather than to create young mathematicians.

We must seek to identify the reference framework for the ideas pupils will meet on their journey through a discipline. This framework must be known by all teachers at all stages so they understand what knowledge a new idea sits upon and the reasons for laying the new idea down – it will become the firm foundation of some other idea later in the curriculum. We must always refer back to the reference framework every time we introduce a new idea and then build the knowledge and the connections to other ideas gradually and unforgettably.

Ensuring that all approaches are always forward facing requires the explicit stating of a coherent, carefully sequenced curriculum, covering the entire journey through the subject. A curriculum planned for progression; a curriculum that ensures everything is taught correctly, first time. It is, therefore, incumbent upon all schools to ensure the curriculum they have at hand is not one limited to a year group or key stage, but is the full curriculum for the entire journey. The stated curriculum must be common to primary and secondary schools so that the forensically planned sequencing is not broken.

Some educators – particularly those who do not or have not ever taught in real classrooms – persistently object that approaches to teaching an idea must be personal to the teacher, that the teacher should be empowered to write their own curriculum and always make their own resources. This is an objection that holds back the teaching profession and prevents other professions from taking the education sector seriously. There are no heart surgeons in training who are told, 'Hey, you come up with your own way of doing this surgery – anything goes, as long as it makes you feel good.' A serious profession, with a canon of professional knowledge, extensively trains new entrants in the tried-and-tested methods that have been shown to work by the entire profession over many years. Of course, as teachers become expert, they too will contribute to the professional canon and it is undoubtedly an important professional skill to be able to design tasks and, perhaps, curricula. But this should not be used as a false empowerment agenda that leaves thousands of teachers flailing and hunting around for ideas as they try to reinvent perfectly good wheels.

In mathematics, we ask pupils to grip around 320 mathematical ideas during their entire time at school (assuming they are to learn everything on school-level mathematics). Surely, then, it should simply be the expectation that every single person who wishes to teach mathematics is instructed in the very best ways our profession knows of teaching every one of those 320 ideas. They should be instructed in the models, metaphors and examples that can be used to bring about meaning-making. They should be taught several approaches to each of those ideas such that they have at their disposal a selection of explanations, allowing them to vary those explanations expertly so that every single pupil has the moment of enlightenment. They should have shared with them the effective questions, prompts, tasks, investigations and activities that we, as a profession, have created and know to be impactful. They should be instructed in the known misconceptions that arise in pupils' minds when encountering each of the ideas and have explained to them the ways in which they can best mitigate those misconceptions. And they should be required to know the mathematics.

Imagine what a difference could be made if, instead of a teacher-training route that is obsessed with pedagogy, teacher training was a serious discourse about the mathematics that pupils will meet and the effective ways to explain it **with meaning**.

Imagine what a difference could be made if we took the view that every single child can grip every single idea, not because of some chance 'gift' of ability but because their teacher is an expert at communicating all of those mathematical ideas.

Teacher training that subscribes to the cult of pedagogy without didactics sells our new entrants short and leaves them with little intellectually rigorous knowledge on how to teach their subject.

I am completely uninterested in the teacher who can teach well. What matters is that they can teach **mathematics** well.

Teaching makes absolutely no sense without considering what is being taught. Yet, across Western countries in particular, over the past 30 years we have created a system that rewards the teacher who is the exquisite performer – the teacher who has the funkiest resources and games, the card sorter, the teamwork facilitator, the teacher who orchestrates the 'active' classroom by asking pupils to do times-tables questions whilst running around bean bags, the teacher with the big personality. A regime of inspection and observation that fetishises pedagogy has seen the performing teacher elevated over the teacher who is expert at enabling pupils to grip the difficult new ideas they need to get their heads around if they are to gain anything meaningful from their schooling, the teacher who knows that thoughts and ideas matter more than feelings, the teacher who demands effort and the truly purposeful grappling with tricky ideas.

The cult of pedagogy has almost entirely wiped out the central importance of didactics and reduced the assessment of the teaching process to one that focuses entirely on style without even a nod to substance.

Pedagogy is, of course, important – it is concerned with the general frameworks, styles, models and assumptions of education – but it is not sufficient. Pedagogy without didactics is a key contributor to the problems faced in many Western education systems.

Didactics is concerned with technical details. Pedagogy and didactics combined strengthen the focus of education beyond simply performing, beyond the style of social interactions in the classroom, to the details of specifically how best an idea can be taught, the prerequisite ideas on which it must build and whether those connected ideas are readily retrievable by the pupil. Pedagogy with didactics moves beyond simple exercise to the design of specific exercises that we know will more likely lead to the pupil making sense of and gripping the novel idea at hand. It moves beyond repetitive practice to carefully varied practice with specific sequences of questions or tasks that extend a pupil's thinking and demands that they grapple with the underlying principles and structures of an idea. Pedagogy with didactics – the technical details that underpin a mathematical idea – forensically brings into existence an associated web of ideas, with correctness and reason, that forces the pupil to consider a novel idea in a broader framework, including problems beyond their current grasp such that they identify the need for further learning and purposeful work.

Mathematics teaching is about generating a long-term change in a pupil's understanding of, and progress with, specific mathematical content. It is not good enough that the teacher plans a lesson on, say, fractions. What specific aspect of fractions should be examined and what specific models, examples and metaphors should the teacher use to explain that specific aspect? And on what specific questions and tasks should the pupils work? And why choose those specific questions – what do they specifically lead to and how will working on those specific questions define the associated web of ideas? Importantly, how will these specific experiences result in the pupils' robust preparedness for subsequent specific content in their journey through learning mathematics?

Getting to grips with the didactics – the technical details – of the mathematics being learnt means that pupils have correct and efficient techniques which they can deploy at any time.

There are those who protest that mathematics education should not be about techniques but instead should focus on problem solving. This is a false dichotomy and the argument that wages eternally between mathematics factions is unhelpful. The reality is that if we want to prepare pupils for a continuing love of and desire to study mathematics, we must integrate the requirement that they become fully proficient with techniques with the requirement to solve problems.

Solving problems makes no sense as a separate activity, but only as an integral part for all pupils of learning to use each technique in its full complexity – which is what is needed if those techniques are to support subsequent mathematics (Gardiner, 2016).

There are many subject areas that have, for a long time, truly embedded a mastery approach to schooling. In art, music, sport and dance, it is the norm for the teacher to carefully and deliberately progress the pupil through the subject. The sport teacher does not demand the pupil who can leap only 80 centimetres to suddenly jump 2 metres. The music teacher knows that the pupil must go through the arduous process of getting to grips with scales as a step towards playing a piece with ease. The outcome of successful art teaching may well be a beautiful and unique sculpture or painting, but the art teacher knows that the pupil must invest many years in perfecting technique before those techniques can come together into something magical. Consider the eloquent professional ballet dancer, who moves with apparent ease in a stunning and profound performance. How wonderful it would be to be able to replicate their achievements – but those achievements are the result of thousands of committed hours rehearsing micro-techniques over and over again until they become behaviours.

Mathematics, too, comes together in an eloquent dance. All of those basic techniques that once stood alone and were practised repeatedly and with purpose form a complex, integrated schema of techniques, understanding and behaviours that combine into something truly beautiful as the mathematician dances their sublime dance. It is only possible because the pupil has been exposed to techniques in a carefully scheduled journey and they have worked hard to perfect those techniques with great accuracy. Each of the techniques that they meet along the way is a doorway to profound and awe-inspiring mathematics.

The didactics of mathematics analyses how the content of elementary mathematics can be arranged into a carefully sequenced succession of ideas and how each idea can be introduced and organised so that all pupils understand its underlying principles and can fluently work with all of its related processes. The didactics of mathematics also examines the main barriers to learning the new idea, meaning the teacher can design better-informed instructional approaches.

This is not a book about didactics, but it is worth taking a diversion into mathematics as an example of how just a small number of ideas might be arranged and introduced. Although the examples are from my own subject area, the central point holds for all subjects: pedagogy without didactics is simply not good enough. We should all be aiming for pedagogy with didactics.

Multiple representations

When Aristotle rejected Platonism in favour of his newly forming epistemological model (an early form of empiricism) he brought to epistemology an additional insight: the real, lived world is important in bringing about meaning when learning a new idea. Aristotle writes, 'All knowledge begins with the senses.'

Enabling pupils to meaning-make is the greatest challenge that teachers face. It is particularly challenging since the teacher is an expert themselves and recalling the emotions of being a novice is difficult. Novices work with new information and ideas in entirely different ways to experts, so the teacher must attempt to strip away their expertise and put themselves in the place of the pupil. Upon first encountering a novel mathematical idea, pupils must be able to assimilate the information into their current schemas in such a way that the new idea makes sense and fits logically with what is already known.

Representational fluency

Kaput (1989) documented the need for, and benefits of, representational fluency in mathematics since mathematics is 'inherently representational in its intentions and methods'.

We must now add this phrase to the shared vocabulary we began to establish earlier. First, let's deal with the word 'representation'. I outlined earlier that to be able to think about a mathematical idea, one must first hold a mental representation of the idea in one's memory. Here are two useful definitions of what such a representation might mean:

> **Representation is any kind of mental state with a specific content, a mental reproduction of a former mental state, a picture, a symbol, or sign, or symbolic tool one has to learn, a something 'in place of' something else.**

Seeger et al., 1998

> **The act of capturing a mathematical concept or relationship in some form and to the form itself.**

National Council of Teachers of Mathematics, 2000

Clearly, there are many forms these mental representations can take for any single mathematical idea. I will take 'representational fluency' to mean having a range of mental representations and an ability to translate across these representations. The NCTM highlights some of the possible forms:

> **a variety of mathematical representations, including graphs, tables, symbolic expressions, and verbal expressions, as well as the interconnections among them**

National Council of Teachers of Mathematics, 2000

Each mathematical idea or concept can be thought of in a range of ways, like looking at it from a range of perspectives. Mathematical ideas, principles and relationships can be expressed verbally, visually and symbolically, with each of these types of representation bringing different meaning to the idea. Naturally the pupil and teacher could hold bias towards or away from a particular representation. If such a bias exists, this bias may not always align with the most efficient, useful or robust representations. Pupils revealnatural tendency to reduce the level of abstraction to a level that is compatible with their existing cognitive structure (Pape and Tchoshanov, 2001) or tend to make the unfamiliar more familiar by 'concretizing' the concepts they learn (Wilensky, 1991).

One interesting large-scale study (Panasuk and Beyranevand, 2011) examined pupils' experiences and preferences towards different representations. There is a preference amongst low-achieving pupils for pictorial representations and amongst high-achieving pupils for the symbolic. However, these preferences do not tell the full story, since pupils (and teachers) are not good at choosing the most effective ways of learning or working. It was observed that low-achieving pupils would often state a perceived preference for the pictorial, yet when actually working on a problem, the images they produced made the task more difficult and they found it clearer to work symbolically. Meanwhile, some high-achieving pupils, who all expressed a very strong dislike of working with pictorial representations and espoused the effectiveness of working symbolically, were unable to articulate an understanding of the mathematical idea when asked to describe more than the algorithmic procedure they were following to arrive at a solution.

Mathematics teachers also seem biased towards symbolic representations, which leads to these being viewed as more valid and worthy by pupils. Teachers very often encourage pupils to work symbolically, even when it is not the most useful approach.

Pictures can be powerful tools for helping pupils to articulate the underlying principles of a concept, but teachers should think carefully about their use and monitor pupils' beliefs. As Pimm (1995) suggests, 'Because diagrams seem so iconic, so transparent, it is easy to forget that they too need to be read rather than merely beheld.' It is also likely that pupils focus on 'surface details' (Diezmann, 1999) rather than the deep structure of the mathematical idea.

When aiming for far transfer – that is to say, for a pupil to be able to apply some mathematical technique or idea in the long term and in a variety of non-isomorphic scenarios – teachers should take note that the Panasuk and Beyranevand study showed that pupils who were able to recognise the same relationship represented in different modes (what Panasuk refers to as 'conceptual understanding') were more likely to perform well on later standardised tests. It would seem, however, that the reverse does not hold. There is evidence to suggest high achievement is not an indicator of good conceptual understanding. This is an interesting dilemma for the mathematics teachers since, yet again, behaviours exhibited in a lesson that may lead to praise by the observer or inspector (all pupils getting correct answers to a set of equations, say) may not be the behaviours that indicate the best chance of far transfer. The classroom in which the teacher is asking the pupil to articulate relationships across multiple representations can appear, on the face of it, chaotic, with pupils having numerous conversations about the different meanings and interpretations of a whole range of ways of looking at a mathematical idea. I have very often seen such lessons criticised by a school inspector who was incapable of seeing beyond the surface-level characteristics of the lesson to the deliberate, difficult thinking that pupils were being made to undertake.

Concrete, pictorial, abstract and language

Now the new idea is to be communicated in such a way that all pupils are able to build meaning and a sense of the idea.

The teacher will use a range of models, metaphors and examples in order to allow all pupils to see how the novel idea is connected to what they already know and how the various representations connect to each other. Haylock and Cockburn presented a useful visual for this 'connective model' in their 1989 book *Understanding Early Years Mathematics*.

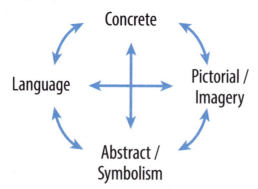

Adapted from Haylock and Cockburn, 1989

One powerful way of bringing about a sense of these connections and meaning-making when meeting a novel mathematical idea is to use mathematical manipulatives.

Manipulatives are objects which have been carefully thought about and designed such that when a pupil handles and manipulates the objects, they will begin to perceive some mathematical idea, concept or fact. They also help the pupil to communicate their thinking and to articulate connections and underlying relationships. This articulation gives the teacher insight into the meaning-making process that the pupil is going through and therefore enables them to respond or guide as appropriate.

Talking about mathematics and new mathematical ideas with increasingly sophisticated language is a key step in learning mathematics. Through articulation of ideas, pupil and teacher can test and refine, extend and connect. The use of manipulatives is, therefore, suitable at any stage of learning mathematics. I have had many a conversation with mathematics PhD candidates as they have tried to explain their thinking through the use of string, plasticine or Lego. Being able to manipulate mathematical models and metaphors in real time, being able to change the variables and conditions, being able to demonstrate the impact of change, and being able to describe boundary conditions or limitations – these all vastly improve understanding. As discussed earlier, understanding is not just about the connections between mathematical ideas, but is about the ability to reason why those connections hold true. Manipulatives, used carefully, allow pupils to do this in a sophisticated and robust way.

Teachers of mathematics have a vast range of manipulatives at their disposal, including:

- Number lines

- Pattern blocks

- Multi-link cubes

- Fraction tiles

- Polydrons

- Balancing scales

- Geoboards

- Tangrams

- Counters

- Rekenreks

and many more.

It is important to recognise that the elements of the connective model do not form a hierarchy and it is not intended as a pathway from the concrete to the abstract. Rather, we can move between the representations as appropriate. It is common that starting with the real lived world can be the most useful, but it is not always the case. Some discussions will begin in the concrete; others as stories or pictures; and others as ideas. Of course, we want all pupils to be able to work with all mathematical ideas efficiently and effectively in the abstract/symbolic form, but there is no need to rush there. Giving pupils many opportunities to examine a mathematical idea from a range of viewpoints enhances their appreciation of the underlying principles behind the idea and the ideas on which it is founded.

A common misconception in the teaching of mathematics is to believe that the most skilled teachers are required as the mathematics itself becomes 'harder'. In fact, it is far more intellectually demanding to work out how to get a pupil to grip earlier mathematics and this is where our most expert teachers are required. It is a more difficult task to enable a human being to gain a sense of number, for example, than it is to get a teenager to solve a quadratic equation.

Yet, often, school systems do not invest sufficient expertise in teaching early mathematical ideas. Without these early ideas securely in place, the whole Jenga tower tumbles down.

Early years and primary settings are faced with a significant conundrum. In the vast majority of cases, teachers are not mathematics specialists and are responsible for teaching a wide range of subject areas. There are most definitely benefits to this approach – teacher-pupil relationships trump everything else when working with young children, so a move to subject-specialist teaching in early-years mathematics is unwise (and is, in any case, logistically impossible given the enormous CPD and recruitment requirement). In a mastery approach, we are working carefully to create homogenised cohorts of pupils, and so, as the approach becomes embedded, it becomes increasingly more possible to predict the mathematical ideas that are encountered over a broad period of time. Instead of subject specialists, it is therefore possible to ask teachers to become stage specialists. This reduces the CPD burden considerably by asking teachers to become highly expert in teaching a smaller range of mathematical ideas (whilst still retaining a professional knowledge of the whole of school-level mathematics).

It would be easy to fill a book – or indeed many books – with a discussion of the various manipulatives available to the mathematics teacher. For the purposes of illustrating the importance of multiple representations and the use of a concrete-pictorial-abstract-language framework, I will include here a short discussion of just three of my favourite manipulatives, beginning with perhaps the most versatile and useful tool for building a sense of numerosity and beyond: the simple Cuisenaire rod.

Cuisenaire rods

Long before many cognitive scientists had begun to engage with the idea that learning requires energy and that learning is really about causing a change to the long-term memory, Caleb Gattegno (1974) suggested that there was an 'energy budget' to learning. He proposed that a unit of energy, which he called an 'ogden', was required to learn a new fact or idea and, crucially, to retain it for later recall. Without the ability to recall the fact at a future date, Gattegno suggested that the ogden had not been fully spent.

With the realisation that learning was truly effortful, Gattegno rightly asserted that we should seek educational approaches that reduced this energy requirement. He began to theorise, test and refine many approaches to teaching mathematics, languages and reading, which could reduce the energy cost. Gattegno noticed that many types of learning were 'expensive', requiring the spend of many ogdens, but that other ways of learning the exact same idea required very little energy budget. He suggested standalone, disconnected facts and ideas were much harder to recall; but when teaching drew on sensory images, the costs vastly reduced.

All of this now seems very familiar. John B. Carroll, in the 1960s, held similar views and the domain of cognitive science today has brought new insight into the mental energy that learning requires and ways of reducing that energy. But in the 1950s, many of these ideas were at the cutting edge. Caleb Gattegno became a hugely influential educator, writing over 120 books and developing pedagogical approaches that have stood the test of time.

During the '50s, Gattegno popularised the use of Cuisenaire rods, named for the Belgian primary teacher Georges Cuisenaire, who invented the rods and used them in his own teaching.

Cuisenaire rods are mathematical manipulatives which pupils can use to learn a wide range of mathematical ideas and knowledge. The use of the rods in mathematics teaching is extensive and a discussion of Cuisenaire rods could easily fill a significant book of its own. Here I will outline just a small number of ways that the rods can be used to teach mathematical ideas.

Cuisenaire rods – play

The first step to using rods with young children (or pupils of any age who are mathematically developmentally at this stage) is to allow them to simply play with the rods. Although this may sound unstructured or even inefficient, the very nature of the rods means that the play is actually quite predictable, with pupils gaining insight into precisely what the teacher has planned they will. Many teachers are tempted to try to shortcut this play phase, choosing instead to tell the pupils about the rods; yet this only serves to reduce, not increase, the rate of learning, particularly as teachers often skip vital emphasis on the relationships between the rods.

The rods come in different sizes and colours.

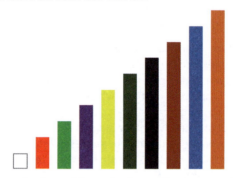

As the pupils play with a box of the rods, the teacher is waiting for key moments to occur.

Initial play will result in some predictable results. Children will make patterns and drawings, build towers, make shapes and group the rods in certain ways. For instance, a pupil might take all of the rods in their box and arrange them into groups of white, red, green, etc. They will often arrange the rods in order of size, perhaps placing them alongside each other like a staircase. Many children will then enjoy the symmetry of continuing the staircase, but now going downstairs.

It is interesting to note that pupils will undertake this sort of arranging behaviour first. That is to say, they are ordering the rods before there is any notion of assigning the rods value.

Ordinality comes **before** cardinality.

This is in keeping with the history of the development of mathematics as a discipline: ordinality arose before cardinality. Ordering comes naturally before learning how to count objects and was historically important for describing the position in a battle, race or hierarchy. Culturally, stating who has come first or second or third has been more crucial in societal systems around the world (and far more importantly, in the early evolution of society) than being able to use cardinal numbers.

And here we are, with a short time of free play, children quickly displaying ordinality and being able to articulate it.

One of the errors that education systems often make is to assume that the day a child arrives at school for the first time is somehow the first moment that child has miraculously popped into the universe. Teachers treat pupils like clean slates. This is true across the age range: we frequently see secondary school teachers behave as though their pupils have not learnt any mathematics to date, so they start afresh and ignore what has come before. This is a great shame since, by age 11, most pupils have actually encountered a great deal of mathematics and their primary mathematics education has often been far more sophisticated than their secondary teacher realises. It is even more pronounced at the beginning of primary education, with the teacher treating their new pupils as though they couldn't possibly have learnt any mathematics before this point. But, of course, by the time a child arrives at school at age four or five, they have existed in the universe for quite some time and have experienced a great deal. They already have a sense of shape and pattern and quantity and direction and so much else. Watch two small children for just a short period of time as they play and you will quickly spot them arranging toys in order of size, trading with their sister or brother ('I will give you two small action figures for that large teddy') playing out fantasy car races in their heads and on the floor with model cars and announcing their positions ('First! Second! Last'), talking about speed and distances, depths and temperatures, describing how one action effects another ('Making the slide steeper makes the Lego car roll down it quicker!').

Children have learnt a lot.

The teacher needs to understand what experiences the child has encountered and what beliefs they already hold so that they can bridge from those beliefs and continue to reveal mathematics to the child from a correct starting point, whilst also unpicking and undoing incorrect beliefs that the child may have.

The expert teacher is alive to (and takes account of) the possible knowledge that pupils have acquired to date. Much of what they have come to believe as true is, in fact, utterly wrong or, at the very least, a seriously unhelpful view of a mathematical idea.

Take, for instance, this simple question: is five bigger than eight?

Now, the teacher may well tell the pupils that five is not bigger than eight and the pupils may well nod and smile in agreement. Sometimes they nod and smile because the teacher is a teacher and they have been told to listen to them and not play up! Sometimes pupils will not protest when the teacher says something they believe to be false; they will instead keep schtum, ignore the teacher's claim, and quietly go about maintaining their erroneous beliefs.

Is five bigger than eight?

Well, perhaps a child walks to school each morning and passes a billboard with a giant five written on it!

Is **5** bigger than 8? It might be!

Clearly, I am using a fairly trivial example here to make the point. But the teacher must not assume that the pupil is a clean slate. There is so much going on in their heads and the teacher needs to elicit from them any misconceptions so that they can be told they are wrong and then taught the correct information.

Cuisenaire rods – equivalence, equality, algebra and arithmetic

As the pupils continue to play with their rods, other predictable outcomes arise, such as this:

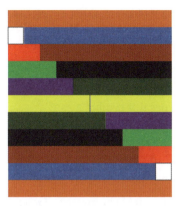

Although we have not yet begun to assign any values to the rods, what we can see here is the beginnings of number bonds. Pupils will find lots of examples where the length of one rod can be made from the lengths of several other rods.

The teacher can circulate the room eagerly watching out for these key moments to occur.

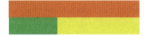

Perhaps the teacher spots a pupil, Poppy, who has placed these rods on their table.

TEACHER: 'Oh! Neat! Can you tell me what you have noticed?'

POPPY: 'A brown rod is the same length as a green and a yellow rod.'

TEACHER: 'Ace! Let's capture that at the board!'

The teacher can use a visualiser to project the pupil's arrangement on to the screen for all the class to see and then ask Poppy to say their sentence again... and again...and again.

As Poppy repeats 'A brown is the same length as a green and a yellow', the teacher carefully and deliberately writes on the board:

$$b = g + y$$

The teacher points to each symbol as the pupil says their sentence, making no fuss about the way in which they have written it. There is no need to explain to class that the letters represent the rods, they will know – they are not stupid!

TEACHER: 'What an interesting thing Poppy has found out. We can make the same lengths with different rods. Do you see how I have written this on the board? Do you see what the symbols mean?'

The teacher has repeatedly pointed at the symbols as the image as the sentence has been said.

TEACHER: 'What does this symbol mean?'

Point at the + symbol.

CLASS: 'And!'

TEACHER: 'OK. Can you tell me more about it?'

PUPIL: 'It's when you put them together. Green and yellow. The symbol means joining them together.'

TEACHER: 'Yes, we **join** the rods together. We **add** the rods together. We get the **total** length of the rods. We have **added** the rods. There is an **addition**. This symbol is an **addition** symbol.'

The teacher then points to the = symbol.

TEACHER: 'What does this symbol mean?'

CLASS: 'Is the same as!'

TEACHER: 'OK. Can you tell me more about it?'

PUPIL: 'It means they have the same length.'

TEACHER: 'Interesting. It looks like it has something to do with making the same length. The lengths are **equal**. There is **equality**. This symbol is an **equals symbol**.'

The teacher then points carefully at the rods and the symbols again.

TEACHER: 'Brown **equals** green **plus** yellow.'

This should be said several times, each time pointing at the symbols and the rods.

TEACHER: 'This is neat. Well done for showing us this, Poppy. When we use the **equals symbol**, we are making **equations**. I bet you can all make equations. Please make as many **equations** as you can. Build them and write them down.'

Pupils will now busy themselves making all manner of equations and happily writing them in the format described. Again, the teacher is waiting for key moments to happen.

Perhaps a pupil, Sam, has on their table:

The teacher can again show the class using the visualiser and ask Sam to describe what he has found.

SAM: 'An orange is five reds.'

The teacher asks Sam to keep saying his sentence over and over, while the teacher writes on the board and continually points to

$$o = 5r$$

timing their pointing with the words Sam says.

Again, there is no need to make a fuss. The pupils can see that there is a short way of writing five reds: 5r.

The teacher now gives them more time to find even more equations. For quite some time, pupils will restrict themselves to equations in which one rod is expressed in terms of several other rods. They seem cautious about beginning with a length that is not just a single rod, but the moment will come and the teacher can be on the lookout for it.

Perhaps another pupil has this on their table:

The teacher can then repeat the show, repeat, point and symbolise process.

$$bk + y = r + p + dg$$

Note that the teacher has proposed some new symbols for black and dark green, which will help avoid confusion with blue and light green. Other formats could be used, of course, but it is the consistency of use that will be important.

As the pupils continue to work with the rods, they will begin to assign values to each rod. Naturally, pupils will decide that the small white rod

should be given a value of one and the numeral '1'.

Once the emergence of oneness arises, the other rods suddenly take on the extra meaning of having given lengths, values and numerals. It will not be long until pupils start to form number sentences of the type:

$$7 + 3 + 4$$

Pupils can continue to find many such number sentences and their numberness expressed in rods. As pupils lay out representations like this, the teacher can choose to simply lay alongside their rods an orange ten-rod. Doing so creates a moment of curiosity for the pupil: **why did they do that?** Pondering for a moment, it is common for a pupil to then select a new rod to complete the length, giving:

$$7 + 3 + 4$$

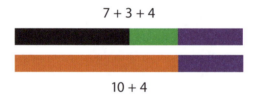

$$10 + 4$$

The pupil can now see that the same length could be created utilising the orange ten-rod. Continuing to lay orange rods alongside the pupils' trains of rods begins to establish the usefulness of representing numbers as a number of ten-rods and an appropriate additional rod to complete the length. This is deliberately subtle. The pupil will begin to see that the ten-rod makes creating numbers easier. They will also notice it is far easier to determine the value of larger numbers.

Interestingly, I have often come across arrangements such as:

$$4 + 8 + 3$$

Alongside this, I have placed a ten rod, expecting the pupil to select the five-rod to complete the length, but found they have instead built:

$$4 + 8 + 3$$

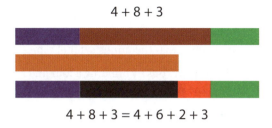

$$4 + 8 + 3 = 4 + 6 + 2 + 3$$

This is a surprising result and can lead to an interesting debate with the pupil, who has clearly given serious thought to their next step. There is certainly a logical explanation for bonding to the ten and then extending beyond in the way the pupil has. However, we want them to utilise the ten-rod, and so place down the final combination:

$$4 + 8 + 3 = 4 + 6 + 2 + 3$$

$$= 10 + 5 = 15$$

The teacher might also introduce the minus symbol and ask the pupils to show a number sentence such as $9 - 4 = 5$. Note: this sentence is 'read nine minus four equals five'. It is not 'nine subtract four', since 'subtract' is a verb and does not fit grammatically. 'Minus' is a preposition and so holds grammatically correct. It should also not be read 'nine take away four', since we want to avoid the misconception that $4 - 9$ is impossible. You might protest: 'Well of course it isn't and nobody would ever suggest that it is.' Yet, watch hundreds of mathematics lessons with Year 1 pupils and you will hear pupils asking questions such as, 'What if it was the other way around? What if we had to do four take away nine?' Sadly, the almost-universal response to this from the classroom teacher is, 'It can't be done.' This might seem like just a white lie to help them proceed with the type of problems they are working with at that moment, but that lie is internalised and remembered by the pupils; it festers and soon becomes an embedded misconception. Teach everything correctly, first time.

There are two helpful ways of thinking about the number sentence $9 - 4 = 5$, firstly as addition and secondly as a difference. Both of these ways of thinking about subtraction are generalisable and will hold throughout school-level mathematics.

Subtraction is not anti-addition; it is not the opposite of addition; it doesn't 'undo' addition. Subtraction is addition. It is just the addition of additive inverses. 9 − 4 is 9 + (−4). It is therefore helpful even at this early developmental stage to communicate to pupils that the minus symbol represents an addition.

We can easily show this with our rods by building a four and a five on top of the nine-rod. We can see that the same length is made from both.

It is also easy to communicate the idea of difference using our rods. Showing the nine-rod and the four-rod, the teacher can ask, 'What is the same and what is different?'

The difference is clearly the gap. The pupils can demonstrate that the gap is the same length as a five-rod.

The teacher should ask the pupils to show many such examples, continually reinforcing the fact that the minus symbol represents addition and difference.

When Cuisenaire rods are joined together to create lengths, we refer to these formations as 'trains'. Trains can be used to show equivalent lengths and are useful in communicating meaning behind equations and number sentences for addition. Another important representation of equivalence using the rods occurs when rods are placed on top of each other, which we refer to as 'floors'.

Suppose a teacher says to some young children (or pupils who are at an early stage of mathematical development, regardless of their age), 'six times four is the same as four times six'. Read that sentence again and hear those words in your head. It's just not true, is it. The teacher is literally saying different things are the same as each other. Most pupils will accept the statement as simply a given fact, but there are plenty of pupils who hear the sentence and think, 'Whoa, wait a minute, that's not right.'

Establishing truth is crucial when teaching new ideas. Rather than simply stating the fact, the teacher could take a moment to demonstrate the meaning behind the sentence by showing six four-rods and four six-rods alongside each other.

$$6 \times 4 = 4 \times 6$$

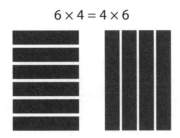

The pupils can then be convinced of the equivalence of these statements by laying the purple rods on top of the green to make a perfect floor of the same area.

Multiplication can also be used as another opportunity to develop a sense of the importance of the ten-rod in expressing values.

TEACHER: 'Please show me 12 lots of 4. Write down a number sentence to represent what you have created.'

Typically, pupils will show:

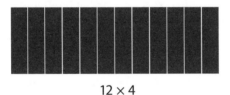

$$12 \times 4$$

TEACHER: 'What is the full value of the rods that make up the rectangle? What is the area of the rectangle? It's tricky to see, isn't it. Could we use different rods to make it easier to know the value?'

Using a visualiser, the teacher can show the creation of a new floor on top of the four-rods, this time utilising the ten-rods. For example, using the ten and the two-rod, the teacher can show the length is equal:

Continuing in this way, a new floor is built:

TEACHER: 'Can you see this is easier to count? 10, 20, 30, 40, 42, 44, 46, 48. Using the tens makes it easier to count to larger numbers. And look what we have here! 4 lots of 12! So, 12 lots of 4 is equal to 4 lots of 12. That is, 12 times 4 is equal to 4 times 12. 12 multiplied by 4 is the same as 4 multiplied by 12. Both products are 48.'

Again, the teacher is establishing the commutative properties of multiplication and can formalise the sentence by writing on the board:

$$12 \times 4 = 4 \times 12 = 48$$

When creating floors of this type, the original multiplier and multiplicand get lost under the new floor or floors that are built. We often want to know the value of these original numbers, since they represent a factorisation of the floors created. One way in which this can be achieved is to build the floors inside a multiplication space, with the original multiplier and multiplicand defining the space to be filled. For example, we might show that 4 times 12 is equal to 48 by first creating a defined space

$$12 \times 4 = 48$$

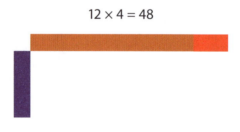

and then asking the pupils to fill in the space in an efficient way. Typically, pupils will create either the same model as previous or

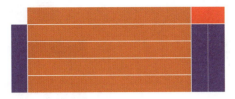

This gives yet another view of 48 that is easily countable.

In line with the use of the field axioms, which we will discuss later, we can think of division as a multiplication process. So, 24 ÷ 6, can be seen as 'How many 6s would be needed to make 24?'

A simple view of this might be

$$24 \div 6$$

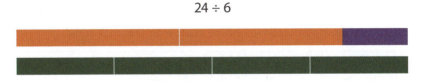

Here the pupils can see that $4 \times 6 = 24$. And because we know multiplication can happen in any order, it must also be true that $6 \times 4 = 24$, which can be viewed as

These could also be considered floors, rather than trains, by showing a range of floors that equate to 24 and then finding equivalent floors made up of 6s and 4s.

Cuisenaire rods – considering primeness

A simple task that the teacher can ask the pupils to explore is to create each of the rod lengths in trains of single colours. For example, the first eight lengths can be created in single-colour trains as follows:

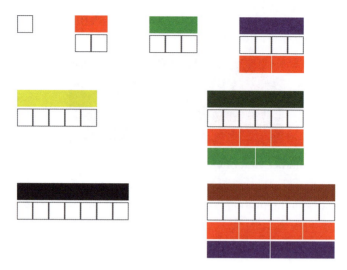

TEACHER: 'What do you notice about the lengths you are able to make?'

CLASS: 'Some numbers can only be made with the white rods.'

TEACHER: '**Only** the white rods?'

PUPIL: 'No. The original rod and the white rods.'

TEACHER: 'Aha! So, some lengths can only be made in **two** ways: the original rod itself and the white rods. Does that work for all of the lengths?'

PUPIL: 'The first one can only be made in one way.'

TEACHER: 'Oh, yes! So that doesn't fit our rule. Find more lengths that can only be made in **two** ways.'

Working in this way, we create a rules-based system for expressing certain types of numbers: numbers which can only be represented as multiples of the 1 and the number itself. As pupils work further with this task, they will gain a sense of the types of numbers where this is the case, which the teacher could choose to now label as prime numbers.

Cuisenaire rods – fractions

Let me start by making this clear at the outset: teaching fractions using metaphors of pizzas is really unhelpful. Stop it.

It is easy to spot pupils who have been subjected to the pizza analogy. They think that fractions are limited and bounded by one. The teacher draws a circle on the board.

TEACHER: 'Here is a pizza. Can you show me half of a pizza?'

PUPIL: 'Yes.'

The pupil cuts the pizza in half with a straight line and points to one half.

TEACHER: 'Can you show me another half of a pizza?'

The pupil points to the other half.

TEACHER: 'Can you show me another half of a pizza?'

The pupil looks bewildered.

PUPIL: 'No. There are only two halves. You can't have more than two halves.'

Pupils taught in this way are, quite understandably, relating the story to their real lived experience. 'Sure, I can cut my pizza into sixths, no problem,' the pupil thinks. When asked how many sixths there are, the pupil can easily state that there are six of them. When asked about seven sixths, the pupil thinks the teacher has lost it – there would, after all, be no pizza left!

Stop using bloody pizzas to teach fractions.

It is of utmost importance that pupils understand that fractions are not bounded and can, in fact, form their own set of images with numberness.

TEACHER: 'Please put in front of you a red rod.'

The pupils lay down the rod:

TEACHER: 'Please show me a rod that is **half** of the red rod.'

The pupils lay down a white rod without any difficulty.

TEACHER: 'Now show me another half of red.'

TEACHER: 'And another.'

Now, this moment does not feel like a big deal to anyone reading this book. You understand fractions; you understand that this is perfectly possible. But for a young child or anyone at an early developmental stage of mathematics, this moment is profound.

The pupil considers for a moment and then lays down

TEACHER: 'Oh! Wow! Look!'

This really is a big moment and should not be underestimated or rushed.

TEACHER: 'Can you say out loud please, how many halves of red do you have?'

CLASS: 'Three halves of red!'

TEACHER: 'Yes! Three halves of red. The white rods are showing three halves of red. Can you show me a rod that is equivalent to three halves of red?'

The pupils lay down:

TEACHER: 'Please describe the green rod.'

Up until this point, the pupils had come to believe that the green rod was the number three. Now, in this profound and important moment, pupils realise, 'Aha! The rods can be any numbers!'

CLASS: 'Green is equal to three halves of red.'

The teacher, without making any fuss, asks the class to chant their sentence a few more times and writes on the board

$$g = \frac{3}{2}\, r$$

pointing at each symbol as the class says the work aloud.

Note that the numberness is in the rods, not the numerals. The numeral $\frac{3}{2}$ is not a number; it is showing the relationship between numbers and only has meaning when expressed as three halves of red. This is one of the reasons that pupils often get confused by the idea of fractions when they first arise – the teacher does not take sufficient time to stress that the fraction is a relationship. Pupils are told very early on that $\frac{1}{2}$ is equal to 0.5. This is not true (until later when we consider the representation as a simple fraction, where the vinculum denotes a division). $\frac{1}{2}$ is not equal to 0.5; $\frac{1}{2}$ of 1 is equal to 0.5. It takes no additional time or effort to always say 'one-half of one' rather than simply 'one-half'. This removes the misconception that one-half is always 0.5. It is only when we know what we are considering as the whole that we know what one-half is. It is not uncommon to see young children respond to the question, 'What is one-half of 20?' by writing down '20.5'. This occurs, obviously, because they have memorised that one-half is 0.5 without any sense of meaning.

We now know that the rods can represent numbers other than one to ten.

TEACHER: 'Please tell me the value of all of the other rods as fractions of red.'

The pupils will see they are able to express all of the rods as multiples of halves. They will also see that every second number forms a whole number.

Let us now hammer the point home.

TEACHER: 'Please place on your desk the light-green rod. Now show me a rod that is one-third of light green.'

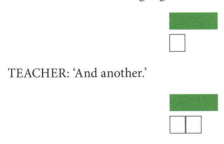

TEACHER: 'And another.'

TEACHER: 'And another.'

TEACHER: 'And another.'

TEACHER: 'And another.'

TEACHER: 'How many thirds of green do you have?'

CLASS: 'Five-thirds of green!'

TEACHER: 'Can you show me a rod that is equivalent to five-thirds of green?'

The pupils lay down the yellow rod.

TEACHER: 'Please describe the yellow rod in terms of the green rod.'

CLASS: 'Yellow is equal to five-thirds of green.'

Once again, the teacher can write the symbolism on the board as the pupils chant the sentence.

$$y = \frac{5}{3} \, g$$

TEACHER: 'Please now express all of the other rods in terms of the green rod.'

We now have the rather pleasing and surprising revelation that fractions go beyond 1 and that the rods can be used to express lots of different numbers.

Pupils are gaining an appreciation of fact that the fraction numeral communicates the relationship between the numbers (the rods in this case). This understanding that the fraction itself is not the number is of such great importance, it is worth further solidifying it in pupils' memories.

Perhaps the teacher asks the pupils to show a rod that is equivalent to one-third of light green:

The teacher can write on the board the symbolic representation of this:

$$w = \frac{1}{3}\, g$$

And then a rod that is equivalent to one-third of dark green:

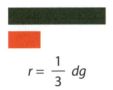

$$r = \frac{1}{3}\, dg$$

One-third of blue:

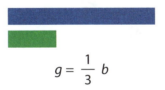

$$g = \frac{1}{3}\, b$$

And how about one-third of orange plus red:

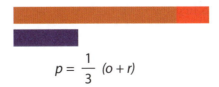

$$p = \frac{1}{3}\, (o + r)$$

Here, the pupil is seeing the symbolism for the numeral one-third appear repeatedly yet with different meaning. This variation in representation of the idea of third-ness will help to avoid the misconception that fractions always represent the same value.

Cuisenaire rods – arithmetic with fractions

Consider the problem

$$\frac{3}{2} + \frac{2}{5}$$

Now that pupils have a sense of fractions and the knowledge that the rods can be used to give meaning to any fraction numeral by considering the numeral as representing the relationships between numbers, they can address problems like this.

There are many ways in which these relationships can be expressed. With extensive use of the rods throughout their mathematical education, pupils become very familiar with the relative sizes and with the factors that each rod has. The teacher will notice pupils making sensible choices for the unit; for example, knowing that we will be thinking about halves and fifths, pupils will recognise that it is easy to cut the orange rod into two equal parts and into five equal parts. Choosing the orange rod as the unit, the pupil can present the yellow as a half and the red as a fifth.

The above question is now trivial, since

$$\frac{3}{2} + \frac{2}{5}$$

is asking the pupil to find the result of three yellow rods and two red rods, giving the number

This number **is** the answer. But how can it be expressed as a numeral?

Placing the answer alongside the unit rod, the pupil can see that this number is greater than the unit but less than two units.

What is the missing gap? The pupil can easily find that adding a white rod will make both lengths equal.

So, now the pupil knows that the length they are interested in defining is one white rod less than two units.

Comparing the white rods to the units, it is clear that each white rod is one-tenth of a unit.

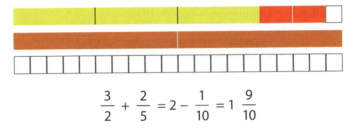

$$\frac{3}{2} + \frac{2}{5} = 2 - \frac{1}{10} = 1\,\frac{9}{10}$$

Alternatively, the pupil might express this as

$$\frac{3}{2} + \frac{2}{5} = \frac{19}{10} = 1\,\frac{9}{10}$$

There is a strong element of calm, purposeful storytelling in solving these problems. The pupil does not know the resolution to the problem as originally posed; but they understand that by attacking the problem and telling the story of what they can see to be true at each stage, a resolution will arise. The rods help to frame the storytelling and help to form a logical path to the correct answer.

Consider the problem

$$\frac{1}{3} \times \frac{1}{4}$$

The teacher can make the pedagogic choice to read this sentence aloud as 'one-third multiplied by one-quarter' or 'one-third times one-quarter' or 'one-third of a quarter'. The words that the teacher chooses here fundamentally change the interpretation that pupils will make when working with their rods. In all cases, the pupil must first consider what unit the thirds and quarters relate to. Once again, because the pupils will have had extensive experience of working with the rods at this stage, they are able to make informed choices about which length to use as the unit. They know that they are considering thirds and quarters, so it will be helpful to use a unit length which is easily expressed in both three equal rods and four equal rods. There are many ways of doing this, but the most common choice I see pupils make is to choose a length equivalent to 12 white rods.

Reading the symbols as 'one-third multiplied by one-quarter' typically leads to pupils thinking back to the multiplication of integers that they have met previously, where they were able to form rectangular spaces and find the areas. The pupil might build a multiplication grid like

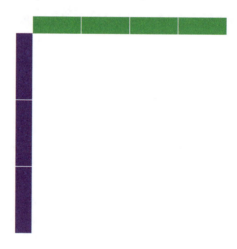

Both the purple lengths and the green lengths are equivalent. This length can be considered the unit. So, when thinking about the fractions of the unit, a

single purple rod represents one third of the unit length and a single green rod represents one quarter of the unit length. If we filled in the area created by the two boundaries, as we did previously, then we would be representing the multiplication

$$1 \times 1$$

Showing the area represented by the fraction multiplication we are interested in is a simple case of filling only the space where one-third and one-quarter intersect, for example

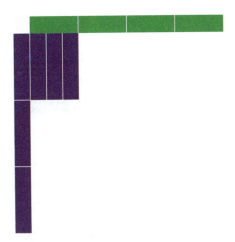

Clearly, we could have also filled this space with green rods. The question now is how much of the total space is filled. It is evident that we need 12 such areas to fill the entire space, so the space filled is one-twelfth of the total area. The total area is

$$1 \times 1 = 1$$

This tells us that the filled space is one-twelfth of 1, which can be represented by the simple fraction

$$\frac{1}{3} \times \frac{1}{4} = \frac{1}{12}$$

Alternatively, the teacher could have chosen to say aloud 'one-third of one-quarter'. This brings to mind a different representation. Suppose we take a length expressed in quarters, such as the following:

Each of the green rods is a quarter of the total length. The sentence 'one-third of one-quarter' suggests the solution – we just have to find one-third of one of the green rods. We have discussed previously that the green rod can be shown as thirds. Doing so gives

We have split the green rod into three equal lengths, so the individual white rods must be one-third of the green rod; that is to say, the white rod is one-third of one-quarter.

But what is the value of the white rod when related to the full length? It is easy to demonstrate that the white rods can make the full length by using 12 of them.

So, each white rod is one-twelfth of the total length.

$$\frac{1}{3} \times \frac{1}{4} = \frac{1}{12}$$

Similarly, we can consider the problem

$$\frac{2}{3} \times \frac{1}{4}$$

Following the same logical storytelling to arrive at the description of thirds of quarters, it is then straightforward to consider two of those thirds (or indeed any number of thirds).

Here, two-thirds of one-quarter can also be represented as a red rod, which is one-sixth of the total length.

$$\frac{2}{3} \times \frac{1}{4} = \frac{1}{6}$$

The teacher can use the opportunity to further reinforce the fact that multiplication is commutative. So, instead of saying aloud 'two-thirds of one-quarter', the teacher could choose to say 'one-quarter of two-thirds'.

This brings to mind a length defined in thirds rather than quarters, for example

Here, we can see that two purple rods represent two-thirds of the total length. Our sentence tells us we are interested in quarters of two-thirds, which we can show using the red rods and finally find one-quarter of two-thirds.

Just as before, we have found the answer – a red rod – is one-sixth of the full length.

$$\frac{2}{3} \times \frac{1}{4} = \frac{1}{4} \times \frac{2}{3} = \frac{1}{6}$$

Let us now consider the problem

$$\frac{3}{4} \div \frac{1}{2}$$

The teacher can choose to view this symbolism as the multiplication of the multiplicative inverse (as we will discuss when considering the field axioms later), which means the problem becomes

$$\frac{3}{4} \times \frac{2}{1}$$

and is trivial to solve using the same methods as the multiplications above.

Alternatively, the teacher might read the problem aloud as, 'How many halves are equivalent to three-quarters?' This pedagogic decision leads to quite a different type of thinking and approach. There are many ways in which the pupil could choose to represent this. Suppose, for example, the pupil thinks of the brown rod as the unit:

Then, it is simple to show that the dark green is three-quarters of the brown and the purple is one-half of the brown. The question spoken aloud is asking how many of the purple rods would be equivalent to the dark green rod. By inspection, the pupil can state that it must be more than one purple, but less than two.

Using the red rod, we can see, in fact, that the length is one and a half purple rods.

The pupil could have chosen to start with other unit lengths and would still arrive at the same conclusion that

$$\frac{3}{4} \times \frac{2}{1} = 1\frac{1}{2}$$

For example, the pupil might have chosen to start with the purple rod as the unit and, through calm storytelling and logic, would end up with the arrangement of rods below:

Cuisenaire rods can be used to bring meaning to potentially intractable problems. They allow pupils to tell stories and use straightforward, logical steps in order to **believe** novel ideas. A discourse on the use of these seemingly innocuous rods could easily fill a book in itself, but here I have tried to give just a glimpse of their usefulness, particularly with early number ideas.

I will end the discussion of Cuisenaire rods by reflecting for a moment on how they might be of use with older pupils or those at a higher level of mathematical development. One sad aspect of much of the mathematics education pupils encounter in schools today is that the use of manipulatives tends to be largely absent from the classroom once they have moved beyond early years education. Yet, pause for a moment and consider adults learning something new – they will very often ask for additional explanations and other ways of looking at the idea; 'Can you draw it for me?', 'Just show me!' or 'I need to actually do it before I can see what's happening' are not unusual objections. Why, then, have we moved so adherently to a mathematics education system that delivers the vast majority of lessons exclusively in the symbolic or abstract?

It is interesting to watch teachers teaching mathematics. They are very often simply teaching ideas in the same way they were taught those ideas at school. The mathematics teacher is often someone who has flourished in an abstract mathematics classroom. They then become successful, become qualified and are able to become teachers who then continue the cycle.

But, of course, it is not a teacher's job to teach mathematics in the way that they would want to learn mathematics; it is to teach mathematics in such a way that every single pupil has a moment where the model, metaphor or example clicks with them and they are able to make meaning and assimilate the new idea into their growing schema of mathematical knowledge.

So, a plea: don't give up on the concrete or pictorial representations. Your pupils can all get to grips with all the mathematical ideas in school-level mathematics as long as they are given the right amount of time to do so and the varied perspectives of an idea required to bring about their own moment of enlightenment.

Suppose the teacher is working with some fairly sophisticated pupils at a good level of mathematical development. Apparently simple prompts can bring about high-level questioning, the benefits of interleaving and spaced study, the testing effect and mathematical behaviour. For example, the teacher tells the pupils that it is possible to make triangles using the rods by touching the corners of rods like this:

Now, the teacher could ask questions such as the following:

- How many triangles can be made? How do you know?

- Are there some triangles that cannot be made? If so, what are their characteristics?

- If you select three rods at random from your pack, what is the probability that the rods will make

  ➤ a scalene triangle?

  ➤ an isosceles triangle?

  ➤ a right-angled triangle?

  ➤ no triangle?

These are not trivial questions and take some serious thought.

One of the triangle types to arise is a right-angled triangle, such as this:

Suppose the teacher wishes to introduce pupils to Pythagoras' theorem for the first time. The teacher could simply explain the theorem and tell the pupils something along the lines of, 'The square of the hypotenuse is the sum of the squares of the other two lengths.' This would not be uncommon to see in the mathematics classroom. Some pupils will accept that the teacher is telling them the truth and, having seen lots of subsequent examples and worked on lots of problems, will be able to move forward with Pythagoras in the bag. Some pupils. But some pupils will be thinking, 'What on earth are you talking about?'

Teachers know this. It is why we see so many teachers doing really good introductions to Pythagoras that include dynamic geometry or a video of the famous water containers where the volumes can be redistributed by turning the wheel of the triangle model.

Teachers could also just take a few moments, having made lots of right-angled triangles with the Cuisenaire rods, to seize the opportunity for a demonstration of the theorem before introducing it formally.

Suppose the pupils have the 3-4-5 triangle on their table in front of them. The teacher could suggest that it is possible to show the triangle as a shape bounded by squares:

TEACHER: 'Can you make a floor using your green and purple rods that is the same as the yellow floor?'

The pupils experiment for a few moments and find that yes, they can. Pupils will find different arrangements, such as the following:

The pupils can then form other Pythagorean triple triangles and undertake the process again. After having completed, say, three such examples, the teacher can ask the pupils to articulate a description of what appears to be happening. Typical sentences I have heard pupils say include 'The two smaller squares always make the same as the big square' and 'Adding the two small squares gives the big square.'

Now that the pupils are beginning to become convinced that there is a relationship between the areas on the sides of triangles, the theorem can be introduced formally, pointing out that the task they have just completed was a demonstration of the theorem at play (although not a proof of the theorem). I suggest that taking this opportunity to allow meaning to be made **before** framing the theorem formally sensitises the pupils to the description of the theorem and allows them to more readily integrate this novel idea into their understanding of the universe.

The use of Cuisenaire rods can, of course, be applied to so many more mathematical ideas than I have discussed here, but I hope that this short exploration of their use is enough to whet the appetite.

In order to build a more formal space or field in which mathematics can exist, I will now turn to my other two go-to manipulatives: algebra tiles and Dienes blocks.

Creating a space (or a field) to do mathematics

Let us consider some of the fundamental ideas in early-stage mathematics which underpin a pupil's opportunity to learn the whole of school-level mathematics – and how we might go about communicating meaning of those fundamentals.

In doing so, I shall use algebra tiles and Dienes blocks to build up a view of number and algebra as one unified idea rather than separate topics.

This brief discussion is clearly not exhaustive – nor is it intended to be, since such a discussion could only be covered in a dedicated book on just this one issue. Instead, I want to give the reader a rules-based system for working with addition and multiplication in number and algebra, which I hope brings a deeper understanding of how these are related. Out of necessity of brevity, I have assumed some knowledge acquisition at some of the steps without explicitly covering the models for that acquisition.

Equivalence, equality and equals

What is an equation? Why do some pupils make basic procedural errors when working with equations?

I suggest that one of the key issues is that the meaning of the equals symbol is almost never taught to pupils in schools. If asked to describe what the equals symbol means, most pupils will respond by suggesting it has something to do with being 'the same as'. This is a problematic, superficial understanding of the meaning of this key symbol.

We began to establish a sense of equivalence and equality through our use of Cuisenaire rods, but now it is time to further formalise this crucial idea.

Equality is the **archetypal equivalence relationship**.

The equals symbol should be examined far more thoroughly by the pupil learning mathematics at an early stage than is typically the case. It is not good enough to tell pupils that equals means 'the same as' – indeed, it is one of the key reasons they struggle with equations.

Let us consider a journey through arithmetic and algebra, starting with equality.

The teacher shows the pupils the following image, points to the equals symbol and tells them that the symbol can be read as 'is equal to'

The next image is shown

and the teacher says aloud 'is not equal to'.

And now the next:

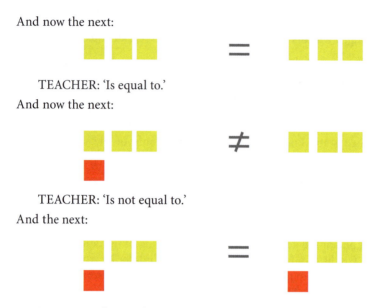

TEACHER: 'Is equal to.'
And now the next:

TEACHER: 'Is not equal to.'
And the next:

TEACHER: 'Is equal to.'

The teacher should continue in this manner, showing the images changing and emphasising the phrases 'is equal to' and 'is not equal to' as the state of the images change. Too often, when introducing the equals symbol, teachers neglect to pair it with the non-example state of **not** equal.

As the images change, the statement changes. The pupils are at this point conjecturing what actions in changing the images bring about one symbol or the other.

The teacher can choose to change the image in any way they like, including more complex changes such as:

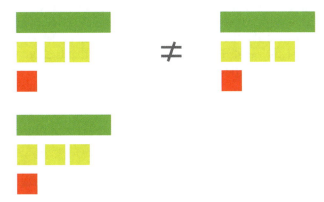

Of course, what we as teachers know here is that a multiplication or doubling has just occurred, but at this stage this will not be highlighted to the pupils, since we do not yet have a field of mathematics in which to perform such operations.

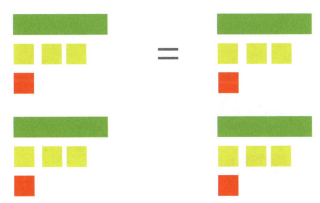

Following a good number of changes and alternating between a verbal articulation of 'is equal to' to one of 'is not equal to' and vice versa, the teacher asks the pupils to describe the meaning of the symbols.

The above sequence has been chosen carefully and deliberately such that it will elicit the response from pupils that the 'is equal to' statement and symbol appear to signify that the separate images are 'the same as' each other.

TEACHER: 'No. That is not correct.'

We want to do this for the same reason we do bridging – the fact is, long before pupils ever arrive in the education system, they have already encountered the words (and probably the symbols), so they have embedded beliefs and invented strategies. Just like the hypercorrection effect, we want to produce an emotional shock in order to shake their misconceptions and lack of deeper insight. We want to sensitise the pupils to an important moment that is about to occur, to make them alert to learning something new.

The teacher now shows this image

and says aloud, 'Is equal to.'

Clearly the images are not the same as each other. This moment is important. The pupils have just moments ago stated their belief that the symbol means the same and now, here in front of them, is a counter-example being stated as true by the teacher. The pupils are shocked by this and a moment of curiosity sweeps through the class. This is hypercorrection at work.

TEACHER: 'Strange, isn't it. I wonder what is going on. Let's look at some more.'

The teacher shows the image

and says aloud, 'Is not equal to.' The next image is shown:

TEACHER: 'Is equal to.'

The teacher continues to change the images on both sides, alternating between the statements 'is equal to' and 'is not equal to'.

The pupils begin to see that the 'is not equal to' statement arises when an action has been carried out to just one of the separate images and that the 'is equal to' statement coincides with the repeating of the same action to the other image.

For example, the following states are all 'equal to':

Both images have been changed through the inclusion of a new green bar.

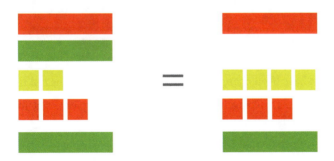

Both images have been changed through the inclusion of a new red bar.

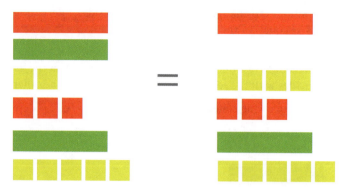

Both images have been changed by the inclusion of some new yellow tiles.

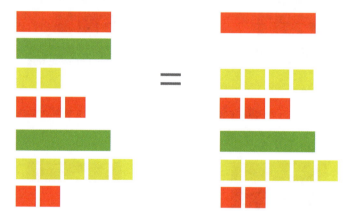

Both images have been changed by the inclusion of some new red tiles.

TEACHER: 'Thinking more carefully this time, please tell me what the symbol means.'

PUPIL: 'I thought it meant "the same as", but it isn't about the pictures being the same as each other. It means doing the same thing to both pictures.'

TEACHER: 'Yes, that is correct. The symbol is telling us that we have done the same thing to both sides. If we only change one side, the pictures are not equal. If we do exactly the same thing to both pictures, they stay equal.'

We are trying to establish a deeper meaning of the equals and not-equals symbols in pupils' minds. If they only have the meaning of 'is the same as', then later when faced with a problem such as $2x + 4 = 10$, the pupil has to additionally recall some process they have been taught for 'solving' these particular types of equations. However, if taught from the beginning that equality is the archetypal equivalence relationship, pupils will be able to understand the equals symbol in a more useful way.

Equals: when given any two expressions, applying an isomorphic function to both expressions will result in equivalence holding true.

Now the teacher can show many more examples and build firmly in pupils' minds the mental representation that the equals symbol gives us permission to break and fix any equivalence relationship we wish to. It is worth taking time to play this game with pupils:

Write the equals symbol in the middle of the board at the front of the room. Invite a pupil to the front to play the game with the teacher. The teacher explains the rule that the equals symbol must always remain true. The teacher draws or writes anything they want on their side of the equals symbol, then pauses. The pupil will usually smile knowingly and then draw or write exactly the same thing on their side of the board. The teacher now alters their side in some way; the pupil repeats the action. This continues for several changes.

The game is then repeated, but this time the initial state is different on both sides, yet the equals symbol still holds true. The pupil has the first move; the teacher repeats the action.

This game can be played at any level of complexity and can include symbolism that the pupil is not yet aware of. For example, the teacher might draw a square, which the pupil repeats. The next action might be to put some brackets around the square, then to write the word 'log' in front of it, to draw a long horizontal line, then draw a circle beneath it, to put a small triangle to the top right corner of the brackets, to draw a horizontal line to the right, then to draw a diamond and so on and so on.

Numerals

With equality in place, it is now time to establish some useful symbolism to help communicate more efficiently in our space of mathematics that we are building.

Using a yellow tile, the teacher can begin to introduce two important aspects of how we can communicate mathematically: numbers and numerals.

Here is an object.

This object is the **archetypal number unit**. The object itself is what we will call a 'number'. Numbers have meaning – a numberness. The object has meaning; we can see it, touch it, move it around, manipulate it. We will call this number the unit and can say this number as 'one'. We will also assign this number a symbol, which we can use to communicate that we are discussing this number without showing the number itself. We will call this symbol a 'numeral'. Here is the number and its related numeral.

All other numbers can be expressed in terms of the archetypal unit. For example, if we have another unit, we can call this number 'two' and assign it the numeral '2'.

Continuing in this manner, we can see that numbers continue to grow. We could always grow our number more by including extra units. This suggests that the list of numbers will not run out; they will go on forever. So, we need an infinite selection of unique symbols in order to represent all of the possible numbers.

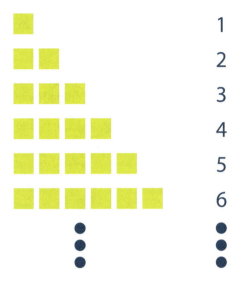

Given that the numbers and numerals never end, it might become tricky to invent enough unique symbols and to remember them all. This is a challenge we will return to later.

Addition

Let us introduce a new symbol, '+'. We can use this symbol to describe a process of combining numbers. We will call this process addition. For example, the two numbers

can be combined together, forming the new number. Pupils can demonstrate this by pushing both of their groups of tiles together on their desk, clearly forming the new group:

This can be written using the related numerals and the two symbols '+' and '='.

$$1 + 3 = 4$$

163

The equals symbol tells us that we can apply the same function to both of the numbers and equivalence will hold true, which can be demonstrated by the teacher multiple times using different actions to change the numbers in the same way on both sides as discussed earlier.

The equivalence is also demonstrated above by pushing the tiles together and forming the new number. It is clear that combining the number represented by the numeral '1' and the number represented by the numeral '3' does indeed result in creating the number represented by the numeral '4'.

The symbolism can be read as the sentence, 'one plus three equals four.'

 $1 + 3 = 4$

Let us now look at some of the interesting patterns that emerge when carrying out additions. The teacher will choose the sequence of additions carefully, such that the next addition is

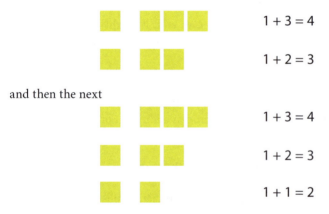

$1 + 3 = 4$

$1 + 2 = 3$

and then the next

$1 + 3 = 4$

$1 + 2 = 3$

$1 + 1 = 2$

TEACHER: 'What do you notice? What do you wonder?'

There is a pattern emerging, with the numeral '1' remaining constant, then a counting pattern in the other two columns.

(At this stage, the teacher can carry out a full exploration of counting, perhaps using Cuisenaire rods as described earlier. For the purposes of this discussion, we shall assume that the counting discussion has occurred and that pupils have in their long-term memory a sequence allowing them to count to nine in both a positive and negative direction. This should include a discussion of the rather tricky concept of zero.)

TEACHER: 'What will the next addition be?'

CLASS: 'It must be one plus zero.'

TEACHER: 'And what must that be equal to?'

CLASS: 'The pattern is four, three, two…so it must be one.'

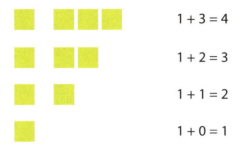

$$1 + 3 = 4$$

$$1 + 2 = 3$$

$$1 + 1 = 2$$

$$1 + 0 = 1$$

TEACHER: 'Ah! So we now know that one plus zero is equal to one. That's interesting! It gives the same number that we started with. Adding zero resulted in the original number. The number did not change when zero was added to it.'

With the pattern continuing, the teacher can again prompt the pupils if required.

TEACHER: 'What must the next addition be?'

CLASS: 'It goes three, two, one, zero…so now it must be to add negative one.'

TEACHER: 'And what must that equal?'

CLASS: 'Zero!'

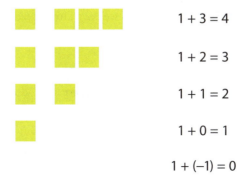

$$1 + 3 = 4$$

$$1 + 2 = 3$$

$$1 + 1 = 2$$

$$1 + 0 = 1$$

$$1 + (-1) = 0$$

The pupils now need a way to represent this number sentence. Here, we introduce a new tile, which we will use to represent negative numbers.

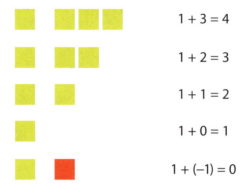

$$1 + 3 = 4$$

$$1 + 2 = 3$$

$$1 + 1 = 2$$

$$1 + 0 = 1$$

$$1 + (-1) = 0$$

This is a profound moment and should be dwelled on.

> TEACHER: 'Wow! Look at that! There was a number that we could add to one to give the total zero. When we add negative one to one, the result is zero. One and negative one form a special pair of numbers, which combine together to give zero. We call this a zero pair.'

The use of zero pairs enables us to represent the additive inverse, which will allow us to build a field of mathematics without the use of the subtraction operator.

One issue that pupils struggle to get to grips with when working with arithmetic is discerning the order in which operations must happen. Many pupils will use an aide-memoire such as BIDMAS. But what if there were no need for this? What if we could build a field of mathematics where this issue does not have to arise? The introduction here of the additive inverse is already hinting at the fact that we do not need subtraction. Perhaps we have already reduced BIDMAS to BIDMA. Perhaps we can go further.

Zero pairs and the additive inverse

With the introduction of the idea of zero pairs – a way of communicating the additive inverse – it is now possible to do some interesting additions. Given that every pair of a yellow tile and red tile is equal to zero, it is trivial to show, for example:

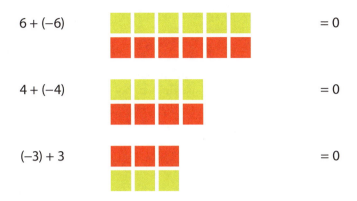

$$6 + (-6) \qquad = 0$$

$$4 + (-4) \qquad = 0$$

$$(-3) + 3 \qquad = 0$$

TEACHER: 'What do you notice? What do you wonder?'

PUPIL: 'When you add these numbers to the same number in a negative direction, the answer is zero. I think that it will work for all numbers. Any number add its negative type will be zero.'

TEACHER: 'Yes, I think I agree. Let's have a better way of describing the numbers. I am going to say that negative one is the additive inverse of one, negative six is the additive inverse of six, negative four is the additive inverse of four, negative three is the additive inverse of three. Can you tell me what you think again, being precise with your language?'

PUPIL: 'Any number add its additive inverse is zero.'

TEACHER: 'Yes, that is correct. Any number add its additive inverse is zero. That is a really important rule in mathematics; it will be very helpful to us as we continue to learn more about mathematics. That rule never breaks; it is always true. You can always use that rule. You have licence to use that rule at any time when working with any problems.'

The pupils can be given lots of opportunities, using their tiles, to show that the additive inverse holds true always. They should be given plenty of time to form and symbolise many number sentences using their zero pairs. When the teacher is convinced that every single child believes the rule and has accepted its logic, the teacher can introduce the next idea as they continue to build up knowledge of the set of important rules they are exposing the pupils to.

Let us introduce a new symbol and have a look at another sequence of additions.

TEACHER: 'I am now going to show you a new symbol.'

The teacher writes the following symbol on the board:

—

TEACHER: 'This is a helpful symbol. It is a short way of saying "addition of the additive inverse". We can use this symbol in number sentences too. For example…'

The teacher writes on the board

$$4 - 3$$

TEACHER: 'Remember: the symbol means the addition of the additive inverse. So, this is a short way of writing an addition. The sentence is saying, "four plus the additive inverse of three". What is the additive inverse of three?'

CLASS: 'Negative three.'

TEACHER: 'Yes, that is correct. So this sentence is saying, "four plus negative three". Let's look at that as numerals.'

$$4 - 3 = 4 + (-3)$$

TEACHER: 'What will the addition result in? Let's look at the addition as numbers.'

 $$4 - 3 = 4 + (-3)$$

TEACHER: 'There are some zero pairs here. What number is shown?

CLASS: 'One.'

TEACHER: 'Let's complete the sentence by showing what numeral this is equal to.'

 $$4 - 3 = 4 + (-3) = 1$$

TEACHER: 'The new symbol means the addition of the additive inverse. The new symbol can be read in this sentence as, "four minus three equals four plus negative three equals one".'

The teacher should spend a good amount of time emphasising the meaning of the minus symbol as the addition of the additive inverse. Now, the teacher can explore with the class another interesting sequence and the pattern that emerges:

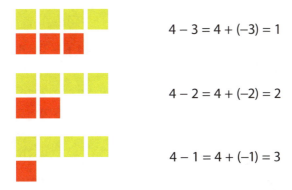

$$4 - 3 = 4 + (-3) = 1$$

$$4 - 2 = 4 + (-2) = 2$$

$$4 - 1 = 4 + (-1) = 3$$

TEACHER: 'What do you notice? What do you wonder? What must the next addition be?'

The pupils are able to see the pattern and conjecture that the next addition will be the case when zero is added and that the result must be four.

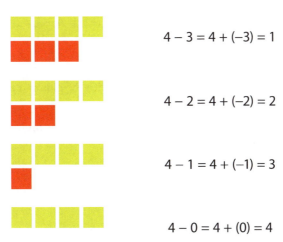

$$4 - 3 = 4 + (-3) = 1$$

$$4 - 2 = 4 + (-2) = 2$$

$$4 - 1 = 4 + (-1) = 3$$

$$4 - 0 = 4 + (0) = 4$$

TEACHER: 'What must the next addition be?'

Examining the pattern carefully, pupils can state that the four is remaining constant, but the other numerals are following a counting pattern, so the next addition is the case 'four minus negative one' and that the result must be five. Using their knowledge that minus means the addition of the additive inverse, it then follows that 'four minus negative one' means 'four plus one (the additive inverse of negative one)', which gives

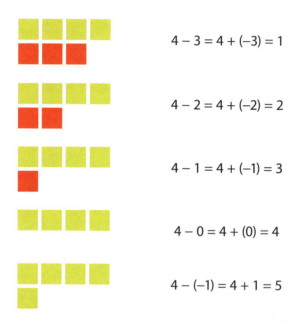

$$4 - 3 = 4 + (-3) = 1$$

$$4 - 2 = 4 + (-2) = 2$$

$$4 - 1 = 4 + (-1) = 3$$

$$4 - 0 = 4 + (0) = 4$$

$$4 - (-1) = 4 + 1 = 5$$

TEACHER: 'Excellent. We can now work with the plus and minus symbols to solve any problems.'

At this stage, pupils can readily work with any additions problems, including those involving negative numbers.

We now wish to move pupils on further and continue to establish the set of rules for addition. By carrying out additions such as

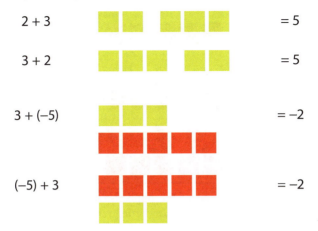

2 + 3		= 5
3 + 2		= 5
3 + (–5)		= –2
(–5) + 3		= –2

the pupils will begin to form a conjecture in their minds.

TEACHER: 'What do you notice? What do you wonder?'

PUPIL: 'It doesn't matter which order numbers are added together, the answer is the same.'

Understandably, but unfortunately, with the above examples, pupils will often state that 'any **two** numbers can be added in any order.' So, it is important to challenge that using additional examples, such as:

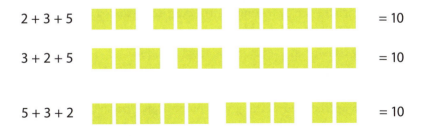

2 + 3 + 5		= 10
3 + 2 + 5		= 10
5 + 3 + 2		= 10

And, of course, examples including negative tiles, such as:

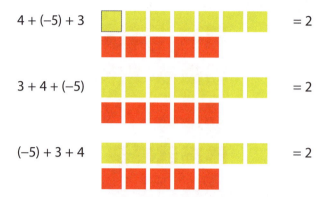

$$4 + (-5) + 3 \qquad\qquad = 2$$

$$3 + 4 + (-5) \qquad\qquad = 2$$

$$(-5) + 3 + 4 \qquad\qquad = 2$$

The teacher can now draw out of the pupil the more general point that any number of numbers can be added in any order, resulting in the same solution.

Quite often, pupils will themselves opt to stop using the tiles, instead introducing a symbolic format such as

$$2 + 3 \qquad\qquad + + \quad + + + \qquad\qquad = 5$$

$$3 - 5 = 3 + (-5) \qquad\qquad + + + \qquad\qquad = -2$$
$$\qquad\qquad\qquad\qquad\quad - - - -$$

I have found that pupils like the speed and recordability of this symbolic approach, which they enjoy writing in their exercise books as a more permanent record of their process and thinking.

We have now established a set of truths about addition.

Just nine properties provide the basis for all of arithmetic and algebra. The axioms of a field – or, as often stated, the field axioms – give the mathematician a rules-based approach to working with number and variables. Knowing and being able to work with the field axioms means that a pupil can attack any arithmetical or algebraic problem they might face in school-level mathematics. These properties always hold true; they are the same properties at the beginning of primary mathematics as they are at the beginning of calculus. They hold for whole numbers, fractions, negative numbers, rational numbers, letters and expressions.

Establishing their truth and utility is therefore the key aim of the teacher of early-stage mathematics.

The nine field axioms are split into properties for addition, properties for multiplication and a property connecting addition and multiplication. It is important to note that none are presented as subtraction or division.

Through our use of the tiles and the discussions and dialogue outlined above, we have now arrived at the first four axioms of a field: the axioms for addition.

Properties of addition

Axiom	Description	Symbolically
1	*Associative property of addition*	$(a+b)+c=a+(b+c)$ Example: $(2+3)+4=2+(3+4)$
2	*Commutative property of addition*	$a+b=b+a$ Example: $2+3=3+2$
3	*Additive identity property of 0*	$a+0=0+a=a$ Example: $3+0=0+3=3$
4	*Existence of additive inverses*	**For every** a **there exists** $-a$ **so that** $a+(-a)=(-a)+a=0.$ Example: $2+(-2)=(-2)+2=0$

These axioms are like a licence to work with addition – they will never break and the pupil has the right to use them whenever they wish. The axioms are a set of fundamental rights to take part in mathematical discussion. But we have not yet built a sufficient field or space in which to do our mathematics. To complete the field, we must now turn to establishing the meaning and truth of a second operator: multiplication.

Multiplication

Let us introduce a new symbol, '×', which we shall say denotes a new operation called multiplication.

The symbolism 1 × 3 can be read 'one times three' or 'one multiplied by three' and we shall say that this is a shorthand way of stating we have one group of three. For example:

2 × 3 would indicate two groups of three. For example:

If the tiles were collected together, they would clearly give the same value as the number six, which is symbolised with the numeral 6. So, we have

2 × 3      = 6

Continuing to look at groups of three we might come across this pattern:

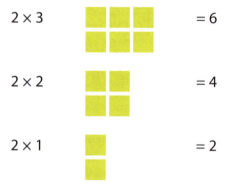

TEACHER: 'What do you notice? What would the next product be?'

The pupils can see the pattern occurring in the columns of numerals and can use a counting strategy to suggest what the next multiplication in the sequence would be.

PUPIL: 'It must be two times zero. The answer must be zero.'

This now gives the following pattern:

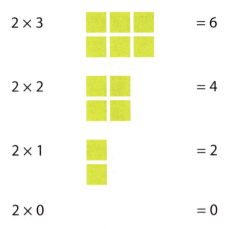

TEACHER: 'What must the next product be?'

CLASS: 'Two times negative one equals negative two!'

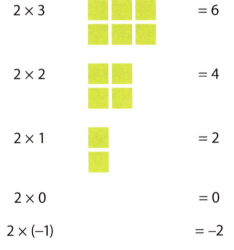

By following the pattern, pupils can state that $2 \times (-1) = -2$. They can then suggest a logical way to represent this as a number, giving

Now that we have a way of representing products as numbers with tiles (including those with negative tiles), let us take a look at another pattern.

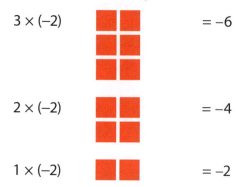

$3 \times (-2) \qquad = -6$

$2 \times (-2) \qquad = -4$

$1 \times (-2) \qquad = -2$

TEACHER: 'What must the next product be?'

CLASS: 'Zero times negative two equals zero!'

$$0 \times (-2) \qquad = 0$$

TEACHER: 'And the next?'

CLASS: 'Negative one times negative two equals two!'

$$(-1) \times (-2) \qquad = 2$$

Which can then be represented by the number.

$$(-1) \times (-2) \qquad = 2$$

Similarly, we could create the sequence

$3 \times (-1) \qquad = -3$

$2 \times (-1) \qquad = -2$

$$1 \times (-1) \qquad \qquad = -1$$

$$0 \times (-1) \qquad \qquad = 0$$

$$(-1) \times (-1) \qquad \qquad = 1$$

TEACHER: 'This is an interesting result. Negative one multiplied by negative one is equal to one. Negative one multiplied by negative one gives the additive inverse of negative one.'

The teacher can make a note of this on the board and draw attention to this particular product.

$$(-1) \times (-1) = 1$$

TEACHER: 'Let us take a look at some other numbers multiplied by negative one.'

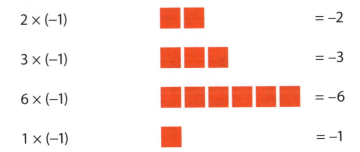

$$2 \times (-1) \qquad \qquad = -2$$

$$3 \times (-1) \qquad \qquad = -3$$

$$6 \times (-1) \qquad \qquad = -6$$

$$1 \times (-1) \qquad \qquad = -1$$

TEACHER: 'What do you notice? What do you wonder?'

PUPIL: 'When a number is multiplied by negative one, the result is the additive inverse of the number. I wonder if that is always true. I think that for any number, multiplying by negative one will give the additive inverse of the number.'

TEACHER: 'Yes. You are correct. That is a really important thing to know. We need to remember that fact carefully.'

As with addition earlier, we now want to establish that multiplication is commutative. Pupils could look at lots of products of the type:

2×3  $= 6$

3×2 $= 6$

By giving pupils plenty of examples of this type, they will come to state that the multiplication can happen in any order. We now have two interesting assertions: that multiplying by negative one gives the additive inverse and that multiplication is commutative. This allows us to build a logical, step-by-step attack on a problem such as $(-2) \times (-3)$.

Firstly, we know that -2 is the additive inverse of 2 and that -3 is the additive inverse of 3. So it must be true that -2 is equal to $2 \times (-1)$ and -3 is equal to $3 \times (-1)$, since any number multiplied by negative one gives the additive inverse of that number. So, we have

$$(-2) \times (-3)$$

$$= 2 \times (-1) \times 3 \times (-1)$$

But we also know that multiplication can happen in any order, so we are free to change the order of our multiplication, giving

$$= 2 \times 3 \times (-1) \times (-1)$$

We know the result of 2×3, giving

$$= 6x \, (-1) \times (-1)$$

And now we have a number being multiplied by negative one, which must give its additive inverse, giving

$$= 6 \times 1$$

$$= 6$$

Using the facts we have established, pupils can follow logical arguments such as the one above. They could now complete several more of the type, presenting their steps logically and accurately.

At this stage, there may be the misconception that only two numbers can be multiplied together in any order, so it is worth now establishing that multiplication is also associative.

Suppose we have 2 × 3 shown as a number

2×3

We can then take that number as its own object and create groups of that object, for example we might show four groups of the object (2 × 3), giving

$(2 \times 3) \times 4$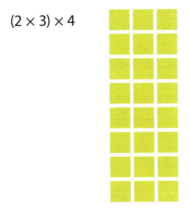

Alternatively, suppose we show the number represented by 3 × 4

3×4

And now show two groups of that object

$$2 \times (3 \times 4)$$

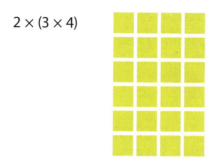

It is a trivial matter to collect up the tiles in both results and demonstrate that they are the same number. So, we have shown that $(2 \times 3) \times 4$ is equivalent to $2 \times (3 \times 4)$.

During the work we have carried out with pupils using Cuisenaire rods, we developed a sense of fraction-ness and introduced appropriate symbolism. Pupils will have learnt, for example, that finding a quarter results in four exactly equal parts. We can use this knowledge to demonstrate a sequence such as

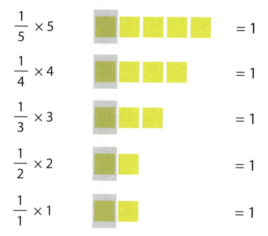

The sequence is chosen carefully and discussed at each step with the class, emphasising correct terminology and asking the pupils what the next product will be in the pattern after the first three have been shown.

TEACHER: 'What do you notice?'

PUPIL: 'I think that multiplying a number by a fraction whose numerator is one and whose denominator has the same numeral as the number always gives the answer "one".'

TEACHER: 'I agree. Can you explain why?'

PUPIL: 'Well, a number will always be made up of that number of units. So, if we split the number in to the same number of exactly equal parts, it must be the unit.'

TEACHER: 'Excellent. Let's make a note of that really important finding.'

The teacher can write on the board something like

$$\frac{1}{anything} \times anything = 1$$

The teacher uses this moment to emphasise and clearly articulate the fact that has now been established.

TEACHER: 'This is called the multiplicative inverse.'

We have now established a set of rules for multiplication.

Properties of multiplication

Axiom	Description	Symbolically
5	*Associative property of multiplication*	$(a \times b) \times c = a \times (b \times c)$ Example: $(2 \times 3) \times 4 = 2 \times (3 \times 4)$
6	*Commutative property of multiplication*	$a \times b = b \times a$ Example: $2 \times 3 = 3 \times 2$
7	*Multiplicative identity property of 1*	$a \times 1 = 1 \times a = a$ Example: $3 \times 1 = 1 \times 3 = 3$
8	*Existence of multiplicative inverses*	**For every $a \neq 0$ there exists $\frac{1}{a}$ so that $a \times \frac{1}{a} = \frac{1}{a} \times a = 1$.** Example: $2 \times \frac{1}{2} = \frac{1}{2} \times 2 = 1$

In establishing these rules for multiplication, it is worth noting and strongly emphasising to the class that an interesting and important pattern has emerged, namely that the multiplication spaces that have come to exist appear to have regions where groups of positive solutions appear and spaces where groups of negative solutions appear. In illustrating this here, I have used numerals that we have not yet brought into existence merely as a way of showing the pattern efficiently to the adult reader.

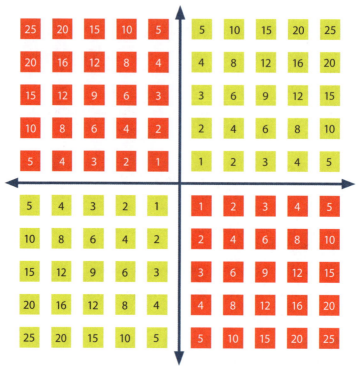

This emerging pattern will be of fundamental importance as the hierarchy of mathematics continues to build into a fuller and more sophisticated discipline.

Connecting addition and multiplication

Consider the addition sentence 3 + 2, which gives the combined number

$$3 + 2$$

Taking the 3 + 2 object as a whole, it is possible to multiply this object as we have established earlier, for example:

$$2 \times (3 + 2)$$

Now consider two separate objects, 2 × 3 and 2 × 2, which form the numbers

$$2 \times 3 \qquad 2 \times 2$$

These products can be considered as individual objects too, which can be combined through addition by collecting up our tiles:

$$(2 \times 3) + (2 \times 2)$$

This gives the same number as our previous calculation:

$$(2 \times 3) + (2 \times 2)$$

In other words, $2 \times (3 + 2) = (2 \times 3) + (2 \times 2)$.

Showing plenty of other calculations of this type, we can now establish the truth of the rule connecting addition and multiplication.

The final field axiom

Axiom	Description	Symbolically
9	Distributive property of multiplication over addition	$a \times (b + c) = (a \times b) + (a \times c)$ $a(b+c) = ab + ac$

The nine properties we have established allow the pupil to express themselves mathematically, to simplify tasks, to solve problems and to undertake mathematical proofs. The teacher must establish with the pupil that these properties are also like fundamental mathematical rights. They have the right to use these properties at any time, in any order and for any mathematics purpose.

Defining area

Let us consider the archetypal unit, the single yellow tile we have been using to express our numbers. We have been able to express any other number as a number of these tiles. Now, we can go further and think about more than just the number of tiles by thinking of other shapes.

The **archetypal number unit** is a square – a single yellow tile. Suppose we thought instead about some rectangles. A rectangle with a length equivalent to that of two of the units would create a space exactly equal to the space created by combining two of the units. We shall call the space created inside the rectangle 'area'.

The square space created inside the archetypal unit shall be considered the **archetypal area unit**.

Thinking about other rectangles, we can see that when the width of a rectangle is the same length as the unit, the area of the rectangle can be found by considering the number of units required to make its length and multiplying this by the archetypal area unit.

So, if the width of a rectangle is the unit and the length of the rectangle is unknown, we would still have an insight into its area. It will be the number of tiles required to create the length lots of the archetypal area unit.

So, all areas, including unknown areas, can be expressed as a multiple of the archetypal area unit, which is the space created by the archetypal number unit.

Comparing areas (solving equations)

Consider an unknown area and a known equivalent area

The equals sign tell us that we are permitted to perform any actions we wish but, to maintain equivalence, the same action must be applied to the expressed values on both sides of the equals symbol. Suppose we break the equality by adding only to one side as such:

To fix the equivalence relationship, we must do the same action to the other expressed value, bringing harmony once more.

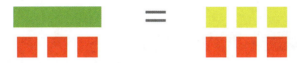

On the right-hand side, we have three sets of zero pairs. We know that each pair has no value – that is to say, each pair is equal to zero – so the pairs combined will also be equal to zero and can be shown with zero number present as such:

We now have an assertion that the combination of the unknown green area and the three negative unit areas is equal to zero. From our work in establishing the rules of addition, we can recall axiom 4:

4	Existence of additive inverses	For every a there exists $-a$ so that $a + (-a) = (-a) + a = 0.$ Example: $2 + (-2) = (-2) + 2 = 0$

So, the only way in which two numbers can combine to be zero is if those two numbers are the additive inverse of one another. We therefore know that the unknown area must be the additive inverse of negative three, which is, of course, three.

We could have stated this at the beginning, but it is a worthwhile exercise to undertake breaking and fixing whenever the opportunity arises, and the logical argument that follows brings about greater clarity.

Let us consider another example. We shall call examples such as this, where we are breaking and fixing the equivalence relationship, 'equations'. Further, we shall call the expressed number values on either side of the equals symbol 'expressions'.

Take the equation

We are permitted to break and fix in any way we choose. The equals symbol gives us licence to do so.

Let's try

This breaks the equivalence. We can re-establish equivalence by carrying out the same action on the other expression.

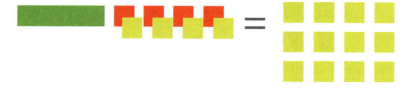

On the left, we can see four zero pairs, which would result in zero number. So we have

Given our work on our first example, we now know that this means that the unknown area must be equal to the area on the right.

Let us look at another example. This time, we will also try to capture a record of our breaking and fixing in a short written format. This means we need a way of communicating the unknown area. Earlier we used a question mark to suggest that the area was unknown. I want to use a symbol for the unknown area, in a similar way to using symbols to represent numbers. I will give the unknown area the numeral 'x'. Therefore, this equation

can be written symbolically as

$$x + 2 = 6$$

We are allowed to break and fix as we please. Let's try

And then fix:

Which can be written symbolically as

$$x + 2 + (-2) = 6 + (-2)$$

The zero pairs will create zero number to give

Which can be written symbolically as

$$x = 4$$

We have found the unknown area in terms of the archetypal area unit and also the value of the length of the rectangle knowing the related number of archetypal number units.

Let us consider another example:

This can be written symbolically as

$$2x + 3 = 11$$

We can break the equation

and then fix it again

This can be written as

$$2x + 3 + (-3) = 11 + (-3)$$

The zero pairs clearly create zero, so

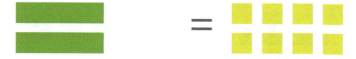

This can be written as

$$2x = 8$$

At this stage, we could seek to create equal groups in line with what we know from our work with Cuisenaire rods and the establishment of axiom 8:

8	*Existence of multiplicative inverses*	For every $a \neq 0$ there exists $\frac{1}{a}$ so that $a \times \frac{1}{a} = \frac{1}{a} \times a = 1.$
		Example: $2 \times \frac{1}{2} = \frac{1}{2} \times 2 = 1$

We can write the equation as

$$\frac{1}{2} \times 2x = \frac{1}{2} \times 8$$

The physical objects can be expressed as two equal groups by doing just that:

We can see here that one of the unknown areas is equivalent to the number four.

$$x = 4$$

Suppose we wished to consider an equation of the form:

$$3(x - 1) = 6$$

We can build this equation step-by-step. First, let's look at

$$x - 1$$

which can be expressed as the number

Taking this to be the object, we can now think of

$$3(x - 1)$$

As a simple multiplication of the object. We will create three lots of the object, giving:

Finally, we recall that we were building the equation

$$3(x - 1) = 6$$

We can represent this in numbers as

On inspection, it is clear that this could also be written as

$$3x + (-3) = 6$$

So we have revealed the interesting and rather pleasing fact that

$$3(x - 1) = 3x + (-3) = 6$$

Let us now break and fix as we wish. We could break the equation by creating the zero pairs

And fix it again

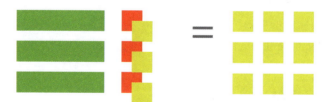

This can be written

$$3x + (-3) + 3 = 6 + 3$$

and clearly results in this situation:

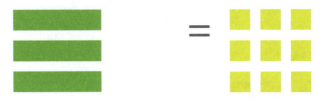

$$3x = 9$$

Considering three equal groups, we can see

$$\frac{1}{3} \times 3x = \frac{1}{3} \times 9$$

$$x = 3$$

Let us consider another example. How might we build up the equation

$$-2(x - 3) = -6$$

First, let us express

$$x - 3$$

as a number:

We can now consider this as a single object, which we are going to multiply by negative two

$$-2(x - 3)$$

We know that multiplying by negative two is the same as multiplying by two and then multiplying by negative one.

$$-1 \times 2(x - 3)$$

Multiplying by two gives

To complete the operation, we must also multiply by negative one. Recalling our work on multiplication earlier, we know that multiplication by negative one will result in the additive inverse. So, we will have the additive inverse of the number above, which is

We have now expressed

$$-2(x - 3)$$

And it is clear to see that this can also be written

$$-2x + 6$$

That is:

$$-2(x - 3) = -2x + 6$$

In our equation, we set this equal to negative six, so the full equation can now be expressed

$$-2x + 6 = -6$$

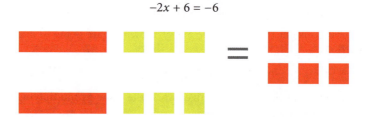

We are now able to **solve the equation** through our process of breaking and fixing.

And now fix

And break

And fix

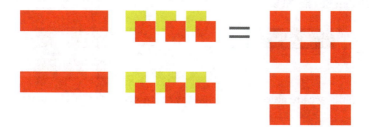

Which can be written as

$$-2x + 6 - 6 = -6 - 6$$

Where the zero pairs will create no number part

Giving the position

$-2x = -12$

Breaking this into equal groups, we can see

$$\frac{1}{2} \times (-2x) = \frac{1}{2} \times (-12)$$

which gives

$$-x = -6$$

And now, as before, we can use our knowledge of multiplication to multiply by negative one, which will result in the additive inverses:

$$-1 \times -x = -1 \times -6$$

Which can be shown as

And, finally, we are able to state what the unknown area must equate to

$$x = 6$$

Given that we have knowledge of fractions, it is worth considering an equation in which the result has a fractional part. For example:

$$3x + 1 = 8$$

As always, we can break and fix however we choose:

The two sides are now no longer equal to each other, so let's fix that:

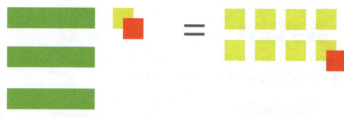

And the zero pairs create no number, giving:

$$3x = 7$$

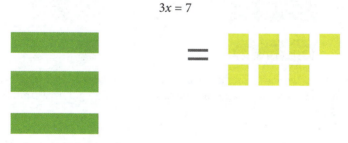

We can isolate one of the unknown areas by considering three equal groups on each side of the equation:

$$\frac{1}{3} \times 3x = \frac{1}{3} \times 7$$

As the pupil attempts to create the three equal groups, they find that one unit tile is stubbornly left out of the groupings. Some teachers will refer to this as a remainder, but this is really unhelpful. The number cannot remain outside of the system; it is integral to it and must be included. We know, particularly from our earlier fraction work with Cuisenaire rods, that anything can be split into equal groups, so let's do that with the unit too:

The unit has been split into three equal parts, creating thirds of the unit, and can now be properly included in our expression:

By inspection, we can see that one of the unknown areas is equivalent to two archetypal area units and one-third of an archetypal area unit. We can symbolise this as

$$x = 2\frac{1}{3}$$

Base systems

Until now, we have had to communicate our numbers using an infinite set of numerals, since every number is considered as a multiple of the archetypal number unit. This is quite a frustrating position and one that would require us to commit to memory an indefinite number of unique symbols, each representing a unique number. This would get rather tiresome!

How else might we arrange our numbers in order to communicate their value more efficiently?

Perhaps we could group the units into convenient and easy to recognise formats. We know, for example, that human beings can readily subitise to five (subitise means to be able to instantaneously recognise the number of objects in a group without the need to count), so perhaps grouping the numbers in fives would be useful. We could then consider a number to be the number of fives and the number of units.

Now, instead of having to remember lots and lots of symbols – or digits – we can represent our numbers by stating the number of fives and the number of units. The number above is one five and one unit, which we could represent using the numeral 11.

This number could be represented with the numeral 43, denoting four fives and three units.

This seems like a useful way of more easily communicating numbers. Perhaps we could even communicate the numbers without having to use the blocks. For example, the above number might be represented like this:

What is the best grouping to use? Perhaps fives are good because it is easy to subitise; or perhaps we should relate our groupings to things that matter to us.

What if we chose to link the groupings to useful things in our culture, like the number of days in a year? There was a time when we believed there were 360 days in a year (hence the number of degrees in a circle). Now that's a lovely number because it has so many factors and is, therefore, highly versatile to work with and can be easily made into lots of combinations of equal groupings, which would make the use of fractions much more straightforward.

But then, that means we need three hundred and sixty unique and memorable symbols, which feels quite tough.

What about a grouping of sixty? Sixty is a nice number too: it has lots of factors and is highly versatile.

No, let's make it even simpler, with fewer symbols to commit to memory. Let's go for twelve. Now that works really well. Easy to represent and easy to count. Yes, let's go with that! It has so many sensible uses and makes factor work really straightforward.

We will call the grouping the **number base**.

And now…wow! We can use just a small number of symbols to represent all possible values. So I don't need a never-ending list of symbols; I can use a small list of symbols – let's call them digits – to create larger symbols – let's call them numerals – which will indicate to me how many of each type of block I have. Amazing!

So, using a small list of digits, I can create all the numerals I will ever need and these can tell me about the 'numberness' of the value by denoting how many objects I have of different sizes. Hey, this is really handy!

This is so much easier than having to count all those yellow units and remember an infinite list of symbols!

Hang on a minute, what about the groups of twelve? We might want to work with really large numbers and will still need countless symbols to represent our groups of twelve. Hmmm.

Aha! We could group the groups of twelve in twelves!

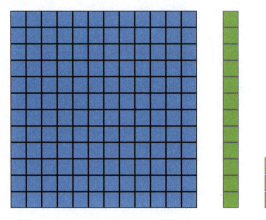

And then we could group those groups in twelves and so on and so on. Now we really do only ever need twelve digits.

Let us look at some numbers:

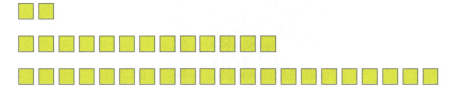

How can these now be expressed in in base 12?

Well, the first number has two units, so can be written simply as '2'. The second number has one lot of twelve and one more unit, so can be written '11'. The third number contains one group of twelve and nine units, so can be expressed with the numeral '19'.

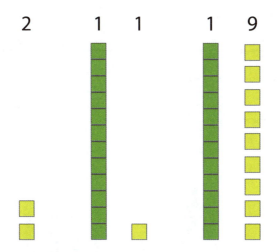

This is one way to express our numbers – using base 12 – which means we can have a short list of easily recallable digits that we can use to form an endless list of numerals, capable of communicating the numberness of any given number.

The choice of twelve is a good choice for our base, since it is an easy number to create lots of equal groupings from, and this makes working with fractions much more simple. But, there is nothing to stop us choosing other groupings. Suppose, instead, we grouped our numbers in sevens.

Base 7 can be shown using blocks, like this:

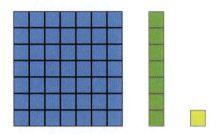

We are beginning to see that, no matter what the choice of base, the archetypal number unit does not vary. All bases are built from the principle of a unit.

Let us look again at our numbers

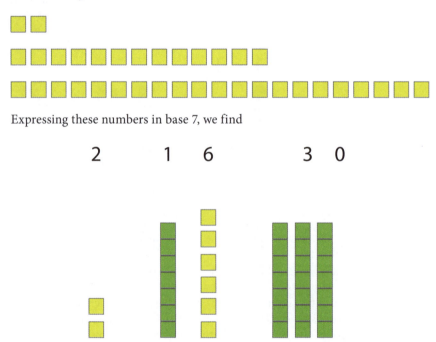

Expressing these numbers in base 7, we find

2 1 6 3 0

So, we can see that, although the numbers are identical, the numerals they are represented by vary depending on the base:

2 base 12 = 2 base 7

11 base 12 = 16 base 7

19 base 12 = 30 base 7

The numeral is not the number. The numeral is a way of communicating the number in a given base system. The value and position of the digits in the numeral indicate the value of the parts of the number in the particular groups – that is to say, the relationship between a digit, a numeral and a number in a given base system tells us about the **place value**.

Given that identical numbers are expressed in different numerals depending on the base, it would be convenient to choose a base that we all work in for a particular purpose. Which base to choose has been an ongoing argument for millennia; but for now, we seem to have settled on using base 10 in most cases. It is far from being a consensus, though. Ten is not a particularly helpful number to use, particularly since it has limited factors and makes many actions more difficult than in some other bases.

Throughout history, different base systems have been adopted by different civilisations and cultures. Adherents to a base-10 system have included Egyptian (3000 BC), Aegean (1500 BC), Roman (1000 BC), Hebrew (800 BC), Greek (pre-500 BC) and Arabic (700 AD). The Babylonians (3100 BC) used base 60, whilst the Mayans (1400 AD), Muisca (1400 AD) and Aztecs (1500 AD) all used base 20.

Different bases are also used for specific purposes, such as: base 2 (binary) in computing and in some early imperial volume measurements; base 4 (quaternary) is used for studying DNA; base 11 (undecimal) is used as the check digit in ISBN coding; base 12 (duodecimal) remains common in many measurement systems including time and imperial measures such as inches and feet; base 14 (tetradecimal) is how pounds and stones work in weights; base 60 (sexagesimal) is familiar to us all when working with hours, minutes and seconds; and base 360 (trecentosexagesimal) is used when measuring angles and turn in degrees.

For most purposes, base 10 (decimal) is at play so we should make our pupils particularly familiar with working in base 10 – though not at the expense of awareness of other bases.

Here are some numbers in base 10 and their respective numerals:

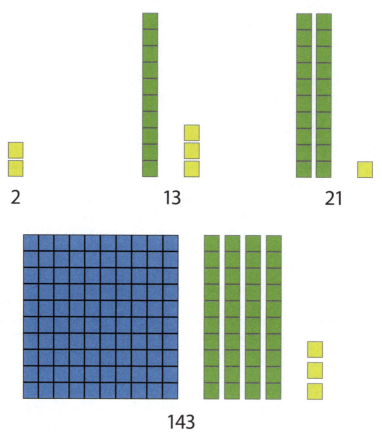

Factorising

Notice that when multiplying a multiplier and a multiplicand, we create an array of unit areas. For example, the multiplication 2 × 3 gives two rows of three, forming the array

This array forms a rectangle. The area is defined, as before, as the number of unit squares. As a rectangle, this area can also be considered as the number of unit squares required to perfectly fill the space of the rectangle.

The values of the multiplier and multiplicand are also equal to the value of the lengths of the two sides of the rectangle.

For instance, 14 × 8 would form an array consisting of 112 unit squares in a rectangle of length 14 and width 8.

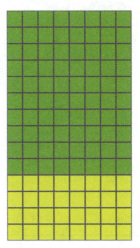

We will call the length and the width of the rectangle 'factors' of the number formed by the rectangular array. A number expressed in terms of its factors shall be said to be 'factorised'.

Suppose we already knew the value of the area but did not know both lengths. We could factorise a number in lots of ways. Taking the number twenty-four, for example, there are many ways we can rearrange the number into a rectangular form. Here are some of the ways that the number twenty-four can be arranged as a rectangular array:

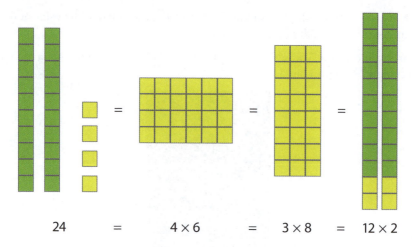

$$24 \quad = \quad 4 \times 6 \quad = \quad 3 \times 8 \quad = \quad 12 \times 2$$

This is not an exhaustive list, but is intended merely to show how a number can be rearranged into different orientations.

What about the case when one of the sides of the rectangle is known and we wish to find the other? That is to say, when we know one factor of the number and wish to find the other factor. How might we express this symbolically? Well, given that we know one side and that we know the number can be arranged into a rectangular array, perhaps we could use the shorthand

$$3 \overline{)12}$$

This symbolism is really helpful in that it tells us precisely what we already know and what we wish to find. Around the world, we sometimes see this symbol written in different ways, but they all have the same meaning.

The symbol is telling us that there exists a perfect rectangle with one length known and the other length unlabelled. The rectangle contains within it a number of unit squares, a property we call 'area'. In our case, we are being told that the rectangle has an area of 12 and that one of the lengths is known to be 3.

So, we know we have the number twelve and that it is to be rearranged into a rectangular form where one of the lengths is equal to 3. Taking the standard format of the number twelve as denoted by the numeral '12', we can see it is not possible to rearrange the ten-rod and the two units into a shape with length three. In order to do so, we must **exchange** the ten-rod for ten units. It is then a simple matter to arrange the units such that one of the lengths is fixed as 3.

The number...   ...exchange...   ...factorise

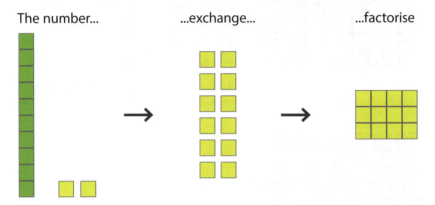

We can clearly see that the other dimension of the array is 4, so the length can be labelled on our symbolism:

$$3 \overline{\smash{)}\, 12}^{\,4}$$

The symbolism and the tiles show everything about the system. It is true that 12 factorises to 3 × 4 or, indeed, to 4 × 3.

Let us look at another example

$$12 \overline{\smash{)}\, 168}$$

The symbolism is stating that there is a perfect rectangle with an area of 168 and one length set as 12. Using our base-10 blocks, we can form the number represented by the numeral 168:

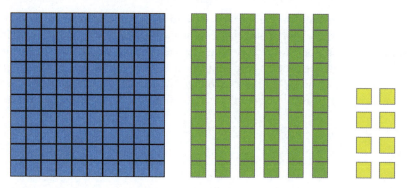

It is now a simple process to set one length as 12 and to form the required rectangle. Notice that we have removed some blocks from our original system.

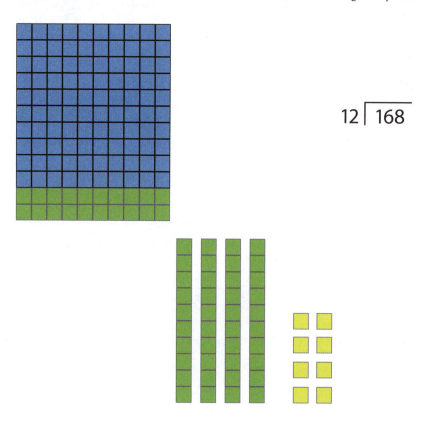

$$12 \overline{\smash{\big)}\, 168}$$

Creating the length of 12 with these blocks has removed 120 from the original system. There remain 48 in the system. We can tell the story of this structural change to the system symbolically:

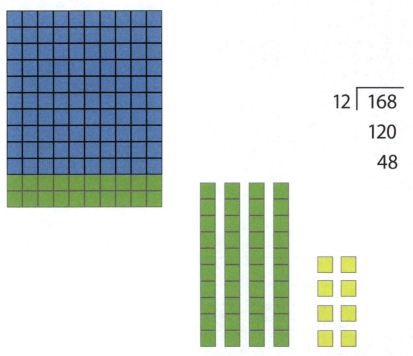

$$12\ \overline{\big)\ 168}$$
$$120$$
$$48$$

We know that the result will be a perfect rectangle, so let's keep building:

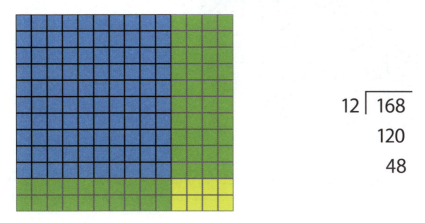

$$12\ \overline{\big)\ 168}$$
$$120$$
$$48$$

Here, we have removed 48 from the original system and there is now no number remaining in the original system. This structural change can be symbolised:

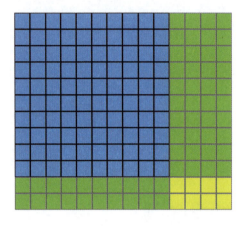

$$12\overline{)168}$$

$$120$$

$$48$$

$$48$$

$$0$$

We now have a perfect rectangle and no number remaining in the original system to take care of. So, we have rearranged 168 into a factorised form and can see the other length is 14, so we can complete the symbolic form

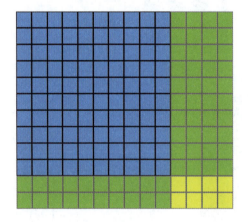

$$14$$

$$12\overline{)168}$$

$$120$$

$$48$$

$$48$$

$$0$$

The reader has probably noticed that this discussion contains no mention of division – we simply don't need it, since we can complete all of our work with just addition and multiplication. We can use the multiplicative inverse from axiom 8:

8	*Existence of multiplicative inverses*	For every $a \neq 0$ there exists $\frac{1}{a}$ so that $a \times \frac{1}{a} = \frac{1}{a} \times a = 1$. Example: $2 \times \frac{1}{2} = \frac{1}{2} \times 2 = 1$

Combing this with our new knowledge of factors, we can reduce BIDMAS even further to simply BIMA.

Generalising the base

When we give numerals numberness, using the blocks, we can see that in base 12, we have a unit block, a 1 × 12 rod and a 12 × 12 square:

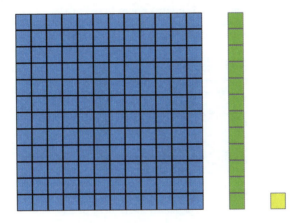

In base 10 we have a unit block, a 1 × 10 rod and a 10 × 10 square:

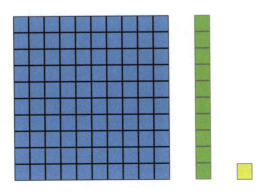

And in base 7 we have a unit block, a 1 × 7 rod and a 7 × 7 square:

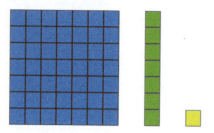

Aha! I can see a pattern!

Suppose the base was unknown. There is, in all cases, the archetypal unit, then a rod, then a square. Let us call the unknown base 'base *x*'.

We would now have a unit block, then a 1 by *x* rod and an *x* by *x* square.

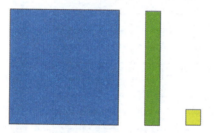

This gives us a new way of writing numbers when the base is unknown which will work for all cases. We have a generalised form of number.

Let us consider the example

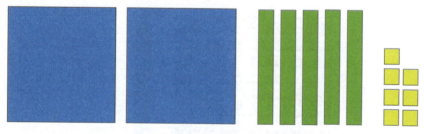

This **is** a number. It has numberness.

What numeral might we use to represent this? Just as before, we can use digits to represent this number as the numeral 257.

How can we make the numeral clearer in its articulation of representing an unknown base such that it better communicates the value? Well, we have two squares, each with area x by x. For short, let us say this as 'x squared' and denote it symbolically as x^2. We also have five rods, each with area x, and then our seven units.

To communicate this meaning, we can write the numeral as a sum of all those parts

$$2x^2 + 5x + 7$$

This is read 'x squared plus five x plus seven.'

So, even when we do not know the base, we can still symbolise the number in a numeral and can communicate the numberness of the numeral further by including the related place value as part of the numeral.

Given our ability to factorise numbers in other bases, it seems likely to be the case that we can factorise these types of numbers that have an unknown base.

We have established that 'factorise' is another way of stating that we are required to find a factor pair that will create the number we are working with – in other words, to find the lengths of the rectangle that make the given area.

Suppose we wished to factorise the number expressed by

$$x^2 + 5x + 6$$

As before, when we are not given one of the factors, we can experiment with the area parts until we make a perfect rectangle.

First, let us translate the numeral into a number:

We know that this number – or expression – can be factorised by arranging the parts of the number into a perfect rectangle. Pupils might spend a short while trying a few arrangements, but all pupils will, in time, be able to find the rectangular arrangement:

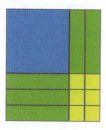

We have seen previously that, when factorised, the value of each of the factors is the same as the lengths of the sides of the rectangle. Here we can see that one of the lengths is $x + 3$ and the other length is $x + 2$. In other words,

$$x^2 + 5x + 6 = (x + 3)(x + 2)$$

Having used this approach with many pupils over the years, I know that it also brings about one of my favourite moments with pupils. After working on lots of these problems and writing the factorised form symbolically, this always happens:

PUPIL: (conspiratorially) 'Sir! Sir! Come here. Look.'

TEACHER: 'What have you found out?'

PUPIL: 'Guess what I have noticed. Look. Whenever I do one of the problems, I find a pattern in the numbers.'

TEACHER: 'Oh? Really?'

PUPIL: 'Yes, it makes it really easy. Look, the two digits that we get in the answer always multiply to give the final digit in the question.'

The pupil will eagerly point out, for example, that in

$$x^2 + 5x + 6 = (x + 3)(x + 2)$$

it is true that $3 \times 2 = 6$.

TEACHER: 'Gosh, that's interesting.'

PUPIL: 'Whoa! You haven't seen anything yet! Guess what! They also always add up to the middle value!'

The pupil points out that $3 + 2 = 5$.

TEACHER: 'Does this always work?'

PUPIL: 'Yes! Every time I do it, I already know what the answer is going to be. Sir, can I stop using the tiles? It's quicker **my** way.'

TEACHER: 'OK, I'll let you do it just with symbols, but only if you can tell me why this must be true.'

PUPIL: 'Oh, Sir, you are so dumb. Look! It's really obvious. The only place that we will get the yellow tiles is where the intersection happens, so it must be multiply. But the green bars happen in two places, so we must add those together to get the full area.'

TEACHER: 'Well I never! Amazing! I wish I had known this – I have been carrying about boxes of tiles for years to solve these problems and now you have just blown my mind with your new strategy. You genius, you. Keep it to yourself for now!'

I really love this moment. They do of course know that I am hamming it up and playing with them, but they genuinely love it too – without instruction, they have truly noticed something of great value and utility.

Let us look at another example:

This number can be expressed symbolically – or **algebraically** – as

$$2x^2 + 5x + 2$$

and can be shown in its factorised form

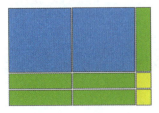

This demonstrates that

$$2x^2 + 5x + 2 = (x + 2)(2x + 1)$$

and is a clear articulation that the initial expression truly can be shown to be the muliplication of two factors.

It is worth pausing here to also consider some alternative language used in re-forming expressions of the type we have been encountering. A common and useful format would be the special case where the rectangular form that the pupil is attempting to create is a square. We call this process 'completing the square'.

We can rearrange our number in an attempt to create a square

The square that is almost formed here is the square of side length $x + 2$, and can therefore be written $(x + 2)^2$. But the square is incomplete – in this case, the shape shown is the square less one. This can be written

$$(x + 2)^2 - 1$$

(I have very often seen pupils being taught about completing the square in mathematics lessons in which the teacher makes no reference whatsoever to either squares or completing them, which has always struck me as odd.)

Let us now consider the problem

$$x + 1 \overline{)\ 2x^2 + 5x + 3}$$

This is known later in mathematical development as algebraic long division, but for our purposes, working with pupils at an earlier developmental stage, we do not have to introduce such a description. Here, the symbolism is clear – there is a system consisting of

$$2x^2 + 5x + 3$$

which can be orientated into a perfect rectangle with one of the lengths set as $x + 1$

Here is our starting number

Let us begin to rearrange our number into a rectangular form with length $x + 1$. For example:

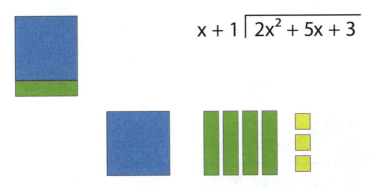

$$x + 1 \overline{\smash{\big)}\ 2x^2 + 5x + 3}$$

To create this shape, we have removed $x^2 + x$ from the system and have $x^2 + 4x + 3$ remaining in the original system, which can be represented as numbers and symbolically:

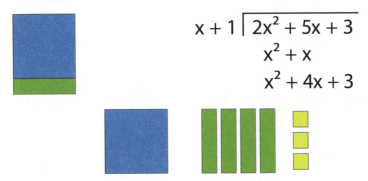

$$x + 1 \overline{\smash{\big)}\ 2x^2 + 5x + 3}$$
$$x^2 + x$$
$$x^2 + 4x + 3$$

Continuing to create the new rectangular form:

$$x + 1 \overline{\smash{)}\, 2x^2 + 5x + 3}$$
$$x^2 + x$$
$$x^2 + 4x + 3$$
$$x^2 + x$$
$$3x + 3$$

And then finally arriving at

$$x + 1 \overline{\smash{)}\, 2x^2 + 5x + 3}$$
$$x^2 + x$$
$$x^2 + 4x + 3$$
$$x^2 + x$$
$$3x + 3$$
$$3x + 3$$
$$0$$

There is now no number remaining in the original system and we have a perfect rectangle, so the factorising is complete and the other factor can be stated in the following symbolism:

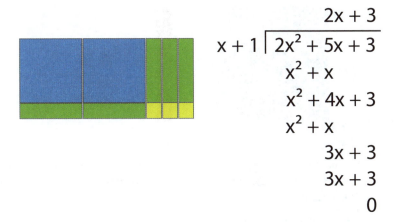

$$\begin{array}{r} 2x + 3 \\ x + 1 \overline{\smash{\big)}\ 2x^2 + 5x + 3} \\ x^2 + x \\ x^2 + 4x + 3 \\ x^2 + x \\ 3x + 3 \\ 3x + 3 \\ 0 \end{array}$$

It is now clear that

$$2x^2 + 5x + 3 = (x + 1)(2x + 3)$$

An interesting question to pose to pupils when the teacher wishes to ascertain their level of understanding is

TEACHER: 'Explain why $168 \div 12$ is the same as $(x^2 + 6x + 8) \div (x + 2)$'

PUPIL: 'If I did $168 \div 12$ with Dienes blocks and $(x^2 + 6x + 8) \div (x + 2)$ with algebra tiles, all the moves I make would be identical.'

PUPIL: 'It's just that the first one is in base 10 and the second one is in base x. If I changed the x to ten, it would be the same question.'

A rules-based system

The examples we have examined thus far have been chosen carefully to introduce pupils to factorising and creating the factor forms of the numbers or expressions in rectangular spaces. Each example lends itself well to being arranged in a rectangle. But the teacher of mathematics must always be expecting the precocious child!

Suppose a pupil wants to consider the challenge of factorising an expression such as this:

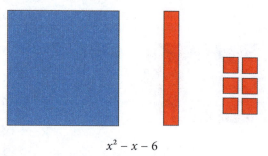

$$x^2 - x - 6$$

There is no obvious way of rearranging this number to create a perfect rectangle, since we are not able to use exchange with these tiles because we do not know the lengths.

However, we can make this shape:

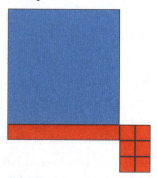

On the face of it, this shape does not appear to have helped us resolve the problem; but what if we could make changes to the system such that we are able to create more tiles?

Here are some tiles. What value do they have combined?

This is clearly a zero pair, which means combined they give zero area. It is an easy case to logically argue that adding zero to a system will not change the system – indeed, we have shown the impact of adding zero earlier when establishing our axioms. So, it is reasonable to state that we can add these tiles into the area without altering the problem. Let us add the tiles like this:

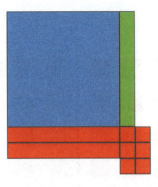

This is still not a perfect rectangle, so let us add another zero pair:

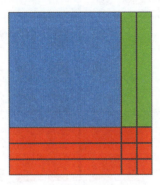

This gives us the perfect rectangle we are looking for.

As before, the rectangle can be represented symbolically by stating the lengths of the sides. Consider the colour of the tiles as we read the lengths. Along the left-hand side, reading from top to bottom we have a length of x in blue then three in red. The red tiles are negative values, so this length can be read as $x -$ 3. Reading horizontally along the top of the rectangle, a length of x in blue and two in green gives $x + 2$.

So

$$x^2 - x - 6 = (x - 3)(x + 2)$$

But how did we know which shape to build initially? And how did we know which sides to read as the lengths?

Recall the interesting result of finding out about multiplication earlier:

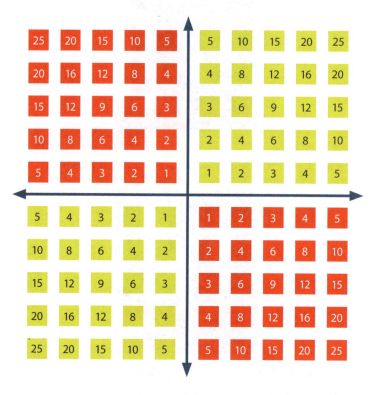

We can see that the results of all multiplications appear to create regions that are populated fully by positive values or negative values. So, there are positive spaces and negative spaces where our numbers can exist.

If we consider our problem again, but this time restrict the positioning of our tiles by placing them on our newly defined spaces, then we can see that the tiles can only take on a limited number of forms. The positive blue square can only exist in quadrant 1 (upper right) or quadrant 3 (lower left); the red negative bars and units can only exist in quadrant 2 (upper left) or quadrant 4 (lower right). Now that we have this rules-based approach to forming our areas, the correct positioning of the tiles becomes obvious and trivial:

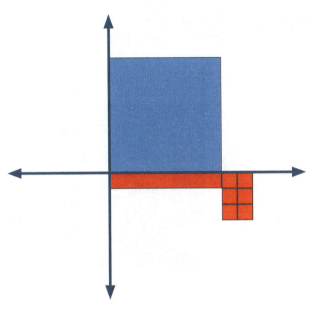

When adding in the zero pairs, clearly the green rods must exist in positive space and the red rods in negative space, giving the model:

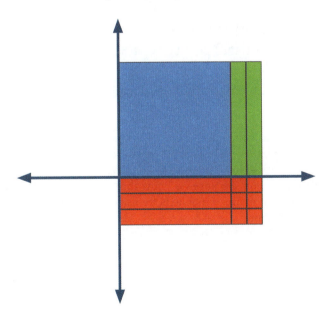

When reading the length of the factors, what we are really doing is reading one length along one axis and the other length along the other axis:

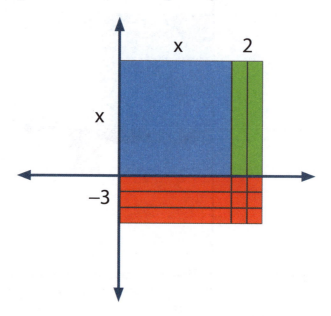

Which gives the same solution as before.

What if we already knew the factors but wanted to find the expression that had been factorised?

Suppose, for example, we know that the factorised form is

$$(x - 2)(x - 4)$$

We can use the same knowledge of our defined space to plot our lengths. The first factor tells us that along one axis there is a length x in a positive direction and 2 in a negative direction. The other factor gives x in a positive direction and 4 in a negative direction. Because we know that multiplication can happen in any order, it does not matter which axis we use for the individual lengths; the result must be the same.

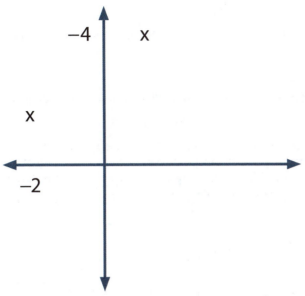

Now we have a rules-based system for representing any factorising or any **expanding** problem.

Combining these directions, we find the shape and the area:

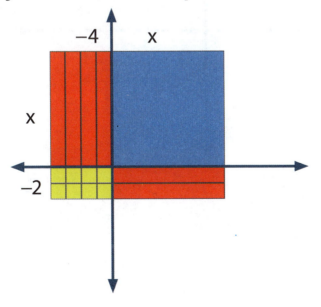

$$x^2 - 4x + 8 - 2x = x^2 - 6x + 8$$

What would this look like in base 10? When the base was unknown, we stated the factors as

$$(x - 2)(x - 4)$$

If we now know that the base is base 10, we can substitute 10 in place of x.

$$(10 - 2)(10 - 4)$$

As before, it is now a matter of showing these lengths on our axes. On one axis, we have length of 10 in a positive direction and a length of 2 in a negative direction; on the other axis, a length of 10 in a positive direction and a length of 4 in a negative direction. This gives:

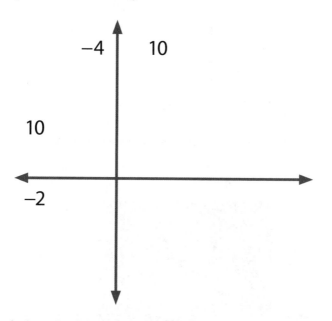

Now that the bounds of the area are known, we can use Dienes blocks to fill the space, giving

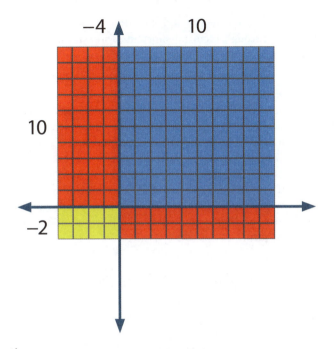

By inspection, we can see

$$100 - 40 + 8 - 20 = 48$$

Looking back at our factors

$$(10 - 2)(10 - 4)$$

and carrying out the operator, this can also be written as:

$$8 \times 6$$

which gives the same result as above: 48.

Given the expression in the unknown base, determining the solution in some given base is a simple process of replacing the unknown x with the known base value.

So, using base x is the same as using the **general** case! Wow! Algebra allows me to deal with all arithmetical possibilities in one go!

We could continue with this journey even further, getting to grips with those expressions that do not factorise and beyond – but that is for another book and another time. Here I merely wanted to sow the seeds for thinking about numberness. The fuller journey would include the move away from the use of tiles and blocks, through pictorial shortcuts and onto the purely symbolic representations that have started to emerge above.

This short exploration of some ideas in the structure of number has allowed us to connect the meaning of numeral, digit, number, base systems, place value and the general algebraic form. Such an exploration is just the very beginning of working with number and algebra as one unified approach. The field axioms give us permission to perform arithmetic with number and algebra in a coherent and rules-based way. Avoiding the introduction of subtraction and division means the avoidance, at an early stage, of embedding misconceptions such as 'two negatives make a positive'. Later, we will indeed introduce subtraction and division in their own right as operators, but only once pupils can work fluently and with deep understanding of equivalence, equality, addition, multiplication and the generalised form.

Designing and doing tasks

Designing tasks is an important activity for teachers to undertake during their careers. Designing, doing, testing and iterating mathematical questions, prompts, activities and problems increases a teacher's awareness of the characteristics of tasks most likely to bring about effective learning in the classroom. However, task design should not be a burden – it is clearly a ridiculous expectation to ask teachers to create all of the tasks that they use. Not only is this an unsustainable position, but it would also result in teachers not accessing and learning from the canon of our profession. Having taught mathematics for millennia, the teaching profession knows a lot about how to do so and has created tried-and-tested teaching materials that individual teachers can draw on.

A very good example of this is the Association of Teachers of Mathematics (ATM) series *Points of Departure*. Each book in the series contains a selection of scenarios or prompts that the teacher can use with pupils to undertake some serious mathematics.

I will take one example from the first *Points of Departure* (Hardy et al., 1977) to illustrate some possible mathematics that can emerge. In the ATM book, the task is titled simply '1089'.

TEACHER: 'Please write down three different **digits**.'

Notice the emphasis on the word 'digits' here. Why has the teacher made this pedagogic choice? As the task progresses, you will hopefully see that we are getting to the heart of what place value means. In defining and gripping place value, we must ensure that pupils understand the difference between 'digit', 'numeral' and 'number'. Each of these has specific meaning and cannot be used interchangeably. The different meaning of these words is critical in establishing an understanding of place value, so the teacher is making the pedagogic choice to over-emphasise the words as they occur.

The pupils now write down three digits of their choosing. Let's suppose they choose:

4, 7, 5

> TEACHER: 'Using your three **digits**, please create the greatest-value three-digit **numeral** you can make.'

The pupils write down their numeral. A numeral is a symbol that represents a number. Numerals are made from digits. So, for example, '7', '87', and '32891' are all numerals. The distinction between digit and numeral is important; they have different meanings and neither of them are numbers. The numeral is a way of communicating a number, which is a concept. When considering the number, there is additional meaning beyond that of just digits and numerals. The number is a relationship between the digits, the numeral and the base system in which we are working. This relationship gives the number its meaning. For example, the numeral 754 can be conceptualised as a number using Dienes blocks in base 10:

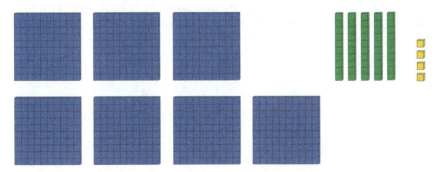

It is only at this moment of conceptualising the meaning of the numeral that we bring about numberness. These distinctions often seem unimportant, particularly to adults who are so familiar with the meaning of numbers and expert in using them that the subtlety has been lost. But these distinctions do matter to the novice who is only just starting to learn about a sense of number.

> TEACHER: 'Underneath, maintaining column position, please write down the least-value three-digit **numeral** you can make with your **digits**. And now, I would like you to perform a **subtraction**.'

This will result in the pupil having on their page something like this:

$$
\begin{array}{r}
\text{Largest} \quad 7\,5\,4 \\
\text{Smallest} \quad -\,4\,5\,7 \\
\hline
 \\
\hline
\end{array}
$$

The assumption here is that our hypothetical pupils have been taught that subtraction is an independent operation of arithmetic and that subtraction will be carried out using an algorithm starting from the right hand side. I will dismantle both of these approaches later, but for this purpose it is useful to imagine these pupils as being typical of real ones we find in our schools.

The pupils will begin at the right-hand side, asking themselves, 'What is four minus seven?' The most common response to this would be to suggest that this is not possible. This type of approach to subtraction is treating the 4 and the 7 as numerals, not numbers. If these were numbers, then of course four minus seven is perfectly possible. But in this approach, the rules do not permit the subtraction to be performed unless the result **of the number subtraction** is positive. Pupils will have been taught to 'exchange' with the digit to the left of the top-row digit we are considering:

$$
\begin{array}{r}
4 \\
\text{Largest} \quad 7\,\cancel{5}\,4 \\
\text{Smallest} \quad -\,4\,5\,7 \\
\hline
 \\
\hline
\end{array}
$$

What does this 'exchange' mean and what is now the meaning of the symbols? Because the 4 and the 7 in this example are being considered as numerals, not numbers, they have no value, so the rules of the algorithm mean we reduce the value of the numeral to the left by one and then this '1' is placed in front of the original numeral.

Of course, what we are trying to communicate is that the number that this numeral represents does indeed have meaning and makes it possible to subtract by considering the relationship between the number, numeral and digits. Let us assume at this stage that the pupils are working in base 10. The numeral 754 represents a number in base 10 made up of $7 \times (10^2)$, $5 \times (10^1)$ and $4 \times (10^0)$. We might consider this using base-10 Dienes blocks, for example:

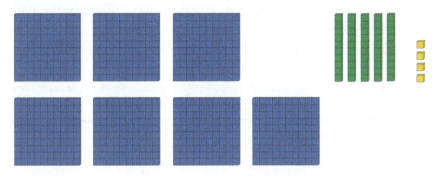

In this method of subtraction, the pupil is considering whether it is possible to remove 7 yellow blocks from this system. Clearly, it is not. However, one of the green rods could be 'exchanged' for 10 of the yellow blocks, leaving us with just 4 green rods and 14 yellow blocks, from which it is possible to remove the 7 blocks represented by the digit on the right-hand side of the bottom numeral.

We now have

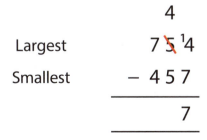

Largest

Smallest

Continuing in this way, we complete the subtraction and find the result:

$$6\,{}^{1}4$$

Largest	$\not{7}\,\not{5}\,{}^{1}4$
Smallest	$-\ 4\ 5\ 7$
	$2\ 9\ 7$

There does not appear to be anything remarkable about this result. Assuming the pupils have long since been fluent in the use of this subtraction algorithm, getting to this point is trivial.

The solution to this simple subtraction problem now acts as a new object in our problem.

> TEACHER: 'Now you have an answer. I'd like you to use that answer for the next step. Somewhere else on your page, write that answer forwards. Then underneath, maintaining column position, write that answer backwards. Now perform an addition.'

Forwards	$2\ 9\ 7$
Backwards	$+\ 7\ 9\ 2$

Our hypothetical pupil will, most likely, deal with this problem by carrying out a column addition algorithm. They will start at the right-hand side and add the 7 and 2 together to give 9.

Forwards	$2\ 9\ 7$
Backwards	$+\ 7\ 9\ 2$
	9

The pupil will then move left, adding the 9 and the 9 together. This gives 18 if we consider these digits as numbers. Typically, pupils will place the '1' digit in the column to the left.

Forwards	2 9 7
Backwards	+ 7 9 2
	8 9
	1

Finally, the pupil will add together the three digits in the left-hand column, treating them as numbers. This gives 10.

Forwards	2 9 7
Backwards	+ 7 9 2
	1 0 8 9
	1

With a classroom of children, I will often ask them to carry out this process on mini-whiteboards. I will tell them to write their final answer in large print and then turn their whiteboard face down so that nobody can see their answer.

TEACHER: 'On the count of three, hold up your answer! 1! 2! 3!'

All the pupils reveal their answers and they all have 1089. This creates a lovely moment of surprise and curiosity in the classroom. Why did they all get the same?

TEACHER: 'Whoa! What on earth has happened here? Did you all choose the same starting digits?'

WHOLE CLASS: 'No!'

TEACHER: 'This is so strange! What is going on? How did this happen?'

As teachers, we use these deliberately created moments of curiosity to create what I call a 'conjecturing classroom culture'. We want our pupils to ask questions of the mathematics that they encounter. Want them to be surprised and have a genuine feeling of wanting to find out what lies behind that surprise. It is important that the pupils truly believe that the questions they are asking are their own questions, that they are conjecturing in a way that is unique to them and that perhaps nobody has ever thought to ask the questions they have asked or ever stumbled upon the revelations they have stumbled upon.

Of course, what is really happening here is that, through careful pedagogic choice, the teacher is manipulating a situation such that the pupils will ask precisely the questions we want them to ask.

It can be tempting to feed them the questions (and sometimes we will choose to do so for specific purposes), but there is gain in creating a conjecturing classroom culture and gain in their belief that they have acted in an independent spirit. I would suggest that part of the gain here is related to the bridging effect discussed earlier – there appear to be significant learning gains in allowing pupils to articulate their theories and invented strategies and approaches. It takes no additional classroom time, and even if one did not believe in the far transfer gains of bridging that have been shown in research – well for goodness' sake it just makes for a damn more interesting classroom and more switched-on pupils!

At this stage in the 1089 lesson, pupils are keen to unpick what has happened. There are lots of directions that this problem can be taken. Here I will suggest one journey through the lesson.

TEACHER: 'This is so weird. I wish I knew what was going on here. I wonder how we can find out.'

CLASS: 'Can we try some more?'

Now, this is an interesting (but, in this case, not uncommon) response. A classroom of children asking (pleading, often) to be allowed to do more calculations.

TEACHER: 'Well, as a class, we have already tried lots of different starting digits, so perhaps we need to try something else. I wonder what would happen if we did it with four starting digits.'

CLASS: 'Can we do it?'

TEACHER: 'Yes. Let's have a go at four digits.'

The pupils work through the same process of largest, smallest, forwards backwards and eventually all find that their answer is 10890. This is a satisfying result.

CLASS: 'Can we try five digits please?'

TEACHER: 'No.'

Why not? Why interrupt this moment of curiosity and deny them permission to follow a line of enquiry that they are keen to pursue? This is a deliberate pedagogic choice. The mathematics teacher wants the pupils to attack problems in a more formal way that might bring about additional gains.

TEACHER: 'You are only allowed to try five digits once you have written down a conjecture.'

Given the two solutions they have available to them – 1089 and 10890 – all pupils will write something along the lines of, 'I conjecture that, using five digits, the answer will be 108900.' This has some merit as a suggestion. It seems there is a pattern emerging and there is a logical explanation for thinking the pattern might be as simple as another zero each time.

The pupils then work confidently through the task, with the expectation that their conjecture will hold true. When they get to the answer, the wave of 'It has broken' will murmur around the room. The answer is not what they expected it to be. This is very frustrating for the pupils and many will go over their work again to check if they have made an arithmetical error. But they haven't. The answer is now 109890.

TEACHER: 'How strange! I thought it was going to be 108900 too. Why are our conjectures wrong? What is happening? Let's find out more! Try six digits, seven, eight – keep going! We can beat this! Remember: before trying each new problem, write down a conjecture.'

Pupils now work with determination to overcome the problem. They are more reserved about their next conjecture – after all, the sequence 1089, 10890, 109890, could suggest a whole range of possibilities. It is not easy to simply guess what might come next.

As the pupils continue to work, the atmosphere in the classroom changes again. As they do eight and nine digits, they begin to get their conjectures correct. This builds a sense of mathematical confidence. In a very short period of time, the emotions in the room have gone from mundane to surprise to curious to conjecturing to frustration to confidence to determination to assurance.

Allow the pupils plenty of time to continue working. After a while, tell the class to stop working. At this stage, I have often heard a pupil yell something like, 'No! Sir! Please, I'm on 37 digits!'

A classroom of pupils has carried out hundreds of calculations from an initial, apparently simple prompt. They did this because they **wanted** to.

TEACHER: 'Stop what you are doing, we are going to start again.'

CLASS: 'What!'

TEACHER: 'We are going to start again with just three digits.'

CLASS: 'Boo! Too easy!'

TEACHER: 'We are going to start again with three digits. But this time, I am going to choose your digits for you and we are all going to work on the same problem. Your digits are...'

The teacher now writes on the board:

$$a > b > c$$

There will be a short pause as the pupils digest this suggestion, but if they have been taught carefully about digits, numerals and numbers and how those things fundamentally bring about a sense of place value in a defined base system, this problem is attackable. The inequality symbolism is an early idea that pupils should have met and got to grips with when learning about equality. On the current English national curriculum, for instance, this symbolism is used with six- and seven-year-olds.

So, the pupils know what to do. They have to create the numeral with the largest possible value and the one with the least. Clearly, to do this, we arrange the digits in descending and ascending order. This gives the new problem:

Largest		a	b	c
Smallest	−	c	b	a

The pupils have an algorithm that they have been using for the previous problems. Nothing has changed; there is no extra demand here. Starting from the right-hand side, pupils ask themselves, is it possible to subtract **a** from **c**?

If **a** and **c** were numbers, the answer would be 'Yes, this is possible.' But here **abc** is a numeral and the individual letters are digits. So, given that **c** is less than **a**, our previous algorithm has a set of rules that forbid us from performing the subtraction. Instead, we follow the procedural steps as before. We look to the left and know that **b** will no longer be the digit:

Largest		a	b̶	c
Smallest	−	c	b	a

The value of **b** decreases by 1.

$$b - 1$$

Largest		a	b̶	c
Smallest	−	c	b	a

Thinking about the meaning of the numeral and giving it numberness, we know that **abc** means there are a lots of one hundred, **b** lots of ten and c units. So, when we reduce the **b** to **b − 1**, we have really removed one lot of ten. This ten is then converted into units. In the units position we therefore have **c + 10** units:

$$b - 1$$

Largest		a	b̶	c + 10
Smallest	−	c	b	a

Looking at the left-hand column, the pupil must consider whether it is always possible to subtract a from $c + 10$. Given that a is a digit and we are working in base 10, we know that every digit has a value less than 10, so $c + 10$ must necessarily be larger than a. This means it must be permissible to perform the subtraction, giving us:

$$b - 1$$

Largest	a	~~b~~	c + 10
Smallest	− c	b	a
			c + 10 − a

The algorithm continues. The pupil considers whether it is possible to subtract b from $b - 1$. Given that b is a digit, $b - 1$ must have a lower value than b, so the subtraction is not permissible.

Again, we look to the left.

$$a - 1 \quad b - 1$$

Largest	~~a~~	~~b~~	c + 10
Smallest	− c	b	a
			c + 10 − a

The a in abc represents a lots of one hundred. When we reduce the value by 1 as the algorithm insists, we are really converting that one hundred into ten lots of ten To represent those additional ten lots of ten, we add 10 to the middle digit. It is worth noting here that many pupils will add 100 rather than 10 at this point – this common misconception arises where pupils have not been taught about digits, numerals and numbers and how they relate in a base system to give meaning to the idea of place value. All too often, teachers' subject knowledge in early mathematics can be superficial, with children being taught convenient tricks or easy-to-regurgitate processes rather than really getting under the skin of a mathematical idea. Watch out for the misconception and, if you spot it, correct it immediately and ensure the pupil understands the correction by demonstrating with Dienes blocks what is happening in the system.

We now have

$$a - 1 \quad b - 1 + 10$$

Largest	a̸	b̸	c + 10
Smallest	− c	b	a
			c + 10 − a

Some pupils will cross out the $b - 1$ and replace it with $b + 9$, but this is fairly rare and doesn't add any additional insight. In many respects the above version is a more useful way of communicating what has happened.

The pupil must now ponder whether or not it is permissible in **all** cases to subtract c from a in this type of algorithm.

When considering the originally digits and the relationships between them, it is clear that c must be smaller than $a - 1$ because at least b lies between them. So, we can consider the subtraction as a legal move.

$$a - 1 \quad b - 1 + 10$$

Largest	a̸	b̸	c + 10
Smallest	− c	b	a
	9	c + 10 − a	

Performing the final step in the overall subtraction gives the answer to the first stage of the task:

	$a - 1$	$b - 1 + 10$	
Largest	a	b	$c + 10$
Smallest	$-$ c	b	a
	$a - 1 - c$	9	$c + 10 - a$

We now have a new numeral: a–1–c 9 c+10–a, which means a number with a–1–c lots of one hundred, 9 lots of ten and c+10–a units.

TEACHER: 'What is the next step?'

CLASS: 'Write it forwards and write it backwards!'

Forwards		$a - 1 - c$	9	$c + 10 - a$
Backwards	$+$	$c + 10 - a$	9	$a - 1 - c$

At this stage of the task, the pupils are performing an addition. They will begin at the right-hand side and ask themselves what the result will be when they add a–1–c to c+10–a. The teacher may have to spend some time with young pupils in discussion about subtracting objects: 'If I subtract a c from a c, what do I have?'

But it is far more powerful if the teacher has spent time when building an understanding of arithmetic to firmly establish the meaning and outcomes of the field axioms. Here we can see an example of the additive inverse, $c + (-c)$. It will have been established that the axiom tells us that the result of this must be zero. So, combining the expressions on the top and bottom through addition, we now have

Forwards		$a - 1 - c$	9	$c + 10 - a$
Backwards	$+$	$c + 10 - a$	9	$a - 1 - c$
				9

Clearly, the middle column here is trivial. The pupils know 9 + 9 = 18 and, if they have been taught well about how digits, numerals and numbers interact in a base system to give a sense of place value, they can see that 18 in this position denotes one lot of one hundred and eight tens. The '1' of '18' (representing 100) can therefore be placed in the column to the left:

Forwards		$a - 1 - c$	9	$c + 10 - a$
Backwards	+	$c + 10 - a$	9	$a - 1 - c$
			8	9
		1		

Looking at the left-hand column, we again see the additive inverse at play: *a* minus *a*, *c* minus *c* and 1 minus 1 (where 'minus' is a preposition meaning the addition of the additive inverse) all result in zero as defined in the field axioms. This leaves 10.

Forwards		$a - 1 - c$	9	$c + 10 - a$
Backwards	+	$c + 10 - a$	9	$a - 1 - c$
1	0	8	9	
	1			

CLASS: 'Oh my God! Oh my God! It's 1089! But…but…we started with letters!'

The class erupts.

I have taught this lesson many times to many hundreds of pupils. They are always, without fail, blown away by this moment.

I like to tell my pupils that there are two types of human beings: the mortals and the mathematicians. The mortals, bless them, would have to do many hundreds of examples to show that if we choose three different digits and follow this process, the result will always be 1089. The mathematician, however – boom! Proof! We prove things; we don't faff about.

Now, when my pupils are later introduced to working more formally with algebra, they do not meet collecting like terms in the guise of fruit salad problems; they say, 'Oh, that's that really cool thing, isn't it, sir? Proof!'

CLASS: 'Can we try $a>b>c>d$, sir?'

TEACHER: 'Oh yes!'

Now allow the class a good amount of time to work in this way. They are honing their skills and refining their understanding of the subtraction and addition algorithms. I have often heard, after around 20 minutes of so, a pupil cry, 'Sir! I have run out of alphabet!' My response to this is always, 'That's OK: there are other alphabets.'

It is exciting to find that working with the digits a, b, c, d, and so on, we are able to show that the results always hold true. To get to this point, working in this way, pupils really do have to understand the differences between digits, numerals and numbers and how they interact in a place-value format to bring about meaning. When the pupil arrives at the answer 1089 in this way, the teacher truly knows they have gripped what it means to work with this algorithm. That's fantastic – but it's not enough.

Does the teacher know they are truly gripping arithmetic? Perhaps they are, but perhaps they are only doing one very specific subsection of arithmetic. Perhaps by only working in base 10, pupils are missing some of the meaning of the digits and numerals and how they relate to the concept of number.

After a good while, stop them from working again.

TEACHER: 'Stop what you are doing. We are going to start again.'

CLASS: 'No way! Why? We have proven it works.'

TEACHER: 'I would like you to start again with just three digits. Perform the activity again – but this time, I'd like you to work in base 7.'

The gains that come from working in multiple different bases are extensive and critical if we want pupils to understand number and understand what they are doing when working with general forms such as $x^2 + 4x + 8$.

Pupils should work with multi-base arithmetic from the beginning and throughout their mathematics education.

Let's look at an example in base 7. Clearly, we now have fewer digits to choose from, since in base 7 the only digits that exist are 0, 1, 2, 3, 4, 5, 6.

Suppose we choose

2, 3, 6

And arrange them as before:

Largest   6 3 2

Smallest   − 2 3 6

What number does the numeral 632 represent here? What does it mean?

To consider the numberness of the numeral 632, let's look at it represented with base 7 Dienes blocks.

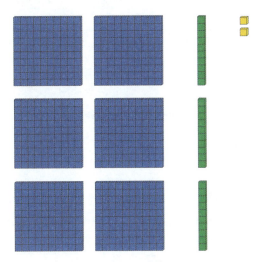

In base 7, the blocks still represent units, then strips of units, then squares made of those strips. We are beginning to discern that the position of a digit in a numeral is related to these shapes. It would seem we always have a one by one, then a one by the base, then the base by the base. We get units, rods, squares. Beyond this, we can show pupils cubes of the base too. Ah! So, from right to left in base 7, we have units, sevens, forty-nines, three hundred and forty-threes and so on. But there is no such numeral as '49' in base 7 because the digit 9 does not exist. Oh, wait! Forty-nine is seven squared! Is there a way to think of these in terms of sevens? Ah! Three hundred and forty-three is seven cubed. Now we're cooking!

These kinds of discussions and challenges will lead to the realisation that place value is really about the relationship between digits, numerals and numbers when considering the base system we are working in.

We can now see that the values of the positions in our numeral 632 are 7^2, 7^1 and 7^0. Assuming pupils have been taught similarly about base-10 place value, this realisation is something they find rather satisfying.

So, the numeral 632 in base 7 means six lots of 7^2, three lots of 7^1 and two lots of 7^0. This gives us the concept of the number.

As before, the first step in the activity is to perform the subtraction. Starting at the right-hand side, pupils must ask if it is permissible in this type of subtraction algorithm to subtract 6 from 2. Determining that it is not, they move to the left and reduce the 3 by 1 to become 2. This '1' that they now have at their disposal represents one lot of 7^1, which they can deconstruct into units and give its meaning in the unit column.

To represent this number in base 7, let's look at the Dienes blocks again:

One of the 7^1 rectangles has been exchanged for seven of the unit blocks.

In the unit position, there were already two units, so placing these new blocks together with the existing ones, we have

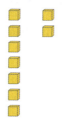

How is this number written as a numeral in base 7? We can see that we have one lot of seven and two units, so the numeral to represent this number is '12'. Note: this is not pronounced 'twelve'!

We now have

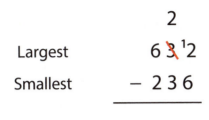

and wish to perform the subtraction of 6 from 12 in base 7.

'12' represents one lot of 7^1 and two lots of 7^0. '6' represents six lots of 7^0. Let's look at these as numbers and consider the subtraction

We can see that this would leave just three units, giving us

Continuing in this way, we find

$$5\,{}^{1}2$$

Largest $\not{6}\;\not{3}\,{}^{1}2$

Smallest $-\;2\;3\;6$

———————

$3\;6\;3$

This gives the numeral to use in the next stage of the process, which we write forwards and backwards:

Forwards $3\;6\;3$

Backwards $+\;3\;6\;3$

———————

———————

We now perform an addition. Starting in the right-hand column, let us consider the numbers and the addition.

Three units plus three units gives a total of six units. In base 7, we can represent this with the numeral '6', so this part of the calculation is trivial.

Forwards $3\;6\;3$

Backwards $+\;3\;6\;3$

———————

6

———————

Moving left and continuing the process, let us consider the numbers and the addition:

Six units plus six units gives one lot of 71 and five lots of 70. This can be expressed with the numeral '15'.

Forwards	3 6 3
Backwards	+ 3 6 3
	———————
	5 6
	———————
	1

As before, following the rules of this algorithm, the '5' is placed in the middle column but the '1' becomes part of the addition to the left.

Adding the three numbers represented by the numerals in left-hand column, we get one lot of 7^1 and no units. This can be represented by the numeral '10'.

Forwards	3 6 3
Backwards	+ 3 6 3
	———————
	1 0 5 6
	———————
	1

At this stage, I find that pupils are quietly satisfied that the answer is similar to the answer in base 10.

The task now continues as before. We ask pupils to choose four digits and repeat in base 7, giving 10560, five digits giving 106560, etc. We then ask them to work with the digits $a>b>c$ in base 7 and so on to ensure they are truly thinking about the use of arithmetic in different bases. I have found that pupils often find it easier to work in the general case $a>b>c$ since the calculations become routine.

After a good amount of time working with base 7, we return to our two answers:

1089... base 10

1056... base 7

Pupils will usually compare these answers without prompting; but if necessary, the teacher can ask if they notice anything of interest about the two answers.

PUPIL: 'It will **always** be 10 followed by the two digits before the base. So, in base 6, for example, it will be 10 followed by 4 and 5.'

The teacher can help the pupils to communicate this more formally. Perhaps something along the lines of

When working in base x, the solution to the three-different-digit problem will be in the form 1, 0, $x-2$, $x-1$

This is an interesting conjecture – particularly the claim of always, which can now be stress tested.

Pupils will generally opt to work on base 8 and base 9 next and find

1089... base 10

1078... base 9

1067... base 8

1056... base 7

Mathematical confidence is growing as the conjecture appears to be holding true.

Carrying on, we have

1045... base 6

1034... base 5

1023... base 4

1012... base 3

Ah! But now there is a problem! At base 2, there is no way of choosing three different digits, since the base only has the digits 0 and 1. Pupils can deal with this by either changing their conjecture to state

When working in base x, where $x > 2$, the solution to the three-different-digit problem will be in the form 1, 0, $x-2$, $x-1$

or by changing the initial conditions from three different digits to allow for any three digits where all digits are not the same.

This moment of realising that their initial conjecture did not hold true for all cases – that is to say that it was not generalisable – is a key moment in the pupil's mathematical development. The teacher can make the pedagogic choice to highlight this moment and draw out further discussion in a way that emphasises the importance of such a significant realisation and to, hopefully, build an emotional reaction that will help the pupil to remember this moment.

At this point, pupils might ask, 'What about base 11?'

Depending on the pupil's experience of working in different bases, the teacher may have to help them to define the digits in base 11, which are 0, 1, 2, 3, 4, 5, 6, 7, 8, 9, a. Once the digits are established the pupils can continue to work.

Nowadays, when pupils reach base 16, they will often have a moment of enlightenment! Pupils have fairly significant experience of coding and will have written in HTML and other languages. When coding a colour in HTML, the pupil will have worked in base 16, where the digits are 0, 1, 2, 3, 4, 5, 6, 7, 8, 9, a, b, c, d, e, f. To enable coders to define very specific colours in the spectrum, each colour is given a six-digit code. This is why, for example, colours will have apparently bizarre codes such as ae1f3d. White is ffffff and black is 000000.

CLASS: 'Hey! We use this in computing class!'

The above is just one example of where to go from a starting point such as the 1089 task. Many teachers take it in different directions, but I have found the sequence described here to be both hugely enjoyable and seriously thought-provoking.

It is important that teachers engage in task design from time to time, but I would suggest it is even more important that teachers engage in actually doing the mathematics. The mathematics teacher should not feel a burden on them to create all the resources they need to teach – they have all already been written! Using tasks like the excellent ones from the ATM Points of Departure series saves time and allows teachers to consider the thinking that other practitioners have undergone in putting together a task. It is crucial, however, that the teacher really does sit down and work through the mathematics themselves. This is a far better use of a teacher's time than to be regularly writing tasks from scratch.

Variation theory

The role of variation in learning mathematics has long since been established. Zoltan Dienes wrote on the impact that variance and invariance can have when encountering new mathematical ideas in his 1971 journal article 'An example of the passage from the concrete to the manipulation of formal systems' (Dienes, 1971).

In the perceptual variability principle, Dienes prescribes the utilisation of a variety of contexts to maximize conceptual learning.

The mathematical variability principle states that children need to experience many variations of 'irrelevant attributes'. For example, there are irrelevant attributes inherent to the concept of like and unlike terms in algebra. Concepts of like terms do not depend, for instance, on the nature of the coefficients or signs. By varying the signs and the coefficients using whole numbers, decimals or fractions, and keeping the relevant attributes constant, pupils will become conscious of what happens to different numbers in the similar situations while ensuring an understanding of like terms and unlike terms.

Dienes considers the learning of a mathematical concept to be difficult because it is a process involving abstraction and generalisation. He suggests that the two variability principles promote the complementary processes of abstraction and generalisation, both of which are crucial aspects of conceptual development.

The role of variation is therefore to reveal underlying relationships and principles, such that the journey to abstraction is both easier for a pupil to attain and one that they have faith in believing as truth.

Dienes continued to work on his theories of variation, with many others picking up the importance of variance and invariance for learning mathematics over the years and contributing to the evidence base.

Notably, Ference Marton in Sweden working with colleagues in China and Hong Kong to further promote the importance of variation led to their work being translated for Western audiences (Gu et al., 2004), which had a great influence on reigniting the discussion around variation theories.

Unfortunately, the translation of their work (or, more accurately, mistranslation) has led to a false distinction being made between procedural and so-called 'conceptual' variation. Prima facie, this makes no sense. Concepts in mathematics do not vary.

This distinction has resulted in much-muddled and damaging assertions being made in the UK about variation. In recent years, even national organisations have promoted the idea of conceptual variation in mathematics – arguing that the teaching of mathematics should include taking a concept and somehow varying it. This clearly makes no sense. Mathematical concepts are not malleable.

However, this confusion should not distract from the important role that variation theory can play in learning mathematics: drawing attention to underlying relationships.

Other notable work on variation includes Watson and Mason (2006). This important article highlights the issue in Marton's theory. Marton suggests we learn what varies against an invariant background. But often what we hope pupils will learn in mathematics is a constant underlying dependency relationship.

Labels of 'procedural' and 'conceptual' variation do not get at the full range of the importance of variation in learning and doing mathematics – that is, to draw attention to the underlying relationships.

Mathematical confidence

A helpful result of careful and intelligent use of variance and invariance can be the building of mathematical confidence, which in turn lowers anxiety and decreases cognitive load.

In order for pupils to become creative mathematical problem solvers, it is necessary that they gain the motivation to want to pursue mathematics and persevere when faced with apparently intractable problems. Motivation – that is, the very desire to continue and go further – is greatly enhanced when pupils are successful and confident.

As described earlier, through examples we can demonstrate to pupils how to attack a type of question, scenario or problem. As teachers, we plan for the problems they will encounter and manipulate the way in which the problem will unfold before them such that, when they are beginning to solve a problem, a pattern emerges from the mist. When pupils notice patterns and relationships, they can begin to conjecture: 'Ah! Look! The pattern is X, so when I do Y, what should happen is Z. Let me try!'

This builds an expectation in the pupil's mind – they believe they have discerned relationship and can continue to work on the problem, but now with an anticipation of what will happen and why. When these expectations are confirmed through experiment and result, pupils gain a sense of mathematical confidence.

Note: we will, of course, also manipulate problems such that the expectation a pupil has and the conjectures they make will not be confirmed. These unexpected results also play a key role in building a pupil's ability to reflect and extend their reasoning.

There are many problems and tasks that mathematics teachers have in their canon that are designed to build such mathematical confidence. Suddenly, an apparently intractable problem becomes addressable and pupils can plot a path through.

Variance and invariance can play a powerful role in building mathematical confidence.

Consider the identity

$$(x - 2)(x + 1) \equiv x^2 - x - 2$$

We could demonstrate the truth of this identity to our pupils in many ways and then ask them to follow our examples to find other such identities. Often, textbooks will contain exercises with random questions for pupils to work through. But what if we used invariance to help build mathematical confidence?

Suppose, as the next example, we looked at

$$(x - 3)(x + 1) \equiv x^2 - 2x - 3$$

Here, the $x + 1$ term has remained invariant. What do you notice?

And perhaps as the next,

$$(x - 4)(x + 1) \equiv x^2 - 3x - 4$$

At this point, pupils may spot a pattern emerging and be able to conjecture what the next example would be.

$$(x - 2)(x + 1) \equiv x^2 - x - 2$$

$$(x - 3)(x + 1) \equiv x^2 - 2x - 3$$

$$(x - 4)(x + 1) \equiv x^2 - 3x - 4$$

Most pupils will look at the $x - 5$ example next and rightly conjecture that the coefficient of x will be -4 and that the constant term will be -5. This confirmation of their expectation builds confidence. As teachers, we would direct them to try 'going backwards' and find the result

$$(x - 1)(x + 1) \equiv x^2 - 0x - 1$$

and so on. The pattern is useful in bringing about confidence but also in revealing the nature of the relationships between the terms in the expressions.

We will see pupils confidently deal with the case where the varying term is $x - 0$:

$$(x - 0)(x + 1) \equiv x^2 + x - 0$$

which then leads, by pattern, to the natural conclusion that the next example will be

$$(x - -1)(x + 1) \equiv x^2 + 2x + 1$$

So, by keeping one aspect invariant, we are able to build mathematical confidence at the point where the task is novel and also begin to reveal underlying relationships.

$$(x - -1)(x + 1) \equiv x^2 + 2x + 1$$

$$(x - 0)(x + 1) \equiv x^2 + x - 0$$

$$(x - 1)(x + 1) \equiv x^2 - 0x - 1$$

$$(x - 2)(x + 1) \equiv x^2 - x - 2$$

$$(x - 3)(x + 1) \equiv x^2 - 2x - 3$$

$$(x - 4)(x + 1) \equiv x^2 - 3x - 4$$

This systematic way of working – of specialising – is what allows the pupils to conjecture. We can then change features and build towards generalisation.

Note: the power of variation here is in revealing underlying relationships and building mathematical confidence at the point of first learning. Later, when the pupil passes through the 'doing' phase to the 'practising' phase (when they are fluent), it is no longer desirable to give such structure. We want the questions to become random so that the pupil has to decide when to use a principle or not.

As another example, take the following sets of subtraction questions, adapted from Mike Askew's fantastic book *Transforming Primary Mathematics* (2010).

Set A	Set B
120 − 90	120 − 90
235 − 180	122 − 92
502 − 397	119 − 89
122 − 92	235 − 180
119 − 89	237 − 182
237 − 182	502 − 397

Which set is the most helpful in building mathematical confidence and revealing underlying relationships?

Clearly, the sets are lists of identical questions, but arranged differently. Set A is more typical of what pupils will encounter in textbooks: the questions are arranged randomly, with no obvious pattern emerging. Set B, however, has been arranged in such an order that pupils will spot patterns and connections. They will notice that performing 122 − 92 is the same problem as performing 120 − 90 and begin to reason why this is the case. Working with set B at the point at which this idea is novel gives pupils the chance for expectation, confirmation and confidence. The teacher may suggest, 'Show me more questions that are the same as 120 − 90. Tell me how you know you are correct.'

As a teacher, what question would you choose to come next in Set B?

Perhaps 500 − 395 or 505 − 400, thus connecting this particular subtraction with other methods of subtraction and giving opportunities to explore relationships and connections.

Variation theory is useful because it gives these opportunities. Variation theory is not about extensive lists of questions where pupils stop expecting, testing and conjecturing and simply become passive in stating obvious next answers. Working with variance and invariance requires the teacher to carefully balance the benefits of confidence and relationships with the danger of long sets of questions that result in pupils no longer thinking about what they are doing.

(Rohrer and Taylor (2007) found some interesting results when looking at how many questions pupils need to work on, which we shall come to later.)

Again, I would suggest that set B is a useful and powerful approach when the mathematical idea is novel; but actually, set A becomes the useful arrangement later once pupils have gripped the idea – the random nature of the questions forces pupils to attend to the principle as a whole and make decisions about how to work on the problems.

Using variance and invariance to reveal underlying relationships is the key purpose of variation theory. Another useful outcome of varying can be for pupils to discern commonalities and differences when working with examples and non-examples.

Ask a pupil to draw a triangle on a piece of paper. Almost all pupils will draw something like

or

This is because these are the triangles that pupils repeatedly encounter. Traveling around the UK over the past couple of decades, observing and inspecting mathematics, I have time and time again seen teachers refer to triangles but only ever use these types. Pupils come to believe that 'triangleness' is like a ladder against a wall or the roof of a house. They believe triangles have one horizontal side. Pupils rarely draw

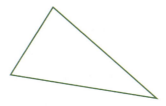

Or

And for many pupils, the following is not a triangle at all

Instead, they will call this an 'upside-down triangle'.

Perhaps even more concerning is that many pupils believe that the following shape **is** a triangle:

It is easy to see why; after all, this does look like the roof of a house.

I use this simple example of triangles to highlight the need, when introducing new ideas, to ensure that pupils encounter many examples and non-examples of the idea. We will return to examples and non-examples later.

A useful way of thinking about variation is to consider three types of procedural variation:

1. Varying the conditions of a problem

2. Varying the method of solving the problem

3. Varying the problems a method is being applied to

Adapted from Lai and Murray, 2012

Varying the conditions of a problem

Lai and Murray suggest that varying the conditions of a problem can assist in dismantling long-held misconceptions. For example, this belief that many pupils have:

Division makes things smaller

This misconception can be broken down by creating a series of carefully sequenced questions. Lai and Murray give the examples:

Problem 1
There are 9L of apple juice and every 3L is put in a jar. How many jars are needed?

Problem 2
There are 9L of apple juice and every 1L is put in a jar. How many jars are needed?

Problem 3
There are 9L of apple juice and every 0.3L is put in a jar. How many jars are needed?

Problem 4
There are 9L of apple juice and every 0.1L is put in a jar. How many jars are needed?

Problem 5
There are 9L of apple juice and every 0.05L is put in a jar. How many jars are needed?

During the journey through this short series of problems, pupils begin to see that the belief they had previously held cannot be true.

Varying the method of solving a problem

It is has always been a wonder to me that teachers have come to regard certain mathematical procedures as 'formal' or 'traditional', often without a great deal of thought as to whether or not they are the best method of working with a problem. Consider, for example, simple subtraction. Almost all teachers I meet believe that the 'correct' way of carrying out a subtraction is to use an algorithm as I shall now describe.

Consider the problem 435 − 258. Most teachers will instruct pupils to write this in the column format:

$$4\,3\,6$$
$$-\,2\,5\,8$$

An algorithm is then followed, starting from the right and working to the left. The pupil asks, 'What is six minus eight?' Immediately a weakness of this algorithm becomes apparent. In this type of subtraction, teachers tell pupils 'You can't do that' and then introduce a process of exchange (or borrowing). This is a problem because, well, you bloody well can do six minus eight! And yet countless numbers of pupils are told it is not possible. Because they trust their teacher, many of those pupils embed this as knowledge and continue to believe that it is not possible to subtract eight from six.

The intention, of course, is to relate the column values and to try to give a sense of the numberness. So, the teacher instructs the pupils that, since six minus eight is impossible (because they are using a 'take-away' metaphor), there is the need to exchange. This requires the pupils to reduce the value of the digit in to the left, meaning our 3 becomes a 2.

$$2$$
$$4\,\cancel{3}\,6$$
$$-\,2\,5\,8$$

The intent here is to communicate that the 3 had represented three lots of ten and now one of those lots of ten has been exchanged for a group of units. Those units can then be added to the other units, represented by the 6, to give enough units in order to make a take-away metaphor work.

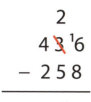

$$2$$
$$4\,\cancel{3}\,{}^{1}6$$
$$-\ 2\,5\,8$$

The pupil is now able to imagine sixteen units and remove eight units, which results in being left with eight units, which can be symbolised as

$$2$$
$$4\,\cancel{3}\,{}^{1}6$$
$$-\ 2\,5\,8$$
$$\overline{\qquad\quad\ 8}$$

Continuing in this way, the solution is found:

$$3\ {}^{1}2$$
$$\cancel{4}\,\cancel{3}\,{}^{1}6$$
$$-\ 2\,5\,8$$
$$\overline{1\,7\,8}$$

The use of this algorithm is widespread in schools. Many problems arise from its use with many pupils. They may, for example, embed the lie that 'you can't do six minus eight' or they may make errors during the exchange process as the symbolism becomes messy (this is a very common problem for pupils). Yet, the algorithm is promoted by the majority of teachers.

There are many algorithms for subtraction. Let us now consider some other methods of solving the same problem.

Subtraction – the equal addition method

Round the smaller number up to the next hundred – what have you had to add to it? Do the subtraction. Now add the same amount to the answer that you had to add to round up the smaller number.

When working with equal addition, the original problem is reconsidered as a new, simpler problem.

$$
\begin{array}{r}
4\,3\,6 \\
-\ 2\,5\,8 \\
\hline

\end{array}
\qquad\qquad
\begin{array}{r}
4\,3\,6 \\
-\ 3\,0\,0 \\
\hline
1\,3\,6
\end{array}
$$

This has required the pupil to know the complement from the smaller number to the next hundred. In this case, the pupil has had to remember they added 42. This is then added to the solution just found to give

$$
\begin{array}{r}
1\,3\,6 \\
+\ \ \ 4\,2 \\
\hline
1\,7\,8
\end{array}
$$

In taking this approach, the pupil no longer has to carry out any exchange. This is a perfectly robust and accurate way of subtracting and is often how people carry out subtraction mentally. An even more common method for mental calculation is to take a chunking approach.

Subtraction – the chunking method

Round the smaller number down to the nearest hundred and subtract. Now take away the original tens and units from the answer.

Again, in this type of approach, the initial problem is changed in to a simpler problem.

$$\begin{array}{r} 436 \\ -\ 258 \\ \hline \\ \hline \end{array} \qquad \begin{array}{r} 436 \\ -\ 200 \\ \hline 236 \\ \hline \end{array}$$

The pupil must now take account of the five tens and eight units they have ignored.

$$236 - 50 - 8 = 178$$

This is how most people carry out subtraction in their head – it is a simple way of breaking down the problem and storing each step, since what has really happened here is that the pupil has subtracted the hundreds, then the tens, then the units.

Subtraction – the Nikhilam sutra method

Write in column form. Replace the digits of the smaller number with the numbers needed to take them up to 9 (i.e. the complements to 9). When you get to the ones column, change the digit to the number needed to take it up to 10 (i.e. the complement of 10). Now add. In the answer, cross out the left-most digit.

Born in 1884 into an orthodox Tamil Brahmin family, Bharati Krishna Tirtha went on to become a spiritual and cultural leader, writing extensively on a wide range of subjects from societal issues, peace, religion, science and mathematics. His book *Vedic Mathematics* was published posthumously in 1965. In it, Bharati Krishna outlines 16 sutras which deal with a range of calculation techniques. The second sutra, Nikhilam Navatashcaramam Dashatah (meaning 'all from 9 and the last from 10'), gives a way of performing subtraction in base 10 using only addition.

The initial problem is rewritten, with the smaller number having its digits replaced with their complements to 9, except for the final digit, which has its digit replaced with its complement to 10. In our example, we have

$$436$$
$$-258$$

$$436$$
$$742$$

The process now is simply to add.

$$436$$
$$+742$$
$$\overline{1178}$$

The first digit of the solution is then ignored.

$$436$$
$$+742$$
$$\overline{\diagdown 178}$$

Which gives the same solution as before: 178. Using this method removes any need to perform any subtraction, which, for some pupils, means the problem is now surmountable.

Subtraction – the pre-algebra digit-by-digit method

Write the subtraction in column form. Take the smaller from the larger for all three columns separately. This gives you three digits. If the top number is smaller than the bottom number, put a minus sign in front of the digit for that column. Now add up the three digits giving them their relevant place value and using their signs.

Using this method, we avoid the possibility of introducing the misconception that 'you can't subtract eight from six'. The digits in each column are treated as separate subtraction problems where the solutions are allowed to be negative values.

$$4\ 3\ 6$$
$$-\ 2\ 5\ 8$$
$$\overline{2\ \text{-}2\ \text{-}2}$$

This gives a numeral, which we can then give numberness by considering its digits' positions. So, the value will be two lots of one hundred minus two lots of ten minus two units.

$$200 - 20 - 2 = 178$$

Again, we arrive at the same answer as before. With the pre-algebra digit-by-digit method, there is no process of exchange and no introduction of an unnecessary misconception. The name of the method also hints at its later utility – this is the method that we use for subtracting polynomials, which we will discuss later in the chapter.

By varying the method being applied to the problem, there is the opportunity to reveal more about the underlying principles behind the idea of arithmetic. We could ask, why do all of these methods result in the same solution? How are they linked?

We could also ask, which is the best method to use when planning for the learning of future mathematics?

For the answer to that question, let us now turn to the third type of procedural variation.

Varying the problems a method is being applied to

Lai and Murray (2012) include a lovely example of this type of variation, stating the following three problems:

Problem 1
In a room with 4 people, everyone shakes hands with everybody else exactly once. How many handshakes are there?

Problem 2
How many diagonals in dodecagon?

Problem 3

In a village there are 20 streets. All the streets are straight. One lamp post is put up at each crossroads. What is the greatest number of lamp posts that could be needed?

On first inspection, the three problems appear unrelated; but a closer examination of each reveals that they are all able to be resolved using the same method (in this case, the drawing of network diagrams).

Another nice example can be found in the What Works Clearinghouse publication *Improving Mathematical Problem Solving*:

Problem

Solve $\frac{2}{10} = \frac{x}{30}$

Context 1

Sara draws 2 trees for every 10 animals.
How many trees will she need to draw if she has 30 animals?

Context 2

Sarah creates a tiled wall using 2 black tiles for every 10 white tiles. if she has 30 white tiles, how many black tiles will she need?

From Woodward et al., 2012

Let us take some time now to consider an example in depth. Suppose we are interested in the resolution to the subtraction problem $754 - 267$. How might we go about finding a solution to this problem and what might that solution mean?

Typically, teachers and pupils will attack the problem using a column method of subtraction, working from right to left and carrying out a procedure known as exchange to give the following steps.

First, the problem is written in column form

$$
\begin{array}{r}
7\,5\,4 \\
-\ 2\,6\,7 \\
\hline
\\
\hline
\end{array}
$$

Then the pupil considers a series of questions, working right to left, asking first 'What is four minus seven?' In this type of algorithm, this is not permitted since the solution is a negative value; so the pupil then moves to the left and carries out the exchange process.

$$
\begin{array}{r}
7\,\cancel{5}\,4 \\
-\ 2\,6\,7 \\
\hline
\\
\hline
\end{array}
$$

The 5 digit in the numeral represents five tens, this is reduced by one to give four tens:

$$
\begin{array}{r}
4 \\
7\,\cancel{5}\,4 \\
-\ 2\,6\,7 \\
\hline
\\
\hline
\end{array}
$$

Which is represented by the digit 4 in the tens position. The ten that has been removed from this position is then added to the four to the right, giving a new numeral: 14. The numeral 14 represents one whole ten and four units.

$$
\begin{array}{r}
4 \\
7\,\not{5}\,{}^{1}4 \\
-\ 2\,6\,7 \\
\hline
\end{array}
$$

This enables the pupil to ask a different question: 'What is fourteen minus seven?' – which is to say, what is one whole ten and four units minus seven units. Clearly, subtracting four units from both leaves the question, 'What is ten units minus three units?' This leaves seven units and can be represented by the digit 7 in the solution.

$$
\begin{array}{r}
4 \\
7\,\not{5}\,{}^{1}4 \\
-\ 2\,6\,7 \\
\hline
7 \\
\end{array}
$$

This process continues in the same manner, until we have the result:

$$
\begin{array}{r}
6\ {}^{1}4 \\
\not{7}\,\not{5}\,{}^{1}4 \\
-\ 2\,6\,7 \\
\hline
4\,8\,7 \\
\end{array}
$$

So, we have a method for solving subtraction problems of this type. But doing so hasn't revealed much about the meaning behind the components or the solution; and nor has it given much insight into the worthiness (or not) of the method being used.

Let us apply the same method again, this time working in base 8.

In the initial problem, we were working in base 10. The position of the digits indicates the numberness of the number by informing us that we have in the first number seven lots of one hundred, five lots of ten and four units making up the complete number.

The digits available to us in base 10 are 0, 1, 2, 3, 4, 5, 6, 7, 8, 9.

Working in base 8, the digits available to us are 0, 1, 2, 3, 4, 5, 6, 7.

So, working through the procedure, we have the following steps. First, the problem is written in a column form:

$$
\begin{array}{r}
7\,5\,4 \\
-\ 2\,6\,7 \\
\hline
\\
\hline
\end{array}
$$

The pupil now asks, 'What is four minus seven?' This is not permitted in this type of algorithm, so they move to exchange:

$$
\begin{array}{r}
4 \\
7\,\cancel{5}\,{}^{1}4 \\
-\ 2\,6\,7 \\
\hline
\\
\hline
\end{array}
$$

In the original numeral, the digit 5 represents fives lots of eight (since we are working in base 8). This is reduced and the eight is added to the right. This gives the new numeral 14, which represents one whole eight and four units. We wish to subtract seven units from one whole eight and four units. First, let's subtract four units from each. The problem is then reduced to subtracting three units from eight units, which gives five units and can be represented by the digit 5.

$$
\begin{array}{r}
4 \\
7\,\cancel{5}\,{}^{1}4 \\
-\ 2\,6\,7 \\
\hline
5 \\
\hline
\end{array}
$$

We continue in this manner until we arrive at the solution:

$$6\,{}^1\!4$$
$$\cancel{7}\,\cancel{5}\,{}^1\!4$$
$$-\ 2\,6\,7$$
$$\overline{4\,6\,5}$$

This is quite a different solution to what was found when working in base 10. We have had to carefully consider the process of exchange and the meaning of the numerals in order to get here. Perhaps there is a connection in the solutions, but at the moment it is tricky to see any link. Let us continue working with the algorithm, but again change the problem. Let's try working in base 11.

In base 11, the digits available to us are 0, 1, 2, 3, 4, 5, 6, 7, 8, 9, a. Working through the problem, we come to the solution:

$$6\,{}^1\!4$$
$$\cancel{7}\,\cancel{5}\,{}^1\!4$$
$$-\ 2\,6\,7$$
$$\overline{4\,9\,8}$$

Let's try another base. How about base 16. In base 16, the digits we have available to us are 0, 1, 2, 3, 4, 5, 6, 7, 8, 9, a, b, c, d, e, f.

As mentioned earlier, base 16 is an interesting base to use with pupils, since they will already be familiar with it and its digit system. In the coding language of HTML, colours are given a unique six-digit numeral in base 16. For example, pure white is 000000 and black is ffffff, with all other colours lying between those values, giving codes such as ff00ff for magenta or 228b22 for forest green and so on. Pupils encounter coding as part of their primary and secondary education and many of them are recreational coders, so it is often the case that this base system is more familiar to the pupil than the teacher!

Working through the subtraction algorithm, we arrive at the solution:

$$6\,{}^{1}4$$
$$\cancel{7}\,\cancel{5}\,{}^{1}4$$
$$-\ 2\,6\,7$$
$$\overline{4\ e\ d}$$

On the face of it, there appears to be little connection between the solutions. This is because we have deliberately chosen bases at random, wanting the pupils to recognise that it is a more fruitful approach of attacking a mathematical problem: work systematically. If we were to do so, we would arrive at this set of results:

Base	Digits	Result
8	0, 1, 2, 3, 4, 5, 6, 7	4 6 5
9	0, 1, 2, 3, 4, 5, 6, 7, 8	4 7 6
10	0, 1, 2, 3, 4, 5, 6, 7, 8, 9	4 8 7
11	0, 1, 2, 3, 4, 5, 6, 7, 8, 9, a	4 9 8
12	0, 1, 2, 3, 4, 5, 6, 7, 8, 9, a, b	4 a 9
13	0, 1, 2, 3, 4, 5, 6, 7, 8, 9, a, b, c	4 b a
14	0, 1, 2, 3, 4, 5, 6, 7, 8, 9, a, b, c, d	4 c b
15	0, 1, 2, 3, 4, 5, 6, 7, 8, 9, a, b, c, d, e	4 d c
16	0, 1, 2, 3, 4, 5, 6, 7, 8, 9, a, b, c, d, e, f	4 e d

And now, through a systematic approach, a pattern presents itself, allowing pupils to conjecture that the solution will be a numeral made up of the digit 4 followed by the second-from-last digit in the list, followed by the third-from-last digit in the list. Pupils can now try other bases as a test of their conjecture.

Let us look at the problem again, this time in an unknown base. Let's call this base x.

Working in base x, the digits available to us will be

$$0, 1, 2, 3, 4, 5, \ldots (x-3), (x-2), (x-1)$$

Since the initial problem involves the digit 7, we must also assert that $x > 7$.

$$7\,5\,4$$
$$-\ 2\,6\,7$$
_____

_____

What do these numerals mean in base x? What number are they representing? What is its numberness?

In base 10, the numeral 754 is representing a number with numberness

$$7 \cdot (10^2) + 5 \cdot (10^1) + 4 \cdot (10^0)$$

In other words, seven lots of one hundred, five lots of ten and four units.

In base x, the numeral 754 is representing a number with numberness

$$7 \cdot (x^2) + 5 \cdot (x^1) + 4 \cdot (x^0) = 7x^2 + 5x^1 + 4x^0$$

So, the numerals in our problem have numberness

$7\,5\,4$	$7x^2 + 5x + 4$
$-\ 2\,6\,7$	$2x^2 + 6x + 7$

Let us work through with the subtraction algorithm. As before, the pupil starts from the right and works left, asking, 'What is four minus 7?' This cannot be done in this type of algorithm, so exchange occurs, giving

$$\begin{array}{ccc} & 4 & \\ 7 & \cancel{5} & {}^{1}4 \\ -\ 2 & 6 & 7 \end{array}$$

The new number 14 represents one whole x and 4 units. We need to subtract seven units from this.

Let us pause for a moment and think about what was happening in base 10. 14 represented one whole ten and four units, from which we had to subtract seven units. We can do this because we can think of the whole ten as being represented by archetypal units. But there is another way to think about this: using the modulo properties of the base system.

The digits in base 10 are 0, 1, 2, 3, 4, 5, 6, 7, 8, 9. These digits are used to represent all numbers in base 10. They repeat in a modulo fashion, as though on a wheel.

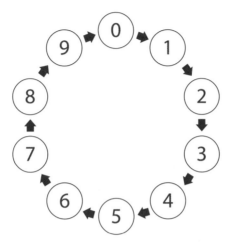

14 means one whole ten – one entire cycle of the wheel – and then four more units. If we move clockwise from zero one full turn and then continue four more steps, we arrive at 4. Subtracting 7 can be seen as moving seven steps anticlockwise around the wheel, which would put us at 7.

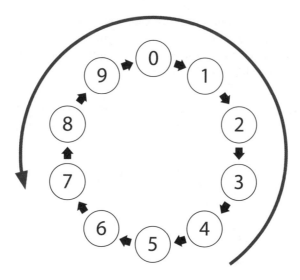

Let's return to base x. This can be thought of as a modulo system too. This time, the wheel will range from 0 to $x - 1$.

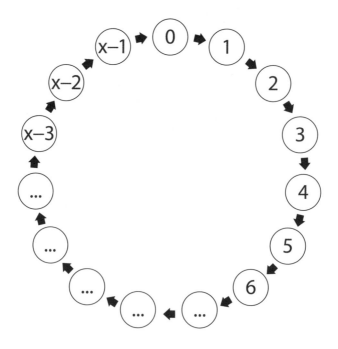

The numeral 14 represents one full turn of the wheel and four more steps, making the starting position 4. Subtracting 7 can be found by taking seven steps back in an anticlockwise direction, giving a final position at $x - 3$.

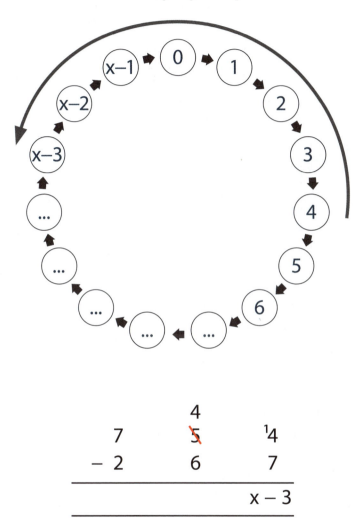

$$
\begin{array}{ccc}
 & 4 & \\
7 & \cancel{5} & {}^1 4 \\
-\ 2 & 6 & 7 \\
\hline
 & & x - 3 \\
\hline
\end{array}
$$

Continuing in this manner, we find

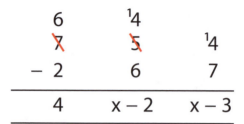

Which matches our pattern and conjecture.

Base	Digits	Result
8	0, 1, 2, 3, 4, 5, 6, 7	4 6 5
9	0, 1, 2, 3, 4, 5, 6, 7, 8	4 7 6
10	0, 1, 2, 3, 4, 5, 6, 7, 8, 9	4 8 7
11	0, 1, 2, 3, 4, 5, 6, 7, 8, 9, a	4 9 8
12	0, 1, 2, 3, 4, 5, 6, 7, 8, 9, a, b	4 a 9
13	0, 1, 2, 3, 4, 5, 6, 7, 8, 9, a, b, c	4 b a
14	0, 1, 2, 3, 4, 5, 6, 7, 8, 9, a, b, c, d	4 c b
15	0, 1, 2, 3, 4, 5, 6, 7, 8, 9, a, b, c, d, e	4 d c
16	0, 1, 2, 3, 4, 5, 6, 7, 8, 9, a, b, c, d, e, f	4 e d
x	0, 1, 2, 3, 4, 5, 6... x–3, x–2, x–1	4 (x–2) (x–3)

We now have the numeral 4 $(x–2)$ $(x–3)$, but what does this mean? What numberness does it have?

Thinking about the position of the digits again, we can see that the numberness will be

$$4 \cdot (x^2) + (x–2) \cdot (x^1) + (x–3) \cdot (x^0)$$
$$= 4x^2 + x^2 – 2x + x – 3$$
$$= 5x^2 – x – 3$$

Thinking about the original meaning of the problem, we see that we could have written the initial problem

$$7\,5\,4$$
$$-\ 2\,6\,7$$

In base x as

$$7x^2 + 5x + 4$$
$$-\ 2x^2 + 6x + 7$$

This can be solved straightforwardly using a standard approach to arithmetic with polynomials to give

$$7x^2 + 5x + 4$$
$$-\ 2x^2 + 6x + 7$$
$$5x^2\ -1x\ -3$$

This is the same answer that we have found using the long-winded – but widespread – approach used for subtraction in most schools. Yes, here the solution is quick and easy. So why on earth use the so-called traditional algorithm for subtraction that schools appear to be so committed to? Why have so many teachers come to unthinkingly accept the algorithm as 'the formal' or 'the standard' method? It introduces lots of possible pitfalls and does not fit with the way we want pupils to do arithmetic with polynomials later, causing a perceived disconnect between number and algebra for most pupils. The majority of pupils do not realise that all that is happening when working with polynomials is the exact same arithmetic they were doing with numbers. The only difference is that the base is now unknown. Polynomials are numerals. They are just numerals for which we do not know (or do not care about) which base is in use.

As discussed earlier, there are many perfectly reasonable methods for subtraction, which give accurate results and can be memorised for use. But the teacher of mathematics must always be mindful about where the mathematics is leading in the future and teach accordingly. Teaching young pupils to use the pre-algebra digit-by-digit method gives them a much stronger foundation for working in unknown bases and for making the now-logical connection from number to algebra without worry or fuss.

Varying the problems the subtraction algorithm was being applied to has led to a much deeper – and, I'd suggest, more interesting and satisfying – exploration of subtraction and the meaning of the algorithm than we would have had had we just applied the same method repeatedly on the same type of problem.

I would suggest that this type of activity exemplifies effective use of variation theory in mathematics and is considerably more powerful in building confidence, reasoning and understanding than simply asking pupils to work through long lists of questions.

Here is another example of using variation in the mathematics classroom, which I would suggest you pause and try. I created this task a while back and have tried it with many pupils and teachers.

$$
\begin{array}{r} 5\,4\,3\,2\,1 \\ +\ 1\,2\,3\,4\,5 \\ \hline \\ \hline \end{array}
\qquad
\begin{array}{r} 5\,4\,3\,2\,1 \\ -\ 1\,2\,3\,4\,5 \\ \hline \\ \hline \end{array}
$$

...in base 10
...in base 9
...in base 8
...in base 7
...in base 6

...in base 11
...in base 12

$$23 \times 25$$

What is the same? What is different?

The initial problems are clearly trivial. But, when the base is changed, the task requires a completely different type of thinking. Working in these different bases in a systematic way, a pattern emerges. This allows for conjecture and, eventually, generalising. Importantly, working on these different bases allows pupils to have greater clarity about working in base 10.

A significant weakness in UK mathematics over the last 30 years is the absence of multi-base arithmetic. I would suggest all pupils learn multi-base arithmetic. After all, how can we, as teachers, be sure that pupils understand arithmetic if they only ever work in one base? All we have shown is that they can perform in one very specialised, limited case.

PART V
PHASING LEARNING

The importance of logic, truth and assimilation

At the point of encountering a new idea, I suggest that two key states must be present in order for learning to occur. Firstly, the pupil must accept the novel idea as true. At the point at which a teacher begins to expose a pupil to a new idea, they quite literally do not know that idea. It is alien. Yet, they do already know a great deal. They exist in the universe and have formed a view of how it operates and what is true. New information, ideas, skills and knowledge disrupt this view of the universe. The pupil is being asked to change the way in which they view life and the very nature of knowledge itself – this is a pretty big deal. Everything they knew until this very moment is about to change. Disrupting reality is tricky. For a pupil to accept this change, the new idea must make sense, it must ring true. The second state that must exist is that of logic. Accepting a new truth can only occur if that new idea fits logically with the pupil's already-held views and understanding. The teacher artfully and deliberately connects the novel idea to already-learnt ideas, so they are able to bring meaning to the new idea and shine a light on it from the perspective of already-embedded truths. Truth and logic matter. A lot. Without both of these being present, the pupil rejects the new information as fantastical or plain wrong and no learning occurs.

Ensuring that a novel idea fits with the pupil's current understanding is a key skill of the expert teacher. Getting it wrong is disastrous. I suggest this is true of all learning and of all human beings, regardless of age or prior knowledge. I have often witnessed the moment when a group of undergraduates in the final year of a mathematics degree are being lectured on some concept – such as the Lorentz contraction – and suddenly lose a sense of truth. A wave comes over the

275

lecture theatre as the students struggle to accept the truth of the new concept because it does not fit with all that they believe about the universe and has no logical progression from earlier ideas. Be careful when teaching: always get the difficulty pitch **just** right.

Jean Piaget called the basic building blocks of intelligence 'schemata' (or schemas). These internal schemata are a way of organising knowledge where interconnected ideas form an emerging picture of the universe and allow human beings to behave intelligently. In Piaget's cognitive theory, a schema is defined as 'a cohesive, repeatable action sequence possessing component actions that are tightly interconnected and governed by a core meaning'.

Mental representations of the world are stored in the memory and can be applied to a new situation when needed by shining a light on the new idea from the perspective of already-embedded and -understood ideas and knowledge. Piaget termed this ability to grip a new idea by connecting it to what is already known 'assimilation'.

Piaget, in his theory of a child being a lone learner – that is to say, the child being able to learn all that they need to learn through discovery – relegated the role of the teacher and attempted to distinguish between teaching and development. Lev Vygotsky further developed Piaget's theories in formulating his 'zone of proximal development' (ZPD) thesis. Vygotsky recognised the difference in what a child is not able to do and what a child is not able to do **without help**. He knew that some knowledge does arise naturally and that children can build and develop new knowledge, but that this development could never advance far if the child were simply left to discover for themselves. Children need to learn from those who are more knowledgeable and educators should ensure that they reveal new knowledge and skills to pupils gradually, keeping the new ideas within their reach.

We now know that there is a great deal wrong in the work of both Piaget and Vygotsky – this is quite a natural step in the evolution of our professional canon – but there is no doubt that both of these great thinkers contributed profound insights. I believe that a blend of Piaget, Vygotsky and modern cognitive science brings us to the following position.

Imagine the whole of human knowledge. Imagine it filling a space. This grey box represents the sum of human knowledge:

Let's imagine the domain of one's own knowledge as a circle in the whole of human knowledge.

As one grows older and learns more, the circle widens, with new knowledge and truth being assimilated into one's current schema. This assimilation can happen because a more knowledgeable other – the teacher – has carefully scheduled the order in which the pupil meets new knowledge to ensure the level of demand is just right. The teacher gives careful and detailed explanations, using a variety of models, metaphors and examples, communicating the novel idea from different perspectives until the pupil is able to meaning-make.

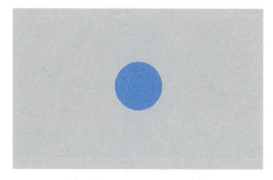

For new knowledge to be assimilated, it must make sense from the perspective of what one already knows. That is to say, the new knowledge can only be **just beyond** the limits of the circle.

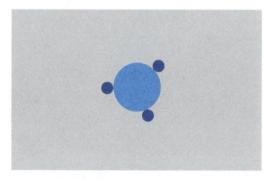

Such ideas can be readily communicated to the pupils through varied models, metaphors and examples, allowing them to assimilate the new knowledge into their schemas.

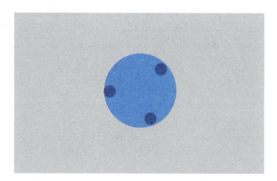

We only learn things that are just beyond our current understanding – this is necessarily the case, since knowledge well beyond one's current view of the universe – beyond one's logic framework and one's own living history and truth – is rejected as incomprehensible or wrong. Unfortunately, it is common to see models of schooling that enforce a situation where pupils are having **presented** to them ideas that cannot be assimilated.

In conveyor belt curriculum approaches, where pupils have presented to them content based purely on their age, it is often the case that large groups of pupils are forced to endure a school diet of content that is either far too easy for them to have any interest or intrigue or far too advanced for them to have any chance of assimilation. We see a situation such as

It is also not unusual to hear teachers talking about 'weaker pupils', when, in fact, they are really referring to a situation where a pupil is being presented with an idea **way beyond** what they are able to assimilate.

I have observed hundreds of lessons where pupils are being asked to, for example, understand how a formula works, and within just a few moments of discussion it is revealed that those same pupils haven't even got to grips yet with, say, basic arithmetic or have a very loose grip of number sense. This happens all too often. Schools that have schemes of work based on a pupil's age (rather than where that pupil actually is, mathematically) continually serve up the wrong mathematics to their pupils. I suggest that the **overwhelming majority** of pupils in conveyor belt systems are being 'taught' the wrong mathematics.

The new idea is well beyond the limits of their current knowledge, leaving the pupil incapable of making any meaning or connecting it to knowledge and ideas they already hold to be true. Without a logical progression from their current understanding, pupils reject the new idea, are unable to form any mental representations of it and, therefore, nothing is committed to memory.

The result, of course, is that the pupil is unable to get to grips with the idea and is labelled as weak or low ability. They are not weak; all pupils can learn well. The uncomfortable truth is that the teaching is not serving their needs.

As John B. Carroll showed many times, all pupils can learn new ideas if they are given the right amount of time and are starting from where they are already secure.

I would urge all teachers to pause a moment before labelling a pupil 'weak' to consider the possibility that they are trying to teach a pupil the wrong level of content.

Bridging instruction

Individuals choose between possible actions when solving a problem (Ohlsson, 1996a; Ohlsson, 1996b) but, when faced with a novel problem, a pupil's initial knowledge is often overly general, leading to them selecting incorrect approaches.

Ohlsson suggests pupils must detect the error, identify the overly general knowledge that caused the error, and explain what additional conditions or features must be added to this overly general knowledge in order to make it correct. This is consistent with overlapping waves theory (Siegler, 1996), which maintains that pupils know and use a variety of strategies that compete with each other for selection when faced with a problem to solve. As the pupil becomes more knowledgeable, correct and efficient strategies gradually replace misconceptions. To increase the rate at which pupils select correct methods, the teacher can manipulate experiences that lead to the pupils **rejecting** their ineffective strategies. This can only happen if it is made clear that their strategy is wrong – and crucially, **why** it is wrong (Siegler, 2002).

It can be shown that inducing **cognitive conflict** along with providing accurate information on why a pupil is wrong (and how to take steps to be correct) can help pupils to build correct conceptions (Diakidoy, 2003).

Several studies investigating pupils' algebraic reasoning (Hall, 1989; Kieran, 1998; Kieran, 1992; Koedinger, 1999; Koedinger et al., 2002; Nathan and Koedinger, 2002a; Nathan and Koedinger, 2002b; Tabachneck et al., 1994) have demonstrated that pupils approach new learning with their own informal and 'invented' strategies for attacking unfamiliar problems. Such strategies appear to have an impact on a pupil's conceptual understanding of more sophisticated mathematical ideas (Nathan and Koedinger, 2000) and should therefore not be ignored.

An error we, as the teaching profession, very often make is to assume that pupils are clean slates. This is at its most extreme in conveyor belt curriculum models, where schemes of work often treat pupils as though they have just this very minute popped into the universe. We see schemes for five-year-old pupils, for example, that appear to make the assumption that children have done no mathematics at all at that point. The reality is that children have encountered a very large amount of mathematics and mathematical thinking by the time they reach age five. They have, after all, existed in the universe for over 1800 days. They have encountered a lot, seen a lot, played a lot. As discussed earlier, if you watch young children playing, you will quickly see them ordering their toys and other items based on size or shape; you will hear them counting and talking about magnitude. Watch them playing with their siblings and it won't be long until you hear them speaking about ordinality and using ordinal numbers: first, second, third and so on – they know who won a race.

All of this experience has already given them a sense of mathematics. Much of this sense will be nonsense and wrapped in understandable misconception.

It is important that teachers do not treat pupils like clean slates. They have ideas and beliefs and invented strategies. The teacher needs to have an awareness of these and to ensure that any of the nonsensical ideas – that is to say, any misconceptions – they believe are carefully and deliberately dismantled and replaced with logical, accurate and correct strategies.

At the point of teaching a novel idea, the teacher should use the opportunity at the beginning of the learning episode to **bridge** from the pupils' invented strategies to the correct approaches we want them to know and continue to use in future.

When beginning each instructional sequence, the teacher can take just a few minutes to address, challenge, dismantle and replace misconceptions with truth and correct approaches. The teacher must establish supportive, positive and trusted relationships with the class. They must establish an explicit contract with the class, an understanding that there is a deal at play:

> I, the teacher, will always, always guarantee that you, the pupil, will be successful in learning every single idea we encounter together. You, the pupil, will understandably not know what you cannot yet know. You will have incorrect ideas, which are completely understandable and natural. I, the teacher, promise you that these incorrect ideas will be overcome and that you will become enlightened, confident and competent with every mathematical idea that I ask you to grapple with. On your part, you, the

pupil, understand that learning requires effort and perseverance. You will not fear being stuck, not fear expressing your thoughts and not fear not yet knowing. Your articulations of your thoughts are what give me, the teacher, the power to help you to always learn. With your effort and courage and my expert teaching, we will guarantee that you will always overcome.

The relationship and the contract enable a rigorous and accurate discourse about a novel mathematical idea.

At the start of teaching a new idea, the teacher might show the class a question of the type that exemplifies the sort of questions and tasks that pupils will be required to work with when applying the novel idea. For example, the teacher might be at the beginning of introducing pupils to Pythagoras' theorem for the first time. On the board, they might show the question

Look at the triangle. The lengths of two sides of the triangle are known. What is the length of the missing side?

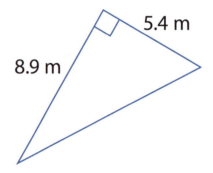

TEACHER: 'Look at this question. Curious, isn't it. I wonder how we can find the missing length. It would be helpful to have a method for finding the length of the missing side accurately. Luckily, there is such a method. Over the next couple of weeks, this is a method you will learn how to use in a lot of different types of problems. Before we look at the accurate method, I would like you to think very carefully about how we might go about finding the missing length. Of course, we haven't yet studied the method, so there is no need to worry about not yet knowing how to do this accurately. That's absolutely OK. I promise that you will all be able to work with the method and that you will all be successful in this unit. I'm really interested in how you might attack the problem now – with all the mathematical knowledge you have acquired to date. Are there approaches you already know and understand that might be useful here? Please think very carefully about this problem and have a go at finding the missing length.'

The teacher now allows the pupils a few moments to attack the problem. If appropriate, the pupils might then discuss with one other pupil what approach they have taken and why they thought it appropriate.

Bridging requires the teacher to elicit from the pupils their invented strategies. The teacher asks the pupils to articulate precisely the approach they have taken.

Many pupils will actually be able to overcome the problems they are shown, using accurate and correct approaches. It is unlikely with Pythagoras' theorem, which is why I use the example here; but on many graphical problems – both linear and nonlinear – pupils very often do state the correct methods, which they have been able to theorise based on knowledge and techniques they have previously learnt. These techniques can be combined into an accurate and efficient way of overcoming the new problem.

As the pupils articulate their approach, the teacher will confirm any correct approaches and reinforce the articulation of those correct approaches. However, when a pupil articulates an incorrect approach, the teacher robustly addresses the misconception.

TEACHER: 'No. That is incorrect.'

The teacher then carefully explains why the invented strategy was flawed. It is this direct and robust dismantling of the incorrect invented strategy that brings about a significant increase in learning and far transfer.

I am, of course, aware that such a challenge of an incorrect suggestion is counter to many school policies that have emerged in the past 20 years or so, which state that all pupil's responses must be considered equally valid and praised. Who does this serve? What value is there in being incorrect and then being praised for being incorrect? I have heard the argument that this approach is a more caring way of dealing with pupils. But is it kind to leave a pupil with a sense that being wrong is OK? Being wrong is not. Pupils have the right to grow into autonomous, successful adults, able to deal with the demands of life and move through their lives knowledgably and able to make informed decisions. There is no social justice in creating an environment where being incorrect is as valid as being correct. This leaves the incorrect pupil ill equipped for the world and the correct pupil bewildered at the teacher's judgement.

TEACHER: 'I really appreciate your serious and careful thinking about how we might go about addressing this question. We have heard some correct statements. This is because you all already know a huge amount. We can always apply our current knowledge and understanding to new problems, even if we can't overcome them at this stage. We now want to know an accurate and effective way of addressing this problem. I am now going to teach you the method…'

I suggest that there are two important insights from cognitive science at play here. Firstly, by showing the pupils the type of question they will be able to overcome by the end of the unit, we are levering the fact that **testing potentiates learning** – we are sensitising pupils to the fact that they have a knowledge gap and that, right now, it requires their attention and effort. Secondly, the **hypercorrection effect** appears to be present here – by asking the pupils to articulate their invented strategies and misconceptions, the teacher is drawing from them a sense of their own confidence in their beliefs and assertions. When the teacher clearly explains why they are incorrect, the same kind of emotional shock that occurs in hypercorrection appears to play a role in dismantling the internally held misconception and alerting the pupil to pay attention and find out the truth.

The 'bridging' aspect of the instruction now comes into play. It is not enough that the teacher has informed the pupils that they are not correct; the teacher must now 'bridge' from their incorrect suggestions to the correct explanation, using any correct and logical elements of the pupils' articulations to segue to an accurate, clear and full explanation.

By first eliciting pupils' invented strategies, the teacher can move from their descriptions and representations in a way that the pupils can accept as logical and that exposes the ineffective strategies the pupils had held before this moment. The pupils also see the benefits of the teacher's formal and more efficient approach – for example, pupils might have chosen to display data in a manner intuitive to them but longwinded and hard for anyone else to interpret; yet, on seeing the teacher's eloquent re-interpretation, the pupil rejects their own approach and buys in to the new method.

Several studies examining the competing or invented strategies that pupils bring to mind when faced with a new problem consistently show the benefit of instructional models that deliberately elicit and dismantle those invented strategies. An interesting study of seventh- and eighth-grade pupils contemporaneously assessed the impact of a bridging instruction approach and the use of multiple representations in mathematics. Compared to a control group (taught by the same teacher to take account of teacher quality), bridging instruction consistently led to better gains (Nathan et al., 2002).

The results on near transfer problems show pupils who received bridging instruction outperforming their non-bridging instruction peers on all types of problems.

Input Representation		Graphical		Symbolic		Worded	
Instruction		Linear	Nonlinear	Linear	Nonlinear	Linear	Nonlinear
Control Group	Pre-test	0.85	0.87	0.29	0.24	0.72	0.17
	Post-test	0.77	0.77	0.47	0.28	0.61	0.15
	Gain	−0.08	−0.10	0.18	0.04	−0.11	−0.02
Bridging Instruction Group	Pre-test	0.87	0.84	0.19	0.18	0.58	0.09
	Post-test	0.88	0.90	0.39	0.25	0.67	0.32
	Gain	0.01	0.06	0.20	0.07	0.09	0.23

From Nathan et al., 2002

More interestingly, the gains on far transfer problems, where pupils had to translate between mathematical representations, remain consistently in favour of a bridging instruction approach.

Output Representation		Graphical	Symbolic	Tabular	Worded
Instruction					
Control Group	Pre-test	0.11	0.19	0.11	0.02
	Post-test	0.10	0.10	0.34	0.05
	Gain	−0.01	−0.09	0.23	0.03
Bridging Instruction Group	Pre-test	0.00	0.12	0.12	0.06
	Post-test	0.30	0.13	0.38	0.21
	Gain	0.30	0.01	0.26	0.15

From Nathan et al., 2002

Overlapping waves theory (Siegler, 1996) asserts that individuals know and use a variety of competing strategies when faced with a problem. If the teacher ignores this, choosing to begin a new unit by stating the method they wish the pupils to follow, the competing method that the pupil already holds – their invented strategy – remains with them. When faced with problems in the future, the overlapping waves of their approach and the teacher's approach interfere with each other, leaving the pupil with a decision to make around which method to use. The expert teacher can calmly, yet robustly, remove this problem by taking just a few moments to debunk false approaches and promote correct ones.

With the pupil suggesting an incorrect approach and the teacher bridging to the correct approach, bridging also brings in the gains of correct vs incorrect examples, which we will discuss later. Having the errors in their invented strategies explicitly pointed out to them forces pupils to attend to the critical features of the problem.

Moving away from non-gain starters

Over a number of years, visiting several hundred schools, I tracked an interesting thought that had played on my mind: are there key differences in the way time is used in different types of schools? I started to record the number of minutes taken up by four key aspects of lessons:

- Transition, entry and settling

- Non-gain starter

- Disruption

- Packing away and leaving

In collecting the data, I also recorded the inspection rating of the school and its GCSE exam results. I was supported in collecting a larger data set by colleagues as we identified its use in a previous project in 2010. The findings show an interesting divergence in the emphasis different types of schools place on the use of starter activities.

The table below shows the average time in minutes per one-hour lesson allocated to different activities in two school categories.

	Average performing	High performing
Transition, entry, settling	8 mins	5 mins
Non-gain starter	12 mins	none
Disruption	5 mins	5 mins
Packing away, leaving	4 mins	1 min
Novel idea teaching	**31 mins**	**49 mins**

It became very quickly apparent that high-performing schools structured their timetabled lessons in a fundamentally different way.

All learning episodes begin somewhere – there has to be the start of revealing a novel mathematical idea to pupils. The learning episode could last for an hour or several days or many weeks. It would, after all, be incredibly fortuitous if every mathematical idea required exactly one hour on a timetable to teach. So, learning episodes typically span multiple individual timetabled lessons. This means that the narrative of a new idea has to occur over different days. In high-performing schools, teachers used bridging approaches to begin a learning episode, but did not include any standalone 'starter' activities at the beginning of individual lessons. Instead, the learning episode continued uninterrupted, with the teacher segueing from the previous lesson naturally into the new lesson. Often, as a way of ensuring a smooth transition, the teacher would begin the lesson with a continuation of discussion about the novel idea and where they had reached in the evolution of that idea. The start of the lesson was a connection between the previous lesson and the new lesson. The instruction focused solely on continuing to teach the novel idea.

Starters that add to the pupils learning of the novel idea are considered 'gain' starters. Starters that disrupt the learning episode and do not add to the learning of the novel idea are considered 'non-gain'.

As we will discuss later, we can lever the gains of the spacing effect, testing effect and interleaving by including previously learnt content in the body of the lesson. There is no need for a standalone, disconnected and disrupting starter activity at the beginning of a lesson. Such non-gain starters interrupt the narrative and contribute to the type of teaching practice where individual lessons are treated as the unit of learning – like the conveyor belt approach, teachers do not see the bigger picture, do not make the necessary connections and treat a curriculum as a list of objectives to be gotten through.

When discussing non-gain starters with teachers – particularly younger teachers who have been trained in three-part lessons – there is a common objection: all the pupils arrive at the classroom at different times, so my starter is a way of settling the class.

I have heard this objection many times, so our team decided to interview pupils in schools that use non-gain starters about their punctuality to mathematics lessons. Undertaking a tally exercise of the transcripts of the interviews, the word that appeared more than any other was the word 'optional'. Pupils repeatedly told us that the lessons had an 'optional' bit at the beginning, which they didn't need to do. They used this as their reason for not having to rush to the lesson. After all, the starter had nothing to do with the lesson and there was no consequence in not engaging with the starter – they would still be able to do everything in the 'real' part of the lesson.

An interesting additional finding was that when schools deploying non-gain starters ceased to do so, punctuality significantly improved. When we went back to interview the pupils in these schools, they described how important it was to get to the lesson quickly because they 'wouldn't be able to do the lesson' if they were late. There was a consequence to arriving late, so the pupils chose to get there in good time and to be alert at the beginning so they could be successful in the lesson.

When scaled up over a year and then over the whole time that pupils spend in the schooling system, the figures indicate significant differences in the amount of instruction received by pupils in these different types of schools:

	Average performing	High performing
Per day	31 mins	49 mins
Per year	69 hours	109 hours
Throughout schooling	827 hours	1307 hours

I suggest that one of the key reasons that high-performing schools are high performing is that the pupils in those schools receive significantly more teaching time. In the data collection schools, pupils in high-performing schools could have received an additional 480 hours of mathematics teaching during their time at school. One can learn a heck of a lot of mathematics in 480 hours.

I suggest that as much curriculum time as is possible should be dedicated deliberately and purposefully to the learning of new mathematical ideas.

Phasing learning episodes

When a pupil encounters a novel idea, I suggest that they pass through four phases as they move first from inflexible knowledge to performance and then to fluency and finally to understanding. They are evolving from novice to expert.

I shall define the four phases:

- TEACH
- DO
- PRACTISE
- BEHAVE

During the TEACH phase, the idea is entirely novel to pupils, though only just beyond their current knowledge and understanding so that it will be possible to assimilate the new idea. The teacher will instruct the pupils, tell them key facts, pass on knowledge, show and describe, use metaphor and model, all in order to bring about connections in the pupil's current schema so that they can meaning-make. This phase is often described as explicit teaching. It is a crucial phase – after all, the teacher knows things and the pupil does not – so we should not shy away from this; the teacher can simply tell the pupils the things they want them to know. We understand that all human beings meaning-make at different speeds and from different models, metaphors and examples, so it is not enough for the teacher to simply state the idea through one example of the type they prefer – after all, our job is not to teach the way in which we would wish to be taught, but rather to teach in such a way that **all** pupils have a moment of meaning-making and can grip the sense of a new idea. This means the teacher's explanations are varied and responsive, such that the teacher is able to spot when individual pupils are failing to make sense and can pivot to a different instructional approach or model.

The end of the TEACH phase does not result in learning. It is merely a first step. At this stage the new knowledge is inflexible and it is our job as teachers to bring meaning and understanding to the knowledge so that it becomes fully flexible and usable as a tool at any time and on any type of appropriate problem – that is to say, we bring about far transfer.

We now ask pupils to DO. At this stage, they do not yet know or understand the new idea; they are merely replicating what the teacher has told or shown them. The DO phase has two important purposes.

Firstly, the teacher is able to observe whether or not the pupils have made meaning of the model, example, metaphor or information they have been given or shown. The teacher can see and act: 'Are the pupils able to replicate what I have demonstrated?' If not, the teacher can change their model, example or explanation, perhaps making stronger and more explicit connections to previous knowledge and understanding. In other words, the teacher is using this responsive, dialogic process to check whether or not the intended curriculum (what the teacher thinks they are communicating) is the same as the received curriculum (what the pupil is actually picking up). This dialogic process enables the teacher to swiftly change their actions where necessary.

The second reason for the DO phase is to give pupils a sense that the idea or task is surmountable – that they, quite literally, can **do** what they are being asked to do. Well-structured TEACH and DO interactions build pupils' confidence and show them there is nothing to be afraid of – the new idea is within their reach. The pupil is able to successfully replicate and use the techniques being described, so it is not a great leap for them to conclude that they will also be able to learn more about the idea at hand.

Again, at this stage no meaningful learning has occurred. The TEACH and DO phases do not lead to long-term learning or far transfer. There is a dilemma here for the teacher. Simple TEACH and DO lessons can be regarded by the lay observer or non-specialist inspector as highly effective – after all, the teacher explained something and now all the pupils can do it; but performance is not the same as learning. Of course all of the pupils can do what they have just been shown – they have **just been shown it**! There is no effort required to regurgitate, so the pupils can simply get through the lesson and get lots of correct answers. They might even feel pretty good about it if their experience of schooling has conditioned them to believe that success means getting questions correct in the moment. But our interests lie elsewhere – we are interested in long-term memory, progress in understanding and far transfer. We want our pupils to be able to call on the ideas of today in the distant future and to put them to good use in a variety of non-isomorphic scenarios. Don't be fooled into thinking that TEACH and DO lessons are sufficient.

Once both teacher and pupil are clear that the pupil is able to DO – that is to say, they can perform in this moment in time – the teacher now creates deliberate, intelligent sequences of questions and tasks which will result in the pupil segueing to the PRACTISE phase.

During the PRACTISE phase, we wish to move beyond simply performing. We want the pupil to gain confidence in working with the new idea, to discern its underlying relationships and principles and to assimilate the new idea into their schema of knowledge, making multiple connections to previously learnt ideas. In order to achieve these more meaningful goals, the pupil needs to be able to attend to higher-level ideas and the deep structure of the tasks. In other words, as described earlier, the pupil needs to have achieved fluency at the performing level first, so that they may attend to connections, relationships and a deeper conceptual appreciation.

So, I shall define the point at which the pupil moves from DO to PRACTISE as the point at which they achieve fluency.

The final phase, BEHAVE, is perhaps the most important phase of all. This is the phase that deepens and embeds a robust and useful understanding of the novel idea.

At this stage, teachers create opportunities for pupils to behave **mathematically**.

Our assumption at this stage is that the pupil has become fluent in the new idea or skill, is able to work confidently with the mathematics and has assimilated the idea into their schema of knowledge. It is tempting, then, to plan BEHAVE tasks that are based on the new mathematical idea which pupils have just gripped; but in learning mathematics – and, in particular, in thinking mathematically – **maturation matters**. The type of thinking and behaving we want pupils to do at this stage requires an embedded sense and understanding of the mathematical ideas that will arise.

When planning for the BEHAVE phase, therefore, we will not be asking the pupils to use the novel idea, but instead the content of the BEHAVE phase will be drawn from well-embedded and -matured mathematical ideas that connect to the new learning. The new learning that has occurred in this learning episode will mature over time as more connections are made and more opportunities are given to see the idea from different perspectives. Later in the journey of learning mathematics, the new idea will be used (many times) in a BEHAVE phase. But, it is not possible to BEHAVE with a novel idea.

It is difficult to determine how mature an idea needs to be before pupils can BEHAVE mathematically with that idea, but a good rule of thumb would be around two years. The assertion that the kind of mathematical behaviour required in the BEHAVE phase requires significant maturation has been around a long time. In 1980, Vern Treilibs suggested a longer maturation process than I do now, stating 'students ability to apply mathematics lags at least three years behind their first learning of it' (Treilibs et al., 1980), but observations have led me to believe two years is a more typical timeframe.

As an example, suppose a pupil is working on a unit with fairly interesting 3D trigonometry being introduced by the teacher. The idea is new to them, but with effort they can become fluent in the techniques that their teacher has demonstrated and can undertake lots of practice, bringing about a greater sense of the mathematics at play. What might the BEHAVE phase look like in such a unit? Rather than attempting to behave mathematically with the novel idea, during the BEHAVE phase, we might be asking pupils to work with ideas of angle facts or simple Pythagoras, which they will have met much earlier on. They can see the connection to the new idea, but it won't demand that they use it (though there is nothing wrong in scenarios that make it possible to use the new idea and ideas beyond). Pupils not only get an appreciation for how their ability to use earlier ideas – which seemed at the time to be complex yet now appear simple and fluent – has become more embedded, but also the positive effects from meeting previous ideas again, bringing benefits of 'spacing' and the 'testing effect', as discussed earlier.

Many teachers find it an uncomfortable – perhaps even illogical – process to plan the BEHAVE phase as one that relates to much earlier learning rather than the new idea, but it is crucial to do so if we want to bring about optimal gains in learning, understanding and long-term recall.

Consider for a moment some learning you have experienced. When did you truly understand the ideas? I would guess you didn't understand them straight away, and probably not even when you first put them to use. We see this happening all the time. The pupil above had once found Pythagoras' theorem somewhat intractable; yet a couple of years down the line, after they have worked with far more difficult ideas, they now find it straightforward. This is because understanding is not just about reasoning why connections to earlier ideas hold true; it also involves reasoning why subsequent ideas are related and appreciating the new light those subsequent ideas shine on an earlier one as the web of ideas grows and becomes ever more sophisticated. As another example, we can see pupils readily perform and resolve interesting problems with calculus when they are first introduced to differentiation and integration, but it is much later – probably when they are undergraduates – that the true meaning of what they were working with two or three years previously starts to dawn on them. The maturation process should not be ignored – so much time can be wasted by attempting to get pupils to undertake meaningful inquiry with novel ideas, which just leads to frustration, failure or – in many cases – superficially completing tasks just for the sake of it. Yet, sequenced carefully with a maturation gap, all pupils can thoroughly engage with and find joy in mathematical inquiry at all stages in their journey through a mathematics curriculum, even from the very first lesson. But we will address that issue later.

Moving from current practice to a mastery approach

It has been some time since mastery was the dominant model of schooling in many Western countries. In England, for example, the introduction of the national curriculum in 1988 resulted in schools almost unanimously adopting the conveyor belt approach described earlier. This approach has resulted in an obsession with coverage rather than learning. Lessons 'cover' content and objectives, but tend not to be concerned with understanding and long-term recall.

Another result of the conveyor belt is the wholly obtuse belief that learning happens in perfectly apportioned pockets of time. It is a common feature of schemes of work to assume that each mathematical idea will be learnt in precisely one hour. How serendipitous this would be and how obviously farcical the notion is on even the most cursory consideration.

Worse, we even hear apparently responsible educators, managers and inspectors talking about pupils 'making progress in 20 minutes'. This is, of course, utter nonsense. Learning is not linear; it is highly complex and involves regressing as well as progressing. These bean counters who travel around our schools pushing their unhelpful agenda (insisting that all pupils must make progress in all lessons or portions of lessons) are a danger to the opportunity we, as a profession, have to take the issue seriously and have an intelligent debate about what learning is, what it looks like and what the implications for the classroom are. The 'progress in 20 minutes' brigade have no place in a grown-up profession – they should be banished from all schools, sent away to cause their damage in places that are not about the serious business of changing children's lives.

I suggest here – as Washburne, Bloom, Carroll and many others have done before me – that a 'learning episode' (the amount of time required to grip a novel idea) has no fixed time period. Yes, some things can be learnt in an hour; but some may take weeks or years – or an entire lifetime.

I take the learning episode to be my measure of learning when talking about the four phases outlined above. The teacher will flow through the four phases during the learning episode, taking the right amount of time necessary, informed by their observations, discussions, questions, experience and the articulations they demand the pupils make.

Let us consider the optimal phasing of a learning episode. I will use the following colour coding:

When one travels around Western countries today, the typical phasing of a learning episode looks something like this:

In other words, what we generally see in conveyor belt schools at the moment is the teacher spending a short amount of time demonstrating and instructing, then asking pupils to work on similar examples. They have to undertake a lot of 'doing' before the ideas start to become clear to them. Eventually, they find they no longer have to give great attention to the surface level and can begin to discern relationships and principles of the concept at hand. At this stage, with fluency, the pupils move to practising, which they are given a large amount of time to do.

In the majority of classrooms currently, most pupils only ever proceed to the PRACTISE phase and the BEHAVE phase is entirely absent. This makes coverage easier – teachers can 'get through the curriculum' – but misses the most important phase, which means pupils do not get the opportunity to reason, understand, reflect, embed and significantly strengthen long-term learning.

It is a common feature of the current education landscape to hear teachers lamenting the fact that pupils have forgotten what they have been taught previously. But without the BEHAVE phase, they have not really been taught; they have just had presentation and practise. Yes, they can perform, but performance is not the same thing as learning at all. If learning did not occur, nor did teaching. Perhaps the lament should more accurately be the rather unsurprising statement, 'My pupils can't recall something they were never taught.'

I suggest that a more impactful phasing could look like this

Notice the increase in time spent on explicitly teaching the novel idea, through modelling, examples, metaphors, stating facts and information and so on. With an increased amount of instruction time, pupils are able to move more quickly from the DO to the PRACTISE phase because the teacher has expertly described the features of the idea at hand and the steps of techniques to be used as well as the potential pitfalls. Now, a good amount of time is reserved for the BEHAVE phase. As discussed earlier, and demonstrated in the McKinsey report, increasing the amount of direct teaching results in greater gains, but only to an optimal proportion. In order to achieve the sweet spot between teacher-directed instruction and pupil inquiry, we can include a BEHAVE phase so that pupils have opportunities for meaningful inquiry in every single learning episode.

This model is more effective than the conveyor belt model, since it takes the pupils into the BEHAVE phase, which requires them to make deeper connections and reason and reflect. The time spent considering the ideas at a deep-structure level (rather than just at surface level) brings about gains in terms of long-term memory and the requirement to reason about the nature of connections significantly improves far transfer.

However, the above suggested phasing can be improved further still. I suggest that the following distribution of a learning episode is even more powerful.

Here the TEACH and DO phases are broken up and intertwined, which helps the teacher to hold their own teaching to account before progressing too far with an idea – a checking activity to ensure the intended meaning is being received by the pupils before attempting to build on it. It also helps to space out the learning of an idea and gives opportunity to disrupt the time spent thinking about one thing. We will examine this important **interweaving** of the TEACH and DO phase in depth later.

Our goal is to get the benefits of the 'sweet spot', the optimal balance between teacher-directed instruction and pupil inquiry. There is no hard or fast rule to the proportion of time spent on each, but a good rule of thumb would be an approximate 80:20 split between the combined TEACH, DO and PRACTISE phases and the BEHAVE phase.

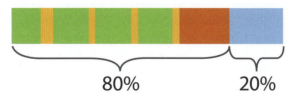

With this phasing, teachers are carefully building up an appreciation of the novel idea, ensuring pupils become fluent in its use, then providing a reflective period in which pupils use earlier – but connected – ideas to undertake serious mathematical thinking.

Combined, this phasing pulls together several key benefits for learning that the field of cognitive science has been confirming over the last 50 years.

Types of examples and questions

Each phase uses carefully planned and deliberate types of examples and questions.

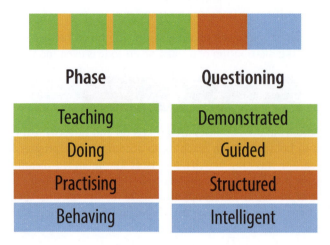

Phase	Questioning
Teaching	Demonstrated
Doing	Guided
Practising	Structured
Behaving	Intelligent

During the first phase, the teacher is teaching. This teaching is carefully considered, planned, well executed and explicit. The teacher uses examples as stories, models and insights into the types of questions that can be addressed with the techniques being learnt. These questions are 'demonstrated' – literally, the teacher is demonstrating what success looks like. They are to the point, accurate and efficient demonstrations of what pupils might encounter when working with the novel idea and how to resolve such problems. At this stage, the novel idea is not known or understood. The most efficient way to get a child to know a new piece of information or idea is to tell them specifically and precisely, using the tried-and-tested didactics we know have the greatest likelihood of ensuring a pupil can meaning-make. As teachers, we hold in our minds a body of knowledge unknown to the pupils. We carefully reveal this knowledge at the right time, taking into account the maturity of their schemas, gradually building up their appreciation of our domain.

The implication is clear: curriculum is the single most important tool we have at our disposal. A carefully planned route through our subject – which is not linear, but complex and takes into account forgetting and unlearning as well as learning – is vital if we are to know when and how to reveal the canon of our discipline. This journey through learning a subject spirals upwards as we mature. Ideas are met and then re-met as we grow older. Earlier ideas suddenly have new meaning as we can view them from the perspective of maturity, integrating them with latterly learnt material, shining a new light on them and revealing underlying relationships that did not seem apparent at an earlier stage. All mastery approaches adopt a spiral or staircase curriculum approach – it is vital in bringing about the gains of maturation and schema assimilation.

Having demonstrated what we know pupils will be able to do, we then ask them to do so. During the next phase, pupils are doing. The questions at this stage still involve the teacher, since pupils have not yet gripped the novel idea. Pupils are replicating, being successful, performing, gaining confidence and articulating. The teacher is a crucial element of this stage, ensuring confidence is being built by continuing to guide pupils where necessary and changing their teaching actions in response to pupils' articulations. At this stage, therefore, I shall call the question types 'guided'.

This transition and mixing of the 'demonstrated' and 'guided' can be instant (for example, the teacher demonstrates a solution and then immediately asks the pupils to do a similar one; show – do) or can take place with greater explanation (for example, the teacher demonstrates a question, takes some questions from the pupils, addresses these in discussion, points out features, then demonstrates a few more examples before asking the pupils to have a go at a few). These pedagogic choices happen in real time – the teacher can judge the impact of their example (perhaps by surveying the class or asking pupils to show the response to a guided question on mini-whiteboards) and then decide the best course of action (more examples, different models or allowing the pupils to do some more of their own).

The teacher is continually monitoring the level of confidence, deftness, accuracy and insight their pupils are showing during these show-do interchanges. With the pupils moving from significant concentration on surface-level issues such as process, the teacher is watching for the transition to procedural fluency. As this is attained, the pupils are slowly, purposefully segueing into practising.

Once pupils progress to practising, the teacher delivers questions designed to reveal underlying relationships and principles such that the pupils are able to gain a sense of the deeper structure of the concept being explored. These questions are well ordered, carefully planned, with deliberate and purposeful variation such that the novel idea is connected to previous learning and assimilated into the pupils' schemas because they are able to appreciate connections, logic and relationship. I shall call these questions 'structured'.

In the final phase of the learning episode, our aim is to elicit mathematical thinking. I shall call such questions 'intelligent'. Questions that elicit mathematical thinking can include scenarios where pupils must evaluate mathematical statements, classify mathematical objects, interpret multiple representations, create and solve problems, analyse, reason and reflect upon solutions and the impact that resolving a problem has had on them.

Crucially, we are seeking to take pupils from a point of specialising, through conjecturing, generalising and then, critically, reasoning and reflecting. The BEHAVE phase is concerned with inquiry rather than simple enquiry. Pupils are being mathematical modellers.

It is these 'intelligent' questions that bring about understanding and make our knowledge truly robust – the ideas have become tools that we have a licence to use any time we wish on any type of problem we deem suitable.

Interweaving the TEACH and DO phases

Alternating examples and problems

As discussed earlier, using worked examples with pupils who are encountering a novel idea helps to reduce the demand imposed on their working memory. This results in more mental energy and attention being available for careful consideration of the new idea and the types of problems they will need to address.

John Sweller has, in several studies, demonstrated the effect in laboratory conditions and John B. Carroll went further – as he so often did – to replicate the benefits of worked examples in real classroom settings.

This appears uncontroversial; teacher demonstration helps. But what if it could be even more powerful?

It is more interesting to consider the alternatives to worked examples. What if, following the teacher explanation of a new idea, the pupil was only given their own problems to work on rather than being shown a worked example? Surprisingly, pupils who do not have a worked example shown to them after the initial steps of the TEACH phase but are instead simply given problems to work on appear to make better gains if given enough time to work with the problem. Najar and Mitrovic (2013) looked at the impact on learning gain from three different approaches:

- Examples only (EO)

- Problems only (PO)

- Alternating examples/problems (AEP)

Pupils working only on their own problems (PO) performed well and, as learning time increased, significantly outperformed pupils working with the other two approaches.

Pupils who were given only teacher-led examples as part of their instruction sequence initially perform well, but both PO and AEP approaches significantly outperform EO as the learning time is increased.

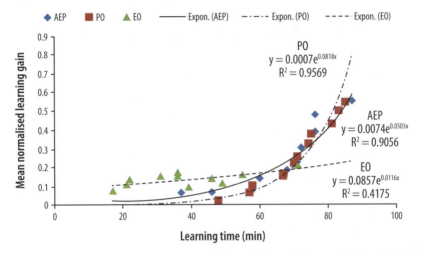

Figure 3 from Najar and Mitrovic, 2013

It is interesting to note that those pupils who were not shown examples apparently made the greatest gains. This would appear to contradict the importance of worked examples. Najar and Mitrovic went beyond just recording a broad learning gain, further distilling their findings to examine problem-solving gain, conceptual-knowledge gain and procedural-knowledge gain. The data reveal a more nuanced picture:

	PO (12)	AEP (11)	EO (11)
Normalised learning gain	.54 (.19)	.55 (.31)	.21 (.35)
Problem-solving gain	.64 (.27)	.58 (.42)	.19 (.37)
Conceptual-knowledge gain	.29 (.39)	.77 (.41)	.54 (.47)
Procedural-knowledge gain	.59 (.22)	.48 (.42)	.13 (.40)

Table 1 from Najar and Mitrovic, 2013

There is no significant difference in the normalised learning gain of PO and AEP and they both significantly outperform EO. However, when looking at conceptual knowledge gain, AEP is a clear winner. So, teachers should seek to alternate examples and problems during their instruction if they wish for their pupils to really grip the deep structure of the novel idea being taught.

This is why I suggest interweaving of the TEACH and DO phases:

The teacher gives clear and precise explanation, using models, metaphors and examples and drawing on multiple representations for meaning-making. The teacher then asks the pupils to complete a problem similar to the ones they have been shown, and this dialogic dance continues for as many repetitions as required for the pupils to grip the meaning of the ideas and to be able to work confidently with them. By interweaving the TEACH and DO phases, the teacher ensures they do not move too far through an explanation without checking if the meaning of their explanations is being received and internalised appropriately by the pupils. By alternating example and problem, the teacher is able to observe the pupils' articulations of the idea being explained and can, therefore, adapt their teaching in real time to address any misconceptions or to build on the correct interpretations that the pupils have made.

The case for alternating worked examples and problems has been made many times in a variety of studies. I suggest that the most powerful form of example is the teacher-led example, but it is also known that giving pupils access to fully worked examples, perhaps with self-study prompts included, also achieves a significant gain, particularly in procedural knowledge. For instance, where half of the practice problems are replaced with worked examples, pupils make significantly more procedural knowledge gain than those who work on twice as many problems (Sweller and Cooper, 1985; Ward and Sweller, 1990). The reduction in cognitive load brought about by seeing the worked examples enables the pupils to focus more of their mental energy on understanding the structure of the problem.

So, alternating examples and problems in this interweaved way should be the aim of the teacher. But what if we could make this even more impactful?

The importance of non-examples

A typical classroom scenario might involve a teacher giving an accurate, clear explanation of a new idea followed by several examples that demonstrate the idea being applied correctly. In doing so, the teacher is giving opportunities to see a number of problems where the idea can be applied and the interactions, structures and underlying principles of the idea are at work. But the pupil does not necessarily gain any sense of the limitations of the idea – where it might break down or where its application is either unnecessary or undesirable.

Many people find it counterintuitive for a teacher to introduce incorrect examples of the idea being taught, but in doing so, the teacher is highlighting the limits of the new idea and ensuring that pupils understand where it does not apply. Further, any range of correct examples can never exemplify the full range of applicability of an idea – to do so would take a rather long time. However, with correct examples and incorrect examples discussed, pupils get a greater sense of the full range of applicable and non-applicable scenarios.

The use of non-examples also levers the benefits of interleaving described earlier. Non-examples can be introduced at any level and might take a simple form such as the following sequence of images that a teacher might choose to show their class when wanting them to grip the idea of triangle-ness.

TEACHER: 'Look at the shapes and listen to my description.'

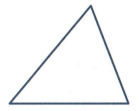

TEACHER: 'A triangle.'

TEACHER: 'Not a triangle.'

TEACHER: 'A triangle.'

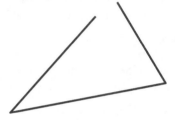

TEACHER: 'Not a triangle.'

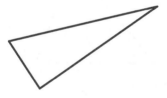

TEACHER: 'A triangle.'

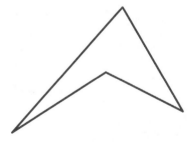

TEACHER: 'Not a triangle.'

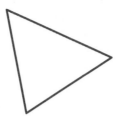

TEACHER: 'A triangle.'

TEACHER: 'Not a triangle.'

And so on. The teacher uses non-examples for the same reason that Bjork suggests interleaving paintings by different artists when trying to discern their individual styles – rather than a sequence showing only correct examples of triangles, which might lead to the pupil being able to comment on aspects that the shapes have in common, the sequence including non-examples gives the pupil the opportunity to see the limits of their descriptions.

For example, showing the pupil lots of triangles might lead to the claim that triangle-ness means to have three sides, but there are plenty of shapes with three sides that are not triangles. Introducing the curved non-example strengthens the description further to three **straight** sides, and then the non-example where the sides do not meet prompts yet another iteration of the description to include that the shape must be closed. Continuing in this manner, non-examples help to define the limits of the description of what it means to have triangle-ness, perhaps resulting in a sentence such as 'A triangle is a closed plane figure with three straight edges and three internal angles.'

Many studies have examined the benefits of including exposition of non-examples, with fairly consistent findings showing gains in both near- and far-transfer problems.

Benefits of explicitly discussing incorrect examples include improved procedural knowledge brought about by pupils having to recognise and accept when they have chosen incorrect procedures (Siegler, 2002). There are also gains in conceptual knowledge since pupils' attention is drawn to the particular features of a problems that make the incorrect procedure inappropriate (Chi et al., 1981).

The use of incorrect examples should be carefully judged by the teacher before use. Große and Renkl (2007) found that very novice pupils do not benefit from incorrect examples when they are expected to locate and identify the error in the example themselves. The teacher can still use incorrect examples as part of the instructional process with very novice pupils, but should do so in a dialogic manner, where the teacher can guide the novice pupil through the flawed aspects of the example.

Good evidence of such gains exists in several studies. For example, when Booth et al. (2013) looked at three separate approaches to instruction with pupils learning elemental algebra, there was a clear benefit to combining correct and incorrect examples.

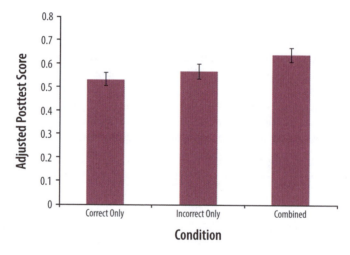

Figure 3 from Booth et al., 2013

The study also considered a more nuanced view of the types of gains being made, showing significant benefits for pupils in terms of far transfer and feature knowledge – that is, an understanding of concepts critical for future success in learning algebra, including the meaning of the equals sign, negative signs, and like terms.

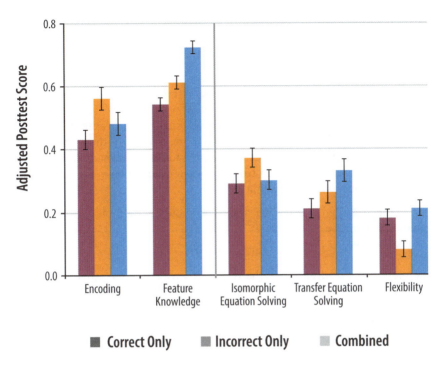

Figure 4 from Booth et al., 2013

In the same study, Booth et al. also considered the effects of self-explanation during the example process and found that including the requirement for pupils to explain the steps in the examples they were working on did have a significant positive impact. The benefits of self-explanation have been replicated in several studies, but for one particularly interesting finding, let us now turn to what happens when self-explanation is combined with prompting and backward fading.

The importance of fading, prompting and self-explanation

We have seen that the teacher can bring about greater gains in both long-term memory and far transfer by alternating problems and examples, including some worked examples that are deliberately incorrect. It is possible to increase these gains even further through the use of two very simple-to-implement pedagogic choices.

Typically, a teacher will work through a full example with a class, discussing and describing each step or annotating it in detail in silence or in full on paper for a pupil to study. All of the steps necessary to overcome the problem are included in the example. For instance, a multi-step equation problem might require five sequenced and distinct mathematical processes to occur in order to find the desired unknown, which the teacher will demonstrate by detailing each of those processes.

Atkinson et al. (2003) examined the impact of removing some of the steps in the worked examples and replacing those steps with prompts. They found that gradually removing the later steps in a multi-step problem example brought about significant learning gains. Furthermore, replacing these steps with prompts for the pupil to read added even more to the gains made. The process of removing one additional step from a worked example on every subsequent example is called 'backward fading'.

For example, suppose a teacher wants to show an example of solving an equation of the type

$$4(2x + 3) = 28$$

For the first worked example, the teacher shows all of the steps (of course, the teacher could decide to show the division first, rather than expanding the brackets):

$$8x + 12 = 28$$

$$8x + 12 - 12 = 28 - 12$$

$$8x = 16$$

$$\frac{8x}{8} = \frac{16}{8}$$

$$x = 2$$

The teacher then shows another example of the same type, but this time omits the final step:

$$2(3x + 1) = 26$$

$$6x + 2 = 26$$

$$6x + 2 - 2 = 26 - 2$$

$$6x = 24$$

On the next example, another step is removed:

$$5(2x - 3) = 25$$

$$10x - 15 = 25$$

And then, finally, no solution steps are shown:

$$6(3x - 2) = 42$$

This backward-fading approach was compared to simply alternating examples and problems in the following way:

Tasks	Solution step	Backward fading	Example-problem pairs
1 and 5	1	Worked	Worked
	2	Worked	Worked
	3	Worked	Worked
2 and 6	1	Worked	Omitted
	2	Worked	Omitted
	3	Omitted	Omitted
3 and 7	1	Worked	Worked
	2	Omitted	Worked
	3	Omitted	Worked
4 and 8	1	Omitted	Omitted
	2	Omitted	Omitted
	3	Omitted	Omitted

From Atkinson et al., 2003

In addition to the backward fading, the missing steps can be replaced by prompts for the pupils to consider. In our example, we might have something like

Example 1	Example 2
$4(2x + 3) = 28$	$2(3x + 1) = 26$
$8x + 12 = 28$	$6x + 2 = 26$
$8x + 12 - 12 = 28 - 12$	$6x + 2 - 2 = 26 - 2$
$8x = 16$	$6x = 24$
$\dfrac{8x}{8} = \dfrac{16}{8}$	Which mathematical operator would enable you to isolate the value of x?
$x = 2$	a) addition
	b) multiplication
	c) subtraction
	d) division

Example 3	Example 4
$5(2x - 3) = 25$ $10x - 15 = 25$ What would help you to find the unknown value? a) factorise the term on the LHS b) isolate the x term in the LHS expression c) break the equivalence of the statement d) place the x term on the RHS *and then the same prompt as shown in example 2*	$6(3x - 2) = 42$ What does the equals sign give you permission to do? a) remove any part of the expression on the LHS b) remove any part of the expression on the RHS c) perform the same operation to both expressions d) perform any operation on one side but not the other *and then the same prompts as shown in example 2 and 3.*

A prompting process was also added to the example-problem pair approach in the trial.

The study found interesting differences in adjusted mean scores:

	Example-problem pairs		Backward fading	
	No prompting	Prompting	No Prompting	Prompting
Near transfer	0.43	0.59	0.58	0.65
Far transfer	0.40	0.50	0.51	0.57

Those who received a backward-fading instructional approach made significant gains in both near and far transfer compared to a standard example-problem-pairs approach.

For near transfer the corresponding effect size (as measured by Cohen's f statistic) was found to be 0.23 without prompting and 0.25 with prompting. This is a medium-size effect produced with almost no additional effort required from the teacher – simply by taking the pedagogic choice to fade out later steps in examples, our pupils can make better progress on similar problems.

The effect size for far transfer – which is, surely, what we are truly interested in – was also found to be really encouraging, with the pattern of effect sizes for the near-transfer problems being repeated in far transfer. So, pupils who receive the instructional approach of backward fading and self-explanation prompts are able to perform significantly better – even on problems that are not similar to the examples they have been shown – than pupils who work only on alternating examples and problems.

The same positive effect from backward fading found in Atkinson et al. (2003) has also been replicated in several other studies, so there is good evidence to support a move to a backward-fading instructional approach in the classroom. The use of prompting had been less well established, so Atkinson et al.

undertook a second experiment examining the impact of prompting on high school pupils in a backward-fading instructional approach.

The adjusted mean score for near transfer was 0.30 without prompting and 0.52 with prompting. For far transfer, the results were similarly encouraging, with a score of 0.23 without prompting and 0.41 with prompting.

This shows an effect size of 0.42 for near transfer and 0.37 for far transfer, both of which would be classified as a large effect.

It is also worth noting that prompting did not increase the amount of learning time required. So, with a simple pedagogic choice, the teacher is able to increase both near and far transfer with little cost in terms of preparation time and no cost in terms of learning time.

Proportioning content

Assimilating new ideas and information into an established, complex schema is difficult. Before the moment of the new idea, the pupil has a perception of the universe – a series of held views, beliefs and truths. Asking the pupil to disrupt that view of the world is a significant burden on them. As discussed, connecting already-established and -understood knowledge and ideas to the new learning enables a pupil to meaning-make more readily – after all, if one can see a new idea from the perspective of already-believed ideas and how it fits with their wider view of the universe, it is much easier to believe the new truth.

It is such a big ask of pupils to believe and grip novel ideas or knowledge that we should take steps to make this process as gentle and effective as possible. An important consideration is to not overwhelm the pupil with novel information. In a conveyor belt curriculum, the content of each lesson is almost entirely novel – this objective-led approach sees teachers racing through new mathematical ideas like a tick list. All of the questions, discussion and exploration in the lesson are concentrated on the new idea. In a mastery approach, a very different structure is used. In each learning episode (rather than lesson), only a small proportion of the content of the PRACTISE phase of the learning episode is novel. The majority of the content is drawn from previously encountered material, with links to the new idea at hand. A good rule of thumb for old:new content is approximately 80:20.

So, in each learning episode, only around 20% of the content of the PRACTISE phase is focused on the new idea. This helps with assimilation, but the real reason I suggest this proportioning of content is to bring about the significant gains that are found in spacing, interleaving and several of the other interventions we have learned from cognitive science in recent decades.

To be clear, the TEACH and DO phases will in all cases be completely focused on the explanation, articulations and replications of the techniques and processes of the new idea at hand. Those phases are carefully designed to ensure that pupils reach a state of fluency and can work unhindered with the new idea on a range of problem types. When fluency has been achieved, the pupil no longer needs to give significant attention in order to perform. But we would not want the pupil to then work in the PRACTISE phase without having to expend serious mental energy – that would be a grossly wasted opportunity.

Rather, we can direct their mental energy elsewhere.

The importance of method selection

When a pupil walks in to an exam hall, takes their seat and turns over the test paper, they are faced with a random selection of questions from a variety of topics. The very first thing they must do, when staring at question 1, is to decide what method they have at their disposal that will help them to unpick the problem and lead to a correct solution. This is also the case for question 2 and question 3 and all subsequent questions. So it is vital that pupils have acquired the skill of selecting an appropriate method for a problem. Indeed, it is key to their development as a mathematician (or whatever discipline they are learning) to know that such a skill exists and that it is the first step in addressing a problem. Yet, in classrooms, the explicit teaching and rehearsal of method selection is almost entirely absent.

Following an interweaved TEACH and DO process, pupils are often asked to then work on a selection of practice questions, all of which require the exact same method as the one they have just been using. The recency of this method means that pupils can, of course, perform and get questions correct. The cue of the teacher – 'Here is a method; here are some questions that all use this method' – means that the pupil can, of course, perform and get questions correct.

Imagine, for example, the teacher has shown the pupils how to find the hypotenuse on a right-angled triangle using Pythagoras' theorem. The teacher and pupils have completed a series of example-problem pairs together as described earlier and the pupil is now fluent in the technique. The teacher then gives the class a worksheet containing 50 questions. Each of these questions requires the pupil to find the length of the hypotenuse in a right-angled triangle using Pythagoras' theorem.

Well, a trained monkey could do that!

There is recency and cue. The pupils do not even have to think; they can just wade through the questions, always knowing precisely which method to apply and how to replicate the technique.

I suggest that this does not qualify as a PRACTISE phase. It is just a waste of time and results in no learning occurring (though lots of performing will certainly take place and the onlooking inspector might leap for joy).

Instead of this mind-numbing experience, we want to capitalise on the fact that the pupil is now fluent and has spare mental energy to give to something serious and challenging.

Suppose that, instead of the worksheet above, the teacher similarly gives a worksheet of 50 questions, but on this worksheet only ten of those questions will require a pupil to find the length of a hypotenuse in a right-angled triangle using Pythagoras' theorem. The other 40 questions will require the pupil to use a method they have met previously, drawing it from their long-term memory. The questions are arranged randomly.

Now what happens? Well, now the very first thing that the pupil must do on every single question is pause, take a step back and ask themselves which method to select in order to resolve the problem.

Method selection greatly improves long-term learning and, crucially, far transfer. The arrangement of the PRACTISE phase can bring about the significant gains of method selection whilst at the same time levering the spacing effect, the testing effect, the hypercorrection effect (the pupil makes a confident assertion about their choice of method and receives an emotional shock if they choose unwisely) and the significant impact on long-term memory brought about by interleaving.

Method selection is not a natural skill. The teacher must teach pupils how to do it and why it is important. The teacher can work this into all of their classroom explanations – whenever the teacher presents an example or problem on the board, they should speak aloud their exaggerated internal monologue.

> TEACHER: 'Hey, I have a problem to solve. I don't know the solution yet. I wonder how I can go about unpicking this problem. What are the characteristics of the problem? What do I know about those characteristics? When I have solved problems with these features in the past, what method was effective at helping me to overcome the problem? Is it a recent method or a method in my toolkit? What is the method? The method I am going to select to solve this problem is X.'

This might feel a little hammed up and perhaps even a little uncomfortable to regularly say in front of the class – but if the teacher does not explicitly articulate their internal monologue in front of pupils, how on earth can we expect pupils to evolve their own powerful internal monitor that will help them every time they are faced with a problem? It does not emerge naturally; it is a key skill that teachers must demonstrate regularly and espouse a belief in.

Interleaving and the Pareto principle

Taking an overview of the curriculum for a subject, we think about the big ideas and themes that we wish to impart along the journey that a pupil will take. To ensure we regularly hold ourselves to account, we arrange the curriculum in manageable units. A unit contains one or more learning episodes, each of which addresses an idea. So, a unit addresses one or more of the ideas we wish pupils to meet. These ideas may be contained to a single unit but will more likely span many units over many years as the curriculum spirals higher and wider.

The TEACH and DO phases in a single learning episode exemplify techniques and approaches solely related to the idea at hand. The PRACTISE and BEHAVE phases draw on multiple ideas, meaning the content in these phases can bring about additional benefits to long-term memory and understanding.

At the very beginning of a curriculum, learning episode 1 begins with the usual TEACH and DO interweaving, building up a fluency with the required techniques. The PRACTISE phase content is necessarily focused on the novel idea too – after all, the pupils have not yet met other content to draw on.

Learning episode 1 does also include a BEHAVE phase. This often baffles some teachers, who question how this can possibly fit with my assertion that pupils cannot BEHAVE with novel content. But this objection is the same trap discussed earlier – that teachers treat pupils as though they are clean slates when, in fact, pupils already know a great deal before arriving in the school system.

Since the problem-solving demand in the BEHAVE phase is high, we must continue to ensure that the content being addressed is drawn from an earlier period in the pupil's life – the mathematical ideas must have matured over approximately two years for the BEHAVE phase to be effective. This remains true even for learning episode 1. So where does this content come from? Well, given that pupils are not clean slates, the content can be drawn from early childhood – this could include, for example, pattern spotting, ordering, simple quantity work, recognizing shapes, etc. Pupils have already experienced a great deal of mathematics by the time they reach school, so there is no reason for the

BEHAVE phase to be absent from the first two years of schooling. What a dull diet of mathematics it would be if the appetiser were completely free of the good stuff. Right from the off, every learning episode will contain a 20% BEHAVE phase – we want to get the pupils hooked on mathematical problem solving from day one.

Learning episode 1 (LE1) would look something like this:

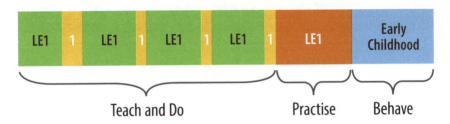

For now, let us ignore the TEACH and DO phases, taking it as read that in every learning episode those phases are focused on the novel idea. Considering just the PRACTISE and BEHAVE phases, in learning episode 1, we have:

In learning episode 2, the content of the PRACTISE phase will be 20% drawn from LE2, but 80% drawn from LE1.

This continues on, with each learning episode consisting of 20% PRACTISE phase content being drawn from that episode and 80% from previous episodes.

So, after the TEACH and DO phases have ensured fluency, the PRACTISE phase is a challenging and purposeful blend of the techniques and methods of the novel idea those retrieved from the long-term memory.

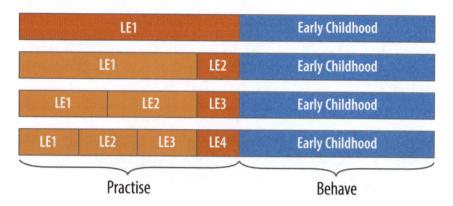

The BEHAVE phase draws many ideas together as the pupils undertake inquiry, but does not include the requirement to work with the novel idea.

I am sure you can imagine how this now unfolds. Approximately two years after LE1, the BEHAVE phase is now made up of LE1 content (and perhaps some other earlier LEs too). By this time, there have been sufficient LEs to allow for a more meaningful mix in the PRACTICE phase – rather than simply previous content, the selected LEs can be related to the content of the current LE, which in itself can be carefully timed and related to the LE that we will use in the BEHAVE phase.

There is no hard-and-fast rule as to the number of learning episodes that can be included in the PRACTISE phase, but four or five episodes appears to be about optimum.

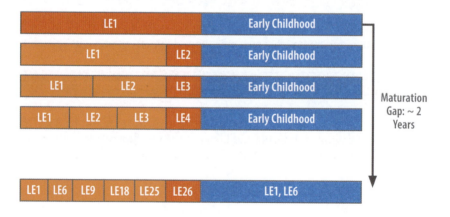

Summary of phased learning

To recap in brief, the TEACH, DO, PRACTISE, BEHAVE phased model consists of:

TEACH	• Eliciting invented strategies and misconceptions • Bridging instruction • Teacher-led instruction • Examples and non-examples • Backward fading and prompting • Precise pedagogic and didactic choice • Forward-facing methods • Stating knowledge and facts
DO	• Replicating and articulating back at the teacher • Responsive teaching – adapting models, metaphors and examples • Developing a dialogic approach – alternate examples and problems • Performing techniques and processes • Re-stating knowledge and facts • Revealing relationships • Continuing to fluency
PRACTISE	• Interleaving content 80:20 old:new • Using variation theory • Revealing underlying principles • Connecting to previous learning • Forming long-term memories • Levering the gains of desirable difficulties • Undertaking mathematical enquiry
BEHAVE	• Knowing that maturation matters • Connecting to previous and subsequent learning • Undertaking mathematical inquiry

This approach to curriculum design – where the unit of learning is not an individual timetabled lesson but rather a learning episode of fluid time, carefully and deliberately structured to plan for teaching for memory and understanding – results in a journey through the subject that gradually and purposefully reveals mathematics and the joy of learning and using mathematics.

Mathematics derives its beauty and power from the way simple techniques combine and interact.

An effective mathematics curriculum must be structured as a carefully planned succession of units, each of which focuses on a web of ideas. Each of these ideas begins with something inflexible, but will build meaning and structure around that initial knowledge such that the ideas being considered today assimilate into the grander universe of related techniques and ideas. And over time, these will all come together in the profound and graceful dance that is mathematics.

PART VI
CONCLUSION

At its heart, a mastery model of schooling is a responsive cycle of teaching in which the teacher continually seeks to build knowledge of a discipline over time in a carefully scheduled, coherent journey that results in a progressively broader and more sophisticated understanding of that discipline and an individual's relationship with it. The teacher is on constant look out for changes in the pupil's knowledge, skills and understanding as indicators for the teacher to take some action, including acting differently to how they have before. The teacher knows and sincerely believes that all pupils can learn well if their pedagogical and didactical choices are carefully considered, intelligent and correct. Each individual pupil in the teacher's charge can be successful. The teacher will use a diagnostic and continuous improvement approach that builds on what the pupil securely knows and understands in order to continue to develop their schema of knowledge in a logical framework of truth.

Washburne was right to explicitly reject the status quo that stated only some pupils could learn well. He was right to consider pupils individually and right to assert that it is critical to start all learning from where a pupil truly is. His tireless development and promotion of a better world in which everyone can succeed has inspired generations of educators to raise the bar and not accept the notion that there are academic and non-academic children. Given the resources and tools at his disposal a century ago, what Washburne was able to achieve was remarkable. But I believe that, as a devotee to learning himself, Washburne would have endorsed the educators who followed and continued to refine his model.

From Carroll and Bloom through to modern retellings by great educators like Guskey and to the present-day integration of the now-established findings of the last 40 years of cognitive science, the development and refinement of Washburne's mastery model of schooling continues to integrate the best of what we can know about the process of learning at any given point in the development of the education canon.

To bring order to the wealth of approaches we know to be highly effective at improving long-term learning, a phased approach to the teaching process can be implemented. The phasing is a framework on which to build truly meaningful learning – from novice to expert. The framework gives structure for the teacher to rigorously develop understanding and ensure the coherent revealing of the web of ideas that constitute a discipline.

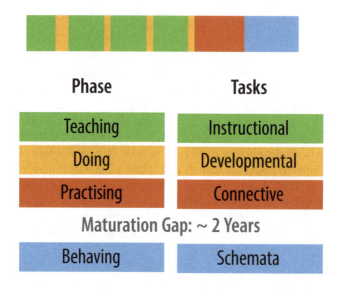

The mastery cycle demands that the high expectation of securely learning each of the ideas encountered is a high expectation for all. No pupil is left behind because the teacher understands that all pupils can learn well.

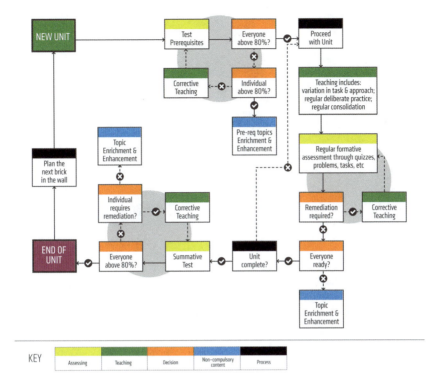

KEY

| Assessing | Teaching | Decision | Non-compulsory content | Process |

The cyclical nature of the model and the duty it places on the teacher to be attuned and responsive to individual pupils' progress is an antidote to the conveyor belt approaches so often seen in schools today. Teaching for mastery is teaching for every child. Teaching for mastery is the unswerving belief that the act of teaching can and will lead to the enlightenment of the determined child.

REFERENCES

Askew, M. (2010). *Transforming primary mathematics*. Routledge.

Askew, M., Hodgen, J., Hossain, S., and Bretscher, N. (2010). *Values and variables Mathematics education in high-performing countries*. London: King's College London.

Atkinson, R., Renkl, A., and Merrill, M. M. (2003). Transitioning From Studying Examples to Solving Problems: Effects of Self-Explanation Prompts and Fading Worked-Out Steps. *Journal of Educational Psychology*, 774-.

Baddeley, A., and Longman, D. (1978). The Influence of Length and Frequency of Training Session on the Rate of Learning to Type. *Ergonomics*. 21, 627-635.

Benjamin, A., Bjork, R., and Schwartz, B. (1998). The Mismeasure of Memory: When Retrieval Fluency Is Misleading as a Metamnemonic Index. *Journal of experimental psychology*, 55-68.

Bjork, R. A. (2009). 'How we learn versus how we think we learn: applications for the design and evaluation of instruction', Carl Wieman Science Education Initiative, University of British Columbia, Vancouver, September 30.

Bjork, R. A., and Bjork, E. L. (1992). A new theory of disuse and an old theory of stimulus fluctuation. In A. Healy, S. Kosslyn, and R. Shiffin, *From learning processes to cognitive processes* (pp. 35-67). Hillsdale, NJ: Erlbaum.

Block, J. H., and Airasian, P. W. (1971). *Mastery learning: theory and practice*. Michigan: Holt, Rinehart and Winston.

Block, J. H., Efthim, H. E., and Burns, R. B. (1989). *Building effective mastery learning schools*. New York: Longman.

Bloom, B. S. (1968). Learning for Mastery. Instruction and Curriculum. *Regional Education Laboratory for the Carolinas and Virginia, Topical Papers and Reprints, Number 1*.

Booth, J., Lange, K., Koedinger, K., and Newton, K. (2013). Using Example Problems to Improve Student Learning in Algebra: Differentiating between Correct and Incorrect Examples. *Learning and Instruction*. 25, 24-34.

Carroll, J. B. (1963). A model of school learning. *Teachers College Record*, 64, 723-733.

Carroll, W. (1994). Using worked examples as an instructional support in the algebra classroom. *Journal of Educational Psychology*, 360-367.

Chi, M. T., Feltovich, P. J., and Glaser, R. (1981). Categorization and representation of physics problems by experts and novices. *Cognitive Science*, 5(2), 121-152.

Cooper, G. (1998). *Research into cognitive load theory and instructional design at UNSW*. Sydney, Australia: University of New South Wales.

Deshler, D. D., and Schumaker, J. B. (1993). Strategy mastery by at-risk students: Not a simple matter. *Elementary School Journal*, 94(2), 153–167.

Diakidoy, I.. Kendeou, P., and. Ioannides, C. (2003). Reading about energy: The effects of text structure in science learning and conceptual change. *Contemporary Educational Psychology*. 28, 335-356.

Dienes, Z. (1971). An Example of the Passage from the Concrete to the Manipulation of Formal Systems. *Educational Studies in Mathematics Vol. 3, No. 3/4, Lectures of the Comprehensive School Mathematics Project (CSMP)* (pp. 337-352). Conference on the Teaching of Geometry.

Diezmann, C. M. (1999). Assessing diagram quality: Making a difference to representation. In J. M. Truran, and K. M. Truran, *Proceedings of the 22nd annual conference of mathematics education research group of Australasia* (pp. 185-191). Adelaide: Mathematics Education Research Group of Australasia.

Dorn, E., Krawitz, M., and Mourshed, M. (2015). *McKinsey Analysis*, OECD PISA. London: McKinsey and Company.

Engelmann, S. (2007). *Teaching Needy Kids in Our Backward System: 42 Years of Trying*. ADI Press.

Estes, W. K. (1955). Statistical theory of spontaneous recovery and regression. *Psychological Review*, 62(3), 145-154.

Feniger, Y., and Lefstein, A. (2014). How not to reason with PISA data: an ironic investigation. *Journal of Education Policy* 29(6), 845-855.

Gardiner, A. D. (2016). Mastery – Confusion and contradiction? Or coherence? *Mastery Symposium.* Nottingham: La Salle Education.

Gattegno, C. (1974) The Common Sense of Teaching Mathematics. New York: Educational Solutions Worldwide Inc.

Gerardo Ramirez, E. A. (2013). *Math Anxiety, Working Memory, and Math Achievement in Early Elementary School, Journal of Cognition and Development,* 14:2, 187-202.

Große, C. S., and Renkl, A. (2007). Finding and fixing errors in worked examples: can this foster learning outcomes? *Learning and Instruction,* 17, 617-634.

Gu, L., Huang, R., and Marton, F. (2004). *Teaching with Variation: A Chinese Way of Promoting Effective Mathematics Learning.*

Guskey, T. R. (2008). The Rest of the Story. *Educational Leadership, Volume 65, Number 4,* 28-35.

Guskey, T. R. (2010). Lessons of Mastery Learning. *Educational Leadership, Volume 68, Number 2,* 52-57.

Hall, R. K. (1989). Exploring the episodic structure of algebra story problem solving. *Cognition and Instruction,* 6,, 223-283.

Hardy, T., Haworth, A., Love, E., and McIntosh, A. (1977). *Points of Departure 1.* ATM.

Haylock, D., and Cockburn, A. (1989). *Understanding Early Years Mathematics.* Paul Chapman.

Hiebert, J., and Carpenter, T. (1992). Learning and teaching with understanding. In D. A. Grouns, *Handbook of research on mathematics teaching and learning* (pp. 65-92). New York: MacMillan.

Hull, C. L. (1943). *Principles of behavior: an introduction to behavior theory.* Oxford, England: Appleton-Century.

Ireson, J., and Hallam, S. (2001). *Ability Grouping in Education.* SAGE.

James, W. (1890). *The principles of psychology.*

Jerrim, J. (2014). *Why do East Asian children perform so well in PISA? An investigation of Western-born children of East Asian descent.* London: Institute of Education, UCL.

Kaput, J. J. (1989). Linking representations in the symbolic systems of algebra. In S. Wagner, and C. Kieran, *Research agenda for mathematics education: Research issues in the learning and teaching of algebra* (pp. 167-194). Reston, VA: National Council of Teachers of Mathematics.

Kieran, C. (1992). The learning and teaching of school algebra. In D. A. Grouws, *Handbook of research in mathematics teaching and learning* (pp. 390-419). New York: Macmillan.

Kieran, C. (1998). Two different approaches among algebra learners. In A. F. Coxford, *The ideas of algebra, K-12* (pp. 167-194). Reston, VA: National Council of Teachers of Mathematics.

Kilpatrick, J., Swafford, J., and Findell, B. (2001). *Adding it up: Helping children learn mathematics.* Washington, DC: National Academy Press.

Koedinger, K. R. (1999). *The real story behind story problems: Effects of representations on quantitative reasoning.*

Koedinger, K. R., Alibali, M., and Nathan, M. J. (2002). *Trade-offs between grounded and abstract representations: Evidence from algebra problem solving.*

Lai, M. Y., and Murray, S. (2012). Teaching with Procedural Variation: A Chinese Way of Promoting Deep Understanding of Mathematics. *International Journal for Mathematics Teaching and Learning*, 1-25.

Lederer, R. (1989). *Anguished English: An Anthology of Accidental Assaults Upon Our Language.* Bantam Doubleday Dell Publishing Group.

Leyton, F. S. (1983). *The extent to which group instruction supplemented by mastery of initial cognitive prerequisites approximates the learning effectiveness of one-to-one tutorial methods.*

Lukianoff, G., and Haidt, J. (2018). *The coddling of the American mind : how good intentions and bad ideas are setting up a generation for failure.* New York: Penquin Press.

Mayer, R. E. (2001). *Multimedia Learning.* Cambridge University Press.

Mayer, R. E. (2005). 'Principles for managing essential processing in multimedia learning: segmenting, pretraining, and modality principles,' in *The Cambridge Handbook of Multimedia Learning*, ed. Mayer R. E., editor. Cambridge, NY: Cambridge University Press, 169–182.

Mayer, R. E. and Moreno, R. (2010). 'Techniques that reduce extraneous cognitive load and manage intrinsic cognitive load during multimedia learning' in *Cognitive Load Theory*, eds Plass J. L., Moreno R., Brünken R., editors. Cambridge, NY: Cambridge University Press, 131–152.

McNiff, J., and McCourt, M. (2010). Professional Education for Teachers in Qatar for Epistemological Transformation in Education Knowledge. *British Educational Research Association Annual Conference*. Warwick: BERA.

Najar, A., and Mitrovic, A. (2013). Examples and Tutored Problems: How Can Self-Explanation Make a Difference to Learning. *Artificial Intelligence in Education: 16th International Conference*. Memphis, TN: AIED.

Nathan, M. J., and Koedinger, K. R. (2000). Moving beyond teachers' intuitive beliefs about algebra learning. *Mathematics Teacher*, 93, 218-223.

Nathan, M. J., and Koedinger, K. R. (2002a). An investigation of teachers' beliefs of students' algebra development. *Cognition and Instruction*, 18,, 209-223.

Nathan, M. J., and Koedinger, K. R. (2002b). Teachers' and researchers' beliefs about the development of algebraic reasoning. *Journal for Research in Mathematics Education*, 31, 168-190.

Nathan, M. J., Stephens, A. C., Masarik, K., Alibali, M. W., and Koedinger, K. R. (2002). *Representational fluency in middle school: a classroom study*. University of Colorado-Boulder.

National Council of Teachers of Mathematics. (2000). *Principles and standards for school mathematics*. Reston, VA: National Council of Teachers of Mathematics.

Newton, L. (1990). *Overconfidence in the Communication of Intent: Heard and Unheard Melodies*. . Stanford, CA: Department of Psychology, Stanford University.

Ohlsson, S. (1996a). Learning from error and the design of task environments. *International Journal of Educational Research*, 25(5), 419-448.

Ohlsson, S. (1996b). Learning from Performance Errors. *Psychological Review.* 103, 214-262.

Panasuk, R., and Beyranevand, M. (2010). Algebra students' ability to recognize multiple representations and achievement. *International Journal for Mathematics Teaching and Learning.*, 1-21.

Panasuk, R., and Beyranevand, M. (2011). Preferred Representations of Middle School Algebra Students When Solving Problems . *The Mathematics Educator*, 32-52.

Pape, S. J., and Tchoshanov, M. A. (2001). The role of representation(s) in developing mathematical understanding. *Theory into Practice*, 40(2), 118-125.

Pimm, D. (1995). *Symbols and meanings in school mathematics.* London: Routledge.

Pociask, Fredrick & Morrison, Gary. (2004). The Effects of Split-Attention and Redundancy on Cognitive Load When Learning Cognitive and Psychomotor Tasks. Association for Educational Communications and Technology.

Ramirez, G., Gunderson, E. A., Levine, S. C., and Beilock, S. L. (2013). Math Anxiety, Working Memory, and Math Achievement in Early Elementary School. *Journal of Cognition and Development*, 14:2, 187-202.

Roediger, H., and Karpicke, J. (2006). Test-Enhanced Learning Taking Memory Tests Improves Long-Term Retention. *Psychological science.* 17., 249-255.

Rohrer, D., and Taylor, K. (2006). The effects of overlearning and distributed practise on the retention of mathematics knowledge. *Applied Cognitive Psychology*, Vol 20, 1209-1224.

Rohrer, D., and Taylor, K. (2007). The shuffling of mathematics problems improves learning. *Instructional Science*, 35(6), 481-498.

Seeger, F., Voight, I., and Werchescio, V. (1998). Representations in the mathematics classroom:reflections and constructions. In F. Seeger, I. Voight, and V. Werchescio, *The Culture of the Mathematics Classroom* (pp. 308-343). Cambridge: Cambridge University Press.

Siegler, R. S. (1996). *Emerging minds: The process of change in children's thinking.* New York: Oxford University Press.

326

Siegler, R. S. (2002). Microgenetic studies of self-explanations. In N. Granott, and J. Parziale, *Microdevelopment: Transition processes in development and learning* (pp. 31-58). New York: Cambridge University.

Simon, D., and Bjork, R. (2001). Metacognition in Motor Learning. *Journal of experimental psychology. Learning, memory, and cognition*, 907-912.

Sparck, E. M., Bjork, E. L., and Bjork, R. A. (2016). On the learning benefits of confidenceweighted testing. *Cognitive Research: Principles and Implications 1:3*.

Swan, M. (2005). Improving Learning in Mathematics: Challenges and Strategies. Sheffield: Teaching and Learning Division, Department for Education and Skills Standards Unit.

Sweller, J., and Cooper, G. A. (1985). The Use of Worked Examples as a Substitute for Problem Solving in Learning Algebra. *Cognition and Instruction Vol. 2*, No. 1, 59-89.

Sweller, J., van Merrienboer, J. J., and and Paas, F. (1998). Cognitive architecture and instructional design. *Educ. Psychol. Rev.* 10, 251–296.

Tabachneck, H. J., Koedinger, K. R., and Nathan, M. J. (1994). Toward a theoretical account of strategy use and sense-making in mathematics problem solving. *Proceedings of the sixteenth annual conference of the cognitive science society*. Hillsdale, NJ: Erlbaum.

Taleb, N. (2012). *Antifragile: Things that gain from disorder*. New York: Random House .

Treilibs, V., Burkhardt, H., and Low, B. (1980). *Formulation processes in mathematical modelling*. Nottingham: Shell Centre for Mathematical Education.

Vockell, E. L. (1993). Why schools fail and what we can do about it. *Clearing House*, 66(4), 200–205.

Ward, M., and Sweller, J. (1990). Structuring Effective Worked Examples. *Cognition and Instruction* 7, 1-39.

Watson, A., and Mason, J. (2006). Variation and mathematical structure. *Mathematics Teaching* 194, 3-5.

White, R. T., and Gunstone, R. F. (1992). *Probing Understanding*. London: The Falmer Press.

Wilensky, U. (1991). Abstract Meditations on the Concrete and Concrete Implications for Mathematics Education. In N. Norwood, *Constructionism.* Ablex Publishing Corporation.

Woodward, J., Beckmann, S., Driscoll, M., Franke, M., Herzig, P., Jitendra, A., Koedinger, K. R., and Ogbuehi, P. (2012). *Improving mathematical problem solving in grades 4 through 8: A practice guide.* Washington, DC: National Center for Education Evaluation and Regional Assistance, Institute of Education Sciences, U.S. Department of Education.